"These essays will make you laugh, cry, and think critically. *Truth's Table* is a must-read for anyone who is in a spiritual rut or demands more from the church."

—Rev. Dr. BRIANNA K. PARKER, CEO of the Black Millennial Café

"People often say, 'Listen to Black women.' Now, with *Truth's Table,* you have your chance. These three friends and sages share about topics as public as mass protest and as personal as singleness and divorce. They do it all from a spiritual lens that remind us of how compassionate and wise church folk are supposed to be. We do not deserve the gift of this book, but, once again, Black women have generously served us all. If we are to actually alleviate the immense burdens our sistas bear, then we must heed their words."

—Dr. JEMAR TISBY, *New York Times* bestselling author of *The Color of Compromise* and *How to Fight Racism,* and co-host of the *Pass The Mic* podcast

"As the son of a beautiful Black woman, and the husband of the same kind, I have wanted many of my peers to know the riches that lie within the mind of Black women. Their unique struggle, indisputable triumph, and interpretation of life's events are the manifesto of time-tested wisdom. In *Truth's Table: Black Women's Musings on Life, Love, and Liberation,* you and I are offered a seat to eavesdrop on the resilience required to build America, the brilliance to birth families, the courage to withstand injustice, and the love that inspires devotion. Our sons and our daughters, our politicians and our preachers, need this work as a core curriculum for making our nation the land of the free and the home of the brave."

—Dr. CHARLIE DATES, senior pastor of Progressive Baptist Church

# TRUTH'S TABLE

# TRUTH'S TABLE

Black Women's Musings on Life,
Love, and Liberation

Ekemini Uwan,
Christina Edmondson, and
Michelle Higgins

CONVERGENT

NEW YORK

Copyright © 2022 by Ekemini Uwan, Michelle Higgins, and Dr. Christina Edmondson

All rights reserved.

Published in the United States by Convergent Books, an imprint of Random House, a division of Penguin Random House LLC, New York.

CONVERGENT BOOKS is a registered trademark and its C colophon is a trademark of Penguin Random House LLC.

All Scripture quotations are taken from the Holy Bible, New International Version®, NIV®. Copyright © 1973, 1978, 1984, 2011 by Biblica, Inc.™ Used by permission of Zondervan. All rights reserved worldwide. (www.zondervan.com). The "NIV" and "New International Version" are trademarks registered in the United States Patent and Trademark Office by Biblica, Inc.™

Library of Congress Cataloging-in-Publication Data
Names: Edmondson, Christina, author. | Higgins, Michelle, author. | Uwan, Ekemini, author.
Title: Truth's table / Christina Edmondson, Michelle Higgins and Ekemini Uwan.
Description: First edition. | New York: Convergent Books, an imprint of Random House, a division of Penguin Random House LLC, [2022] | Includes bibliographical references.
Identifiers: LCCN 2021060336 (print) | LCCN 2021060337 (ebook) | ISBN 9780593239735 (hardcover) | ISBN 9780593239742 (ebook)
Subjects: LCSH: African American women—Religious life. | Christian women—Religious life.
Classification: LCC BR563.N4 E385 2022 (print) | LCC BR563.N4 (ebook) | DDC 277.30089/96073—dc23/eng/20220207
LC record available at https://lccn.loc.gov/2021060336
LC ebook record available at https://lccn.loc.gov/2021060337

Printed in Canada on acid-free paper

crownpublishing.com

2 4 6 8 9 7 5 3 1

First Edition

*Book design by Caroline Cunningham*

*To our grandmothers, daughters, mothers, sisters, mentors,*

*aunties, cousins, play cousins*

*And for Black girls who considered leaving the church when*

*their* imago Dei *wasn't enough*

I been working all night I been working all day
I done seen a lot of things, I done felt a lot of pain
I can see it in your face, girl I know you feel the
    same
I got something to say

If you're wanting somebody to sit down and tell you
    the truth
Sit right here at the table, we have got some tea
    here for you.

—Nabil Ince, *Truth's Table*

# Contents

# Introduction

HEY, Y'ALL! WELCOME TO *Truth's Table*! Midwives of culture for grace and truth. We are Ekemini, Michelle, and Christina! This table is built by Black women and for Black women. So welcome to the table, sistas! How y'all doin'!?

For five years now, we have had the honor and pleasure of building this table. We sit with our Black sistas to discuss politics, culture, and race through the lens of our collective faith in the Gospel of Jesus Christ. By God's design, the three of us had already formed a friendship that began before *Truth's Table* podcast came to be. Between the three of us, there are two MDivs and one PhD at the table. We love Black women and theology, but above all else, we love Jesus.

When we started this podcast in March 2017, we had no idea about all the work it would entail. And we certainly didn't know about the impact and reach *Truth's Table* would have. We are three Black women who'd never listened to podcasts, and suddenly we were spotlit by *The New York Times* and won Black

Podcasting Awards' 2021 Best Black Religion and Spirituality Podcast award (slight flex).

*Truth's Table* began as a humble and hilarious group chat. We'd talk about politics, memes, funny tweets, church people behaving poorly. Whenever we'd gather together to catch up at conferences and events, we knew this much: There was a void and underappreciation for Black women's voices, *especially* when it came to the religion and spirituality category. Podcasting became a way to get a microphone fast—without dealing with the gatekeepers. Several trusted friends took note, too, and encouraged us to create a podcast together to amplify the faith perspective of Black women.

And so *Truth's Table* was born.

We started with the express purpose of centering the issues, concerns, and care for Black women exclusively while glorifying God through it all. When we say, "This table is built by Black women and for Black women," we mean that literally. Black women are our priority here at *Truth's Table,* and they are the ones who get to have a seat at this table. Everyone else outside of that demographic of Black women are welcome to gather around the table in the standing-room section.

By God's grace, we have remained faithful to that commitment. At the table, we talk about dating, friendship, and disagreement; life with our families; resistance and reparations. Through hearty cackles and cathartic tears, we have poured out our lives over the course of six seasons. And in the same way that we pour out our lives on the show, we've poured out our stories into a book for the very first time.

In the midst of social, political, and religious upheaval—and a pandemic, to boot—we got together in an attempt to stay grounded by harnessing the power of community among Black women. It is an actual power. A bona fide force that even surprised us.

Listen close.

Our cackles, tears, frustrations, dreams, and fears have weaved together our three distinct voices. We are not a monolith. Each of us comes with a social location and hard-wrought interpretive lens.

*Truth's Table* podcast listeners go from learning how to distinguish our voices by accents, cadence, and vernacular to eventually being able to *truly* distinguish our voices by passions, convictions, and burdens. What has glued us together at the table isn't our homogeneity of thought, although our Black Christian female identity takes center stage, but our two fierce devotions. We are devoted to who Brother Malcolm calls the most disrespected person in America, the Black woman. We are devoted to the One who is devoted to us, Jesus Christ.

Read close.

We are raised church girls. We are churchwomen. We each have clergy roots. We each have scars and insights from higher education. We have headaches and heartaches. We each have our stories of becoming grown women. We also have the unique ways we understand and wrestle with the Christian tradition. We even reach different conclusions at times—maybe even more so in this book than you hear on the podcast. As you read our words, our musings on life, love, and liberation, we hope that you hear us each and appreciate your own voice even more along the way.

*Truth's Table* is a show about wordy women. Together and separately, we are all much more than co-hosts of the podcast.

Ekemini is a public theologian, Christina is an educator, Michelle is an organizer. We write speeches, sermons, songs, and prayers. We exist as Black women who live by and because of God's word, in Jesus, who we know as the Word of God: the Word who made all things in the beginning, the Word through whom everything was made.

We all work through words every day, in ministry, in our communities, and in lives that interface speech and action. It made sense to us—and the many listeners who have asked for a book!—to set words to the three most-talked-about themes in the podcast: life, love, and liberation.

In these pages you'll read stories we're sharing for the first time. You'll see our responses to the questions we get asked the most. We get in our wheelhouse of expertise in these chapters: Christina talks about trauma, Michelle gets into worship and activism, and Ekemini delivers the theology. We're talking about skin bleaching. Futuristic Blackness. The Ferguson Uprisings. Black movement. Church hurt. Unforgiveness. Black love. You will know us better by reading the book.

We talk about life with our families. Living as people who love. And stories that have marked our individual and collective freedom journeys.

So, sistas, pull up a chair and have a seat at the table with us!

# PART I

# Life

EKEMINI: Hey, y'all! Welcome to *Truth's Table*. We are mid-wives of culture for grace and truth. I'm Ekemini.

MICHELLE: I'm Michelle.

CHRISTINA: And I'm Christina.

EKEMINI: This table is built by Black women and for Black women. So welcome to the table, sistas! How y'all doin'!?

MICHELLE *(to the tune of "My Life" by Erykah Badu):* Welllllllll, well!

EKEMINI & CHRISTINA: *(\*cackle\* \*cackle\* \*cackle\* \*snort\*)*

CHRISTINA: I'm out here living in these life streets! This grown-up life is for suckas!

EKEMINI: You ain't lyin', C! M, how you doing?

MICHELLE: As Langston Hughes said, "Life for me ain't been no crystal stair."

CHRISTINA: How you doing, E?

EKEMINI: I'm yet holdin' on! But I'm glad to be at the table with y'all. *(In my Prince voice)* Dearly beloved, we're gathered here to get through this thing called life.

# The Audacious Perseverance
# of Colorism

## By Ekemini Uwan

Across cultures, darker people suffer the most. Why?

ANDRÉ 3000

LISTEN, SISTAS! OR BETTER YET, READ. I feel like I have the hardest subjects to write about in this book. I know that's not true. All three of us have difficult topics we discuss on the show and now are unpacking in this book. But still, why do I have to talk about all the hard things?

Truthfully, out of all the chapters assigned to me, this is the one I dreaded writing the most. It's the first chapter I attempted to write, and for a whole week, I stared at my computer screen with a blank Google document staring back at me. But I'm committed to truth-telling, and that includes telling the truth about myself. So it seems appropriate for me to name the source of my dread. There is power in naming it. This is my attempt at harnessing this power in ways that are productive.

I feel some trepidation about this subject because trauma lives here. Colorism is a scourge in our community here in America, on the African continent, and within the African diaspora. As a dark-skinned Black woman, I have been deeply impacted by colorism in innumerable tangible and intangible ways. And because of that, this topic requires a level of vulnerability that is uncomfortable, yet necessary.

Colorism is a complicated subject because of our varied experiences with it. Far too often, this conversation defaults to the oppression Olympics about valid yet anecdotal experiences from our light-skinned sistas at the table who have experienced the painful intrapersonal impact of colorism—bullying, caricatures, and taunts like "light, bright, and damn near white!" that call their Blackness into question. Some may cite these as an exception to disprove the rule. But outliers are just that—outliers. Exceptions do not disprove the rule, because colorism is not merely interpersonal; it is a structural reality.

Here is the rule of colorism: dark-skinned Black people are impacted in more significantly negative ways than light-skinned Black people. As bell hooks says, "There is a particular trauma that visits itself upon dark-skinned Black people that those of us who are lighter can't even name." The data bears this out. Denying this reality results in gaslighting dark-skinned Black people.

To be sure, there is real trauma regarding colorism that many of us have experienced, regardless of where we are on the color spectrum. However, this chapter is not *School Daze*—which is one of my favorite Spike Lee joints—in written form; we are not the "jigaboos" versus the "wannabees." Just in case I'm dating myself with that Black culture reference, allow me to translate: this is not about dark-skinned Black folks versus light-skinned Black folks. Not every dark-skinned Black person hates their complexion, and not every light-skinned person thinks they are better than dark-skinned people.

I'm not interested in causing division, but I'm equally disinterested in denial. The facts are the facts. Colorism maps onto dark-skinned Black people especially in ways that are profoundly traumatic and discriminatory. On this we must agree if we are to uproot it from our minds and souls and dismantle it from our churches, systems, and other Black civic institutions.

How is it that I have been saved for over fifteen years and a member in a variety of different Black churches but have never heard one sermon about colorism? It is in the Bible, and it needs to be addressed within the Black church. We address racism with ease, but when it comes to colorism, mum's the word. Could it be that the fingers rightfully pointed out there toward racists and racist systems suddenly start pointing back at us when it comes to colorism, because we are implicated in this intraracial dynamic? It's not enough to be antiracist; we must also be anticolorists, because both evils are byproducts of white supremacy. And what is colorism but white supremacy persevering?

If you've been sitting at the table with us for some time now, you know I believe in defining terms. We've all encountered colorism—whether to our detriment or benefit, depending on where you are on the color spectrum. But I don't want to assume that the term is understood by all of us.

Black feminist author Alice Walker coined the term "colorism" back in 1983 to describe the intraracial discrimination against people with darker-skinned complexions in preference for people with lighter-skin complexions.[1] Dr. Sarah Webb, professor, researcher, and founder of Colorism Healing, defines colorism in this way: "Colorism is bias, prejudice, discrimination, or inequity based on the relative skin tone, hair texture, and facial features among persons of the same race. Colorism is an international phenomenon with regional and cultural differences. However, the commonality across cultures is that lighter skin is systematically privileged while darker skin is devalued or disadvantaged. Some people affected by colorism may even develop a dislike for their own skin and features."[2] As a consequence of colorism, dark-skinned people experience disparity when it comes to socioeconomic status, income level, healthcare, the criminal justice system, education, housing, jobs, and marriage markets.

Colorism is the offspring of white supremacy, and like its parent, it's global: this phenomenon is at work within African, Asian, Caribbean, and Latine communities as well. Suffice it to say that non-Black people of color grapple with colorism, too. Nevertheless, for the purpose of this chapter, my focus centers on dark-skinned African American and African women's experiences of colorism.

Within the American context, sociologists and historians locate the genesis of colorism in chattel slavery, particularly with its "one-drop rule." Theologically, I posit that colorism predates that horrific time in history. But first, let's explore what this one-drop rule did to us.

According to Dr. Yaba Blay,

In the United States, historically, a Black person has come to be defined as any person with *any* known Black ancestry. Although this definition has been statutorily referred to as the "one Black ancestor rule," the "traceable amount rule," and the "hypodescent rule," it is more popularly known as the "one-drop rule," meaning that one single, solitary drop of Black blood is enough to render a person Black. Said differently, the one-drop rule holds that a person with *any* trace of Black ancestry, however small or (in)visible, *cannot* be considered White. Unless that person has other non-White ancestry they can claim—such as Native American, Asian, etc.—they *must* be considered Black. A method of social order that began almost immediately after the arrival of enslaved Africans in America, the one-drop rule became a legal reality in the state of Virginia in 1705, and by 1910, it was the law of the land in almost all southern U.S. states. At a time when the one-drop rule functioned to protect and preserve White racial purity, Blackness was both a matter of biology and law. One was either Black or White. Period.[3]

This rule animated the period of colonial enslavement. According to economists William Darity, Jr., Darrick Hamilton, and Arthur H. Goldsmith in their journal article "From Dark to Light: Skin Color and Wages Among African-Americans," "During the era of slavery, light-complexioned blacks, often the offspring of white slave owners and enslaved Africans, were given preferential treatment through assignment to housework while darker-skinned blacks were typically assigned to outdoor or hard-labor tasks. Moreover, skin shade played a profound role in the acquisition of social status for black Americans following the abolition of slavery."[4]

Allow me to park here for a moment and say something about chattel slavery. When we talk about colorism in our community, we often reach back to the historical dichotomy between light-skinned enslaved women who worked in the homes of enslavers and dark-skinned enslaved women who worked the fields, because it's a conspicuous historical example of colorism. However, it is important to wrestle with historical tension when recounting this dynamic, for there is an aspect of this history that is not as simple as it is often made out to be.

There is a prevalent and ahistorical narrative, believed by far too many of us, that light-skinned enslaved women who worked in the house had it easier than dark-skinned enslaved women who worked the field. That is categorically false. The work of light-skinned enslaved women was just as grueling—albeit in different ways—because they had closer proximity to their enslaver and his mistress. As such, they lived under the constant threat of sexual assault, as well as emotional and physical abuse. Sistas, slavery was bad all the time, and all the time slavery was bad. We must complicate the narrative and respect the interior lives of our enslaved ancestors and relatives, no matter their relative status within the system.

Post-slavery, colorism continued apace. In the 1890s,[5] educator, civil rights pioneer, and public intellectual Nannie Helen Burroughs was systematically denied a teaching position due to colorism. Kelisha B. Graves, editor of *Nannie Helen Burroughs: A Documentary Portrait of an Early Civil Rights Pioneer, 1900-1959,* writes, "Although Burroughs applied for two positions, as an assistant to the domestic science teacher at M Street and as a typist and stenographer at Tuskegee Institute, neither of these opportunities materialized. It was suggested that her dark skin and lack of pedigree had everything to do with it."[6] Burroughs went on to start her own school, the National Training School for Women and Girls.

Sadly, the Black church was not exempt from such colorist

practices. Kathy Russell-Cole, Midge Wilson, and Ronald E. Hall, authors of *The Color Complex: The Politics of Skin Color in a New Millennium,* write, "Many historical African-American churches . . . had congregations with noticeably lighter skin tones, and were known to actively turn away darker-skinned Blacks. . . . During Reconstruction, Black families interested in joining a congregation—or an individual simply wanting to set foot inside a particular church on Sunday morning—might first be required to pass a paper bag test, a door test, and/or a comb test."[7] Imagine walking up to the church as a visitor and having your arm inserted in a paper bag to see if your skin is lighter than the paper bag. Or visiting another church with its door painted light brown. If you're darker than the door, you're not allowed to worship at that church. And if your kinky hair does not pass through the hair comb at the next church you visit, you're barred from entry. Colorist admission policies were a common practice at historically Black colleges and universities as well. "In 1916, it was estimated that 80 percent of students attending HBCUs were light-skinned and/or of mixed ancestry. A principal mission of an HBCU was to groom the mulatto elite in the genteel mores of the bourgeoisie while delivering a strong traditional liberal arts education. Many academic administrators of these schools considered it a waste of time to educate dark-skinned Negroes for paths of life that would be closed to them."[8]

History is replete with examples of the structural impact of colorism on dark-skinned people, individually and collectively. At face value, you might be tempted to think that because these examples of colorism took place long ago, it's no longer an issue; but colorism persists today.

At this juncture, I offer up my own story of colorism's impact on me. As I mentioned earlier, not every dark-skinned Black woman grew up hating their skin tone. I wish I could say this was my experience, but that is not my testimony; so I'm going to tell the truth and shame the devil.

I am the first-born daughter of Nigerian immigrants, which makes me Nigerian American, second generation here in the United States. It's important to lay out my origin story, because lurking beneath it are the histories of the transatlantic slave trade, colonialism, and Christian imperialism. Slavery because, in terms of ethnicity, I descend from the Ibibio ethnic group, from which upward of 1.2 million[9] Ibibio and Igbo people were stolen during the transatlantic slave trade and brought to the United States, South America, and the Caribbean. Colonialism because "Nigeria" is a colonial name. Christian imperialism because of the forcefulness with which this religion was imposed.

Colorism is a global phenomenon, though it manifests differently across countries. As one who was born in the United States, I've found that colorism maps onto me bilaterally, through both the legacy of American chattel slavery and the legacy of colonialism in Nigeria.

The intensity of one's colorism experience varies regionally in the United States. Nevertheless, from my experience as a Black girl who was born and raised in California, I can say with confidence that California is not safe for a dark-skinned girl, as it is rife with colorism—perhaps it's because it is the home of Hollywood, which is notorious for its colorist practices, including the ways that it traffics colorism and broadcasts it through the media and into our televisions and phones. Maybe it's because of the way California is home to the quintessential "California Girl," idolized by the masses—adults and children alike. For some, this is a woman with blond hair and blue eyes. For others, it's a racially ambiguous woman whom they consider "exotic." Their description, not mine. But either way, as early as I can remember, *this* California girl—who lived in the Bay Area and Los Angeles—hated her dark skin tone. Growing up, I thought I was ugly. To borrow words from Laura Pritchard, an antiracism trainer and former *Truth's Table* guest, I was surrounded by a "wall of whiteness," with the exception of my neighborhood block, which was Black.

But even in Black spaces, the colorism continued to stalk me when playing the dozens (the colorist edition) with neighborhood friends. In this regard I was not innocent, as I returned colorist fire for colorist fire.

"You so Black, cockroaches scatter when you come into the room!" someone would say to my teenage self.

And I would clap back, saying, "*You* so Black, the whites of your eyes glow in the dark!"

I stayed ready to aim colorist jabs at whoever wanted the smoke, because I didn't love myself. And if I didn't love myself, then I damn sure didn't love them, either.


In my home, my family of origin was my base of comparison. My dad was very light-skinned, with light eyes; he resembled James Earl Jones. My youngest sister was light. My mom is medium brown—some would say she was dark-skinned, but to me she had medium-brown skin. And my other sister had about my same skin tone. I often compared and contrasted my skin tone with my dad's and my youngest sister's because they were lighter than me. No one in my immediate family ever made any colorist remarks about my skin tone, nor did anyone in my extended family—but they didn't have to. The bleaching cream on my mother's vanity did all the talking. The implicit message communicated to me was that "darkness is badness."

At our family functions, an aromatic amalgamation of afang soup, jollof rice, and pepper soup came wafting through the front door of my uncle's house. Soukous, dancehall, and highlife music blared through the speakers. The sounds of the continent and the diaspora were the backdrop to the aunties' triumphant entrance into the party. The auntie team wore the finest Nigerian lace, with bright and big head ties, known as *ofong iwot* in Ibibio, that seemed to graze the ceiling. They would bust into parties with their gap-toothed smiles, announcing their arrival. We'd all run up to hug each auntie—or else there'd be wahala. Their outfits were always on point. I mean, they *ate*, y'all! Matching shoes, matching purses, dressed to the nines. They understood the assignment. I learned from the best.

But with some of them, you couldn't unsee their yellow faces—and in some cases, pink faces. The moment I'd reach for a hug, their ebony hands, arms, and knuckles returned my embrace. The contradictory skin tones were clear evidence of habitual skin-bleaching-cream use. Message received.

At African food stores, you can get a bag of farina and Caro White. At Black beauty-supply stores all over this country, you can get a pack of Kanekalon braiding hair and Nadinola skin-bleaching cream. Another message received. Nadinola would eventually become my bleaching cream of choice, as it was already in my home because my mother used it as a body lotion. Message received—and applied.

Among the African and Caribbean immigrants I know, skin-bleaching cream in the household is a given. This is a vestige of colonialism. Even now, according to the *International Business Times*, "75% of the population in Nigeria, 52–67% of the Senegalese population, 59% Togo, 25% Mali and 35% of South African women use skin-lightening products."[10]

And according to Kathy Russell, Midge Wilson, and Ronald E. Hall, America is no better: "Currently, America's skin-bleaching market is estimated to be worth over $5.6 billion."[11] Listen. African Americans are bleaching their skin, too. Sistas, it's possible that someone you know is bleaching.

During my freshman year of high school, my self-loathing over my dark skin tone reached its peak as I saw that my light-skinned friends were getting favor and attention while I was ignored, passed over and invisible. So I began to bleach my skin, using Nadinola bleaching cream because it was at home. Their advertisement from the decades prior reads: "The nicest things happen to girls with light, bright complexions. Has your phone quit ringing lately? Perhaps your complexion is to blame. Is it dark, dull and unattractive? Then for goodness sake *do* something about it."

In my colonized adolescent mind, I detected no lies in that ad. I wanted the "nice things" that were happening for my light-skinned friends to happen for me, too, so I started bleaching

my skin. In the words of Fela Kuti, from his infamous song about skin bleaching among Nigerians, I caught "Yellow Fever."

I was chasing lightness in a bottle of bleach. Or was I chasing whiteness?

That's a hard question to answer. Truthfully speaking, when I was bleaching my skin, I honestly didn't want to be white—that wasn't my goal. But I wanted the privileges of *lightness* that the bleaching cream dangled in front of me.

And so, every day, I slathered my face with this cream. Every morning and night, after washing my face, I'd use it as a moisturizer. But at night I'd add a concentrated dab to the darker spots and scars. This went on for around two years. In that time, my skin was lightening significantly. But since I was only applying it to my face, the rest of my body was still dark—and after a while, I began to look like a science experiment gone wrong. Which is to say that I started to look like my aunties. Remember, I learned from the best.

But the skin on my face was not only lightening; it was getting thinner. It would burn when I applied the bleach. On the one hand, I thought I was becoming prettier because my face was lighter. But on the other, I began to realize I was physically harming myself.

I was hustling backwards.

At the time, I didn't know what permanent damage this cream could do, but the burning and thinning was enough to concern me. I concluded that no amount of desirability was worth the cost.

In the words of De La Soul, the stakes is high.

So, after experiencing these persistent side effects from my habitual skin bleaching, I stopped.

What I didn't know back then was that I was harming not only my face but my entire body with these toxins, as there are serious health risks associated with skin-lightening products. Using them can lead to liver and kidney failure or to hyperpigmentation—dark skin patches forming on the area where the product is used. There is also a risk of skin cancer, because the melanin synthesis that protects the skin against ultraviolet radiation is inhibited by hydroquinone. I shudder to think how poisonous this bleaching cream is—the same cream I willingly absorbed, day and night.

When I reflect on this time with a critical analysis, I realize that this white supremacy in a bottle had not only penetrated my skin but my mind and soul as well.

When I recount this memory, I don't condemn my younger self for doing this. I see it less as a choice I made and more an inevitability: I was hard-pressed on every side—from the ubiquity of bleaching creams in West African grocery stores, to the aunts and uncles bleaching their skin, to the United States where the love interest in music videos was always a light-skinned woman.

One thing was clear about that time: I wasn't loving myself. It would be years until I learned to truly love myself, and in turn, love my neighbor as well. But at the time, the best I could do was to simply not harm myself in this way.

I wish I could say that it was the church that led me to this epiphany, but there were no answers in my white church. Several years later, when I got saved in the Black church and became a true Christian, there were no answers there, either. So I had to find a way to love myself fiercely, because back then, darkness was synonymous with ugliness.

Sometime after I stopped the bleaching, I began to notice more dark-skinned women in movies and music. I realized that these women didn't need to change their darkness to be celebrated. The more I saw darkness celebrated, the more I became intentional about looking for images and representations of dark-skinned women, like the supermodels Naomi Campbell and Iman, who had the industry on lock in the nineties. I started listening to music that affirmed my Blackness. Mary J. Blige's *My Life*. Sounds of Blackness. Soul II Soul. Arrested Development. *Baduizm* by Erykah Badu. *The Miseducation of Lauryn Hill*. I watched *Sister Act 2*, in which Lauryn Hill starred, dark and beautiful. I played this movie like it was my duty. I was dogmatic about this regimen, and I knew I had to be in order to uproot the internalized white supremacy. Over the years, it took a lot of prayer, writing daily affirmations, and reciting those affirmations over myself. But eventually, in my mid to late twenties, I began to love myself fully, without a tinge of self-loathing.

Thankfully, by then my dark, melanin-rich skin tone had returned, and I came home to myself for the first time in my life.

Colorism, like every other sin, doesn't remit with time. The systemic oppression of dark-skinned people solely based on their skin tone is not only a historical reality but a present one, too. We see it in movement spaces and in the workplace. Conversations about colorism often live in the realm of the interpersonal and boil down to desirability politics. As you read my story, you saw those dynamics in play.

However, if those are the only aspects raised when talking about colorism, the conversation is reductive, because colorism is also a structural issue. Some of the historical examples I shared make this apparent. Nevertheless, there are modern examples and data that illustrate the many ways colorism impacts dark-skinned people on a structural level.

In "Skin Color Differences in Stratification Outcomes," sociologist Eona Harrison writes, "Numerous empirical studies reveal the greater social and economic achievements attained by lighter-skinned Blacks. It has been invariably found that lighter skin toned individuals have higher earnings, education, occupational prestige, and experience better marriage markets when compared to darker individuals of the same ethnicity."[12] Additionally, Harrison's own study found that "Light-skinned Blacks, on average, earned $6,800 more than their dark-skinned counterparts." Marital status did not change the income disparity.

Color stratification persists in the educational system. Villanova researchers found that "Black girls with the darkest skin tones were three times more likely to be suspended than Black girls with the lightest skin."[13]

And in the criminal justice system, colorism plays a significant role. *The Root* published an article noting that "Villanova
researchers studied more than 12,000 cases of African-
American women imprisoned in North Carolina and found
that women with lighter skin tones received more lenient sentences and served less time than women with darker skin tones.
The researchers found that light-skinned women were sen-
tenced to approximately 12 percent less time behind bars than
their darker-skinned counterparts."[14] Colorism is categorically
punitive to those of us with dark skin tones.

Here is as good a place as any to say that non-Black people
also perpetuate colorism at structural and interpersonal levels.
At *Truth's Table* we have experienced this on an interpersonal
level from people in the "standing-room section" (our non-
Black women listeners). We've seen the DMs, emails, and conversations from people who think Christina is warmer and
kinder because she is light, and peg me as mean and cold because I'm dark. Of course, they don't admit this explicitly, but
the message is heard loud and clear at the table.

I would be remiss if I did not talk about the ways that we see
colorism presently operating in Hollywood. Take Vanessa Bell
Calloway, for example, who played Imani in the cult-classic
movie *Coming to America*. During a press tour for the sequel,
*Coming 2 America*, Calloway revealed that colorism foreclosed
her opportunity to play Lisa, who was Eddie Murphy's light-
skinned love interest in the movie.[15] "When you have white
people hiring Black people in movies, sometimes a certain look
is wanted," Calloway told Page Six. "I just wasn't light enough,
even though Eddie had the final say on who played Lisa. [But]

I didn't want the part of Imani, I wanted to be Lisa—I had read the script and I wanted the bigger role." Examples like this abound.

And in 2020, around the time *Lovecraft Country* debuted on HBO, Amber J. Phillips, a filmmaker, caught wind of a colorist incident that went down on set and broke down the analysis on Instagram. Phillips shared a video taken by the actor Kelli Amirah, who played an extra on the show. Amirah took to TikTok to share what she noticed as she sat in her hair-and-makeup chair.

"I'm just, like, on my phone reading a book, texting my friends, not really fully paying attention . . ." Amirah starts, "as I notice that the makeup's getting a little bit darker. I remember texting my friends and saying, 'What should I do? Should I say something?' I had no idea they were going to do this to me beforehand. And if I knew beforehand, I would not have accepted this job. Who thought this was a good idea?" she asked in what would become a viral video.

Amirah adds that she wishes she would have said something, wishes she would have taken a stand. But in the moment, she thought she should just be professional. "I didn't say anything, and I just kind of let it continue," she says of the incident. "Even like, down to the point of painting my hands to match, because I'm in a wedding photo and I'm wearing a wedding ring. It was a very conflicting, uncomfortable kind of experience to be in."

Wanna know something else? The whole role was for a *wedding photo*. A framed wedding photo on a mantel at Ms. Osberta's house. In *Lovecraft Country*, this photo served as a prop. Ms. Osberta tells Tic, the main character of the show, over dinner that she was married to her husband for thirty years—and points to the old wedding photograph. Kelli Amirah was cast as young Ms. Osberta in the wedding photo.

See how colorism works? Instead of casting a dark-skinned actor for this role, the casting team deliberately chose to erase the presence of a dark-skinned person on set. That this role of a dark-skinned Black woman in a black-and-white photo framed in the *background* of a scene was cast with a light-skinned woman who was painted in blackface for this role makes this erasure all the more glaring and disturbing.

Because blackface on a Black face is still blackface.


In the prophetic words of Nannie Helen Burroughs, "There is no denying it, Negroes have colorphobia. Some Negro men have it. Some Negro women have it. Whole families have it, and somebody tells us some Negro churches have it. Saviour, keep us from those churches, please. Some social circles have it, and so the disease is spreading from men to women, from women to families, from families to churches and from churches to social circles. The idea of Negroes setting up a color standard is preposterous."[16]

Indeed, it is preposterous. What then shall we say to all these things? Color stratification, hierarchy, self-hatred, systemic inequities, and the white supremacy that animates all of the above. Does the Bible have anything to say about colorism, or is it silent on this issue?

I posit that it is not silent. If you all recall, when I began this chapter, I said that, contrary to what the sociologist and economist I cited posited, colorism began long before chattel slavery and colonialism. In fact, it has its origins in Genesis. In order for us to chart a way forward, we have to go back to Eden.

## GENESIS 1

So, in Genesis 1, God created the heavens and the earth and filled the earth with birds and sea creatures, a host of beasts, and livestock. Then we come to verse 26, which reads, "Then God said, 'Let us make man in our image, after our likeness. And let them have dominion over the fish of the sea and over the birds of the heavens and over the livestock and over all the earth and over every creeping thing that creeps on the earth.'"

Notice that there is a marked distinction here. Man is made in God's image and likeness. The animals are not, the plants are not, the fish are not, the creeping things are not. Only human beings are made in the image of God. Not only that, God gave them dominion over everything that was made.

So even before sin entered the world, we see a clear hierarchy that is set forth by God. I call this a "Godward hierarchy," because all human beings are uniquely set apart and placed above the fish, vegetation, beasts of the field, etc. We are made in the image and likeness of God, and were given dominion over all that was made. Adam even named the living creatures, according to Genesis 2:18–21, which confirms the dominion and Godward hierarchy in this context. We were given dominion over every living thing that moves on the earth *except* for one another. We were not made to dominate one another.

One mo' 'gain.

We were not made to dominate one another.

## GENESIS 3

But something happened in Genesis 3: the serpent deceived Eve, and she and Adam sinned against God by eating of the fruit of the tree of the knowledge of good and evil. We see that part of the curse was pronounced upon Eve in Genesis 3:16, which says, "I will surely multiply your pain in childbearing; in pain you shall bring forth children. Your desire shall be for your husband, and he shall rule over you."

The Godward hierarchy that God set forth in Genesis 1–2 has been wholly corrupted in this post-Fall context, due to the entrance of sin. As a consequence of Adam and Eve's sin, *sinful hierarchy* has come in its stead, resulting in domination of some image-bearers over others and enmity between parties—in this case, Adam and Eve.

So, what does this have to do with colorism? Well, colorism, like all sin, has its roots in the Fall, and it is precisely sinful hierarchy that keeps colorism intact. I recognize that it is anachronistic to import a modern category like colorism into the Bible.

The Bible predates white supremacy. Period.

In fact, it predates the construct of whiteness and race. And as we know, there aren't any white people in the Bible. All of which were the precursors to colorism in the United States.

Nevertheless, the social dynamics that underlie colorism are certainly in the Bible, like the way one is socially perceived and identified by phenotype, and how that social perception is internalized and acted upon to one's own advantage or disadvantage.

Consider Moses, who was born a Hebrew—the very people who were enslaved by the Egyptians—yet he was raised as the son of Pharaoh's daughter. According to Exodus 2:19, he was socially perceived as an Egyptian. Yet when Moses came of age, he relinquished his privilege, embraced his ethnic identity as a Hebrew, and chose to be mistreated and oppressed along with his kinsmen according to the flesh (Heb. 11:24, 25). Thereby, he embraced the image of God as it was reflected in his ethnic identity, along with its attendant sufferings. Moses could not bear to see his people—fellow image-bearers—subjugated under the weight of an unjust system. Called by God (Exod. 3), he liberated his people through confrontation and protest, demanding that Pharaoh let his people go.

Similarly, Esther had to choose whether or not to continue concealing her Jewish ethnic identity so that she could reap the spoils of the empire or forsake it all to keep her people alive by identifying with them in every respect. Esther chose the latter.

In Song of Solomon 1:5–6, we meet a young woman, whom I affectionately call "Sista Mahogany," who says,

> I am very dark, but lovely,
> O daughters of Jerusalem,
> like the tents of Kedar,
> like the curtains of Solomon.
> Do not gaze at me because I am dark,
> because the sun has looked upon me.

Here we see that Sista Mahogany forbids her lover to look at her because she is dark. The "but" in verse 5 is up for some translation debate, as it could also be rendered "I am very dark and lovely," acting as a defense for her dark skin. Nevertheless, both translations confirm the negative connotations that accompany people with dark skin when Sista Mahogany tells her lover explicitly not to even look at her because she is dark.

Now, this is *descriptive*, in that this scripture describes how Sista Mahogany *perceives herself*. It is not *prescriptive*, meaning that this passage of the Bible is not setting a colorist standard that ascribes goodness to light skin and badness to dark skin. That is not what is happening here—but I love that the Bible reveals the internal and external battles that we face as human beings in this fallen world.

For most of my life, I identified with Sista Mahogany and wrestled with my dark hue. I'm sure some of my sistas at the table have, too. Sometimes we need to know that we are not alone in this. For me, seeing someone in the Bible articulate the dynamics that underlie colorism was pivotal while I was doing the work of accepting, embracing, and loving my embodied Blackness.

One of the critical ways that the Black church can begin to deal with colorism is to confess its own complicity, whether by commission or omission. Repent and repair the damage that's been done. Then the church can begin to tackle this issue, from the pulpit first and then through discipleship curriculum. The Black church can speak, because God has spoken through His Word and through His Son, Jesus Christ. Colorism was nailed to the cross along with white supremacy and every other sin that plagues us.

But we live in the tension of the "already" finished work of Christ on the cross and the "not yet" expectation of the complete arrival of God's Kingdom, where all sin—including colorism and white supremacy—has no power and is cast into the pit of hell. White supremacy and colorism will both bow their knees to King Jesus.

Know that.

Until then, the church must do the Spirit-empowered work of uprooting this stronghold of colorism and self-hatred from the minds and hearts of Black people. If we don't love ourselves, we can't love our neighbor well, and that is the second-greatest commandment Jesus gave us. This, too, is spiritual warfare.

Not only is colorism a spiritual stronghold, it is a sociological issue that is structural in nature. Because this is the case, the church is not exempt.

It's high time for our people, our churches, and our institutions to divest from this white-supremacist jig, because the joke is on us; and sistas, ain't nothing funny about colorism.

# Protest as Spiritual Practice

## By Michelle Higgins

I WAS BORN ON A SATURDAY in July, at noon, in St. Louis City Hospital. The place operated like a segregated hospital at the time of my birth, because very little structural or policy change on segregation had ever been pursued in my hometown.

My parents and my aunt, who was my mom's nurse, say that I "came without a sound," though I opened my eyes right away. For minutes, I refused to cry. Instead, I looked around the room. When another delivery nurse handed me to my mother, she said, "She's been here before."

> she's half-notes shattered
> without rhythm / no tune
> sing her sighs
> sing the song of her possibilities
> sing a righteous gospel
> let her be born

let her be born
& handled warmly

NTOZAKE SHANGE, *for colored girls who have*
*considered suicide when the rainbow is enuf*

## PART 1: PROTEST IN THE FERGUSON UPRISINGS

St. Louis in the summer is something else. The season is thick with heat, to the point that you can't remember what cool weather feels like. We make the most of it, with festivals and barbeques and all that jazz.

But the city also becomes haunted in the summers.

In 1917 during the month of July, my city faced a bloodbath when a mob of white men murdered hundreds of African Americans. This became known as the lynching season—but not for long. St. Louis police quickly thereafter rebranded this massacre as "riot season," which they used as an excuse to deputize their finest and stretch out lynching season across the years. And years. And years.

Michael Brown, Jr., was murdered on Saturday, August 9, in 2014, at noon, by police officer Darren Wilson in Ferguson, Missouri. After Officer Wilson killed the unarmed young man, Michael Brown, Jr., was left on the ground, uncovered, for four hours. Wilson, like so many other police officers, was not charged for this murder.

It happened on a residential street, between two buildings of an apartment complex from which the street was highly visible. People of all ages witnessed the event, traumatized.

About nine miles away, on the same day, I was leading a worship conference centered on multiethnic artistic inclusivity and representation. At the conference, I was excited by the global styles and ethnicities represented. There was a great deal of talk about racial reconciliation, but there were no extensive discussions of racial justice. I didn't know that the latter was necessary. Justice was taught as an aspect of Christian ministry that happened in conversation with charity. For instance, I was discipled to feel validated by providing food rations to the unhoused, rent and utilities assistance to working class and poor people. In defense of these well-meaning missions, this support was just that: support—it wasn't a cover-up for proselytizing. But at the time, I did not realize that these missions were void of public justice. Nor did I realize that public justice should factor into the gospel we preached. I sensed that our urban missions were accompanied by an increasingly "colorblind," anti-Black theology of suffering—but I ignored these suspicions. I knew in part but had not fully appreciated the truth that reconciliation was different from justice.

I was nine miles away from Ferguson that day, but I was light-years away from the theological implications of what was taking place.

In many ways, the Ferguson Uprisings—what Black movement would eventually name the events that took place over the course of roughly sixteen months following the murder of Michael Brown, Jr.—is my story of being born again, again.

At every turn of protest, I saw the protective shadow of Black liberation history holding hands with the Afro-future of thriving that my people deserved. All the Black women in us have been here before.

By the time I got home from the worship-and-inclusion event, I was hearing from people around the city that the police killed a teenager in Ferguson, on Canfield Drive, near the apartments where my grandpa lived. On Sunday night, August 10, I drove to Ferguson to check on Grandpa. I spoke with him and a few of his neighbors before I went to a candlelight vigil. During the vigil, police took advantage of the rage and mourning of residents and supporters. The Ferguson Police Department deliberately escalated an already tense atmosphere, arrested dozens of people at random, and threatened many more with mass arrest.

I stayed on the street until almost dawn.

By early morning of August 11, the Ferguson Uprisings had begun.

Within days, I grew accustomed to fearing for my life and carrying an undying rage about the disenfranchisement of Black people that brought about death. I was detained by police seventeen times. I was ticketed for jaywalking. Protesters set up makeshift medic stations to tend all the wounds possible. Pepper spray, rubber bullets, and Mace brought personal physical pain, which hardly compared to the stinging sight of armored vehicles and the fog of tear gas in a small town where my grandfather lived, in a retirement community a few blocks from the apartment complex where Mike Brown, Jr.'s blood was crying out from the ground.

This was the same town where I'd visit family members when I was little, the same town where my parents preached at churches up the street from where military-grade weapons and vehicles were now being used to threaten and attack Black people. I remembered visiting with my grandmother before she passed away, in the same rooms where I now tried to clear the tear gas smoke that was preventing my grandpa's rest. It was bizarre to witness and experience, but never was I surprised by the truth: police were attacking the very municipalities that they were paid to protect. That reality was never lost on me, and so it never had to occur to me. Each time I was harassed by a police officer in Ferguson, I remembered the way my family taught me to carry myself around police: be polite but get out quick. Whenever we drove through Ferguson and various St. Louis counties, my dad would slow his speed to a crawl, knowing that Ferguson police would pull us over for any small thing.

For every slow drive on that road through Ferguson, I spent a slow night into morning holding space on that road, joining with protesters demanding an end to police terror.

One night I thought to myself, My people were right. I have been here before.

Every day I went up to Ferguson, I'd spend time on West Florissant, the main road through the town. I thought about my family and my faith community. I thought about the church I worked with, and the ways that they were speaking about the uprisings. I was working in spaces that are squarely evangelical. And I deeply grieved the way many people of faith referred to the murder of Michael Brown as an unfortunate incident.

At that time, I had adopted the label "evangelical" for myself. So, like a good African American evangelical, I hesitated to tell my church family that I was supportive of the uprisings. I selfishly dreaded the thought of speaking to anyone about my reasons for being present in the streets. I felt that I had been through this before, two years before, after Trayvon Martin was murdered. I was so undone and deflated by previous discussions concerning the right of any citizen to stalk and kill someone that I kept my full opinions to myself when I was speaking to church folks. I thought it would save me the headache of arguing, or the frustration of being talked about but not listened to.

Over time I realized that I had to repent of that attitude.

Because the more I trained and engaged with activists who were being radicalized in the traditions of organizing for Black power, the more I read the words and work of Black people of faith. And in my learning I was confronted with and convinced of the dangers of complicity. When I read and reread histories of the Civil Rights Movement, I was reminded of the determined resistance that was required of my own ancestors in the faith who shared my cultural heritage.

The church was not new to the freedom struggle.

We had been here before.


On Wednesday, October 8, 2014, around 8 P.M., a teenager named Vonderrit Myers, Jr., was murdered by an off-duty police officer in the Shaw neighborhood of St. Louis. Vonderrit and his cousins were stalked by officer Jason Flanery through the Southside neighborhood to a grocery and convenience store called Shaw Market on the corner of Shaw Boulevard and Klemm Street. Flanery was off duty that evening, working a second job as a security guard for a wealthy area of the ethnically and economically diverse Shaw neighborhood.

This happened five blocks from the church where I was working at the time.

Word went out through Twitter and organizers' group chats. Over the next few days, hundreds of protesters held space at the place where Vonderrit was killed. Police arrived like an army, surrounding us. I watched the neighborhood where I worked and worshipped become haunted with the ghosts of police-state violence and legalized erasure of Black people. From the fires of Ferguson in the north to the fog in Shaw on the Southside, there were now two battlefronts in the St. Louis area. The corridors between them were occupied by militarized police forces, moving in small and large waves, mostly along roads in Black neighborhoods, which had become sites for random checkpoints and targeted arrests. Activists were disappearing, and police had full immunity from accountability for their own oath to serve and protect. St. Louis was the latest city to once again expose the reality of a police state.

In 1989, Congress granted the Pentagon temporary authority to give local police departments military equipment that was no longer being used. In 1996, Congress made that temporary authority permanent.[1]

Black erasure is not public safety. Yet in most cities, the public safety department is filled with racist policies sanctioning "hotspot" policing resulting in unconstitutional debtors' imprisonment. For example, in St. Louis, when police arrest people who cannot afford bail, they are sent to the St. Louis Medium Security Institution (also called the Workhouse) to await a hearing behind bars, without a court date, for sometimes up-ward of eighteen months.

This is as much a psychological attack as it is physical torture.

As daily protests and standoffs with police were waged like war through late summer, into fall and then winter, mass meetings were held regularly at one of the churches that opened their building to organizers leading training sessions in Ferguson. At each meeting, lead organizers would invite and encourage par-ticipants to join an organization, in a way that reminded me of an invitation to join the church at the end of a worship service. A few hundred people filled the sanctuary—many from the St. Louis region, but also plenty of folks who had relocated or were in town to write about the uprisings. Some were there to honor or dishonor the place where Michael Brown, Jr., was murdered. Some were government agents, others were undercover police. At the time, I was serving as worship director for a PCA (Pres-byterian Church in America) congregation, and I was one of about twelve people from an evangelical worship tradition. Out of that group, four of us followed the invitation to receive train-ing in the traditions of Bayard Rustin of the SCLC (Southern Christian Leadership Council) and Ella Baker of SNCC (Stu-dent Nonviolent Coordinating Committee).

That small group began to meet together and developed a bridging curriculum for people in our church communities who were on some spectrum of interested-to-unsure. We realized that some of our church family were not simply "unable to at-tend" mass meetings in Ferguson. They did not want to attend.

They were afraid that the movement for Black liberation was not part of God's Kingdom work.

The question that many fellow Christians asked us was: Is it biblical to protest?

We began to develop our apologia of protest and the fight for public justice as the continuing story of biblical activism. From this group, who met weekly to pray and share soup (we weren't wealthy by any stretch), the organization Faith for Justice was founded.

The central purpose for our service in the movement was to show God's people that Christian ministry included Black movement, and that the movement for Black lives was a part of the mission of God.


I still hear the Spirit saying, "I've been here before, too. Before you."

In protest I experience a spiritual connection, a living and dynamic presence of both worship and warfare.

I feel myself found, in a place I recognized as a home I had been searching for, even though it was a place I had not been before.

Through the witness and work of Black women on the front lines of Ferguson, we heard the Holy Spirit tell the world to move, and we moved. For the core group of Christians and Muslims who served as Faith for Justice, we went wherever we saw the need for support. We stood outside jails to bail out community members and protesters who had been targeted by police then required to pay inordinate sums for bail. We stood

in front of police stations and courthouses where unconstitutional and inhumane treatment was happening within the halls
of so-called justice. Our neighbors were refused medical care
just because they were in jail. Their families were not permitted
to hear updates on their conditions. Court dates were not being
assigned to people who had been in jail for months and had yet
to see a judge.

We served the mission of the movement by agreeing with
God that humans are born with dignity. And wherever we went,
we heard the Spirit say, "I have come ahead of you, and I have
put my spirit in you, so that you will not be shaken, you will
hold this ground and raise your voice for the glory of God and
the liberation of God's children."

Protesters were a threat to the police and the systems of local
government, so we were targeted on every possible level. At
least three Ferguson protesters disappeared over the course of
the uprisings, their bodies later found in suspicious circum-
stances. Others passed away from health issues that were associated with stress and trauma. We continue to speak their names
as we pursue transformative change.

As I write these words for you, over eighty anti-protest bills
are being presented in state legislatures around the United
States. Considering the constant use of law to attempt to stifle
freedom movements, I find myself frustrated and enraged, but
unsurprised and undeterred.

The work is never done, but Black liberation history—
whether ancient or recent!—reminds us that so much of the
journey is leading us through places that God's spirit has already come to before.

## PART 2: PROTEST IN BLACK
## CHRISTIAN TRADITION

If we were in person, dear reader, I would invite you into the call and response tradition of the Black church: look at your neighbor and say, "Neighbor! We've been here before." Protest is not new for Black people of faith.

One of the largest Black denominations was born from protest. Rev. Richard Allen began preaching at the predominantly white St. George's Methodist Episcopal Church in Philadelphia, which had welcomed him as a member. His preaching became so popular that church attendance began to skyrocket. Soon, though, church leaders decided to force all the Black people who were coming to hear him to sit in the balcony, giving the best seats in the house to the whites. In what was basically a walkout, Reverend Allen opened the first African Methodist Episcopal church, called Mother Bethel, so that his people would have a place to worship in peace.

This story of the Black church is a continuation of a long history of building safe places for Black people to be themselves without explaining themselves. For many, these places were the hush harbors that were built "for us by us."

Hush harbors were gathering places for enslaved people to meet and worship without the gaze of white oppressors who claimed ownership of plantations and the Black people forced to work them. They would gather away from the main plantation house, having shared the exact location with friends and family in a coded song, chant, or variation on a common phrase. Some historians have recorded testimony of enslaved people setting up branches as archways to make the space feel like a church in the middle of a forest or a field. This grounding, ancestral activity is still traceable in the foundations of the Black worship space. Congo Square in New Orleans, altars and shrines set apart in fields that Black families purchased. Gardens and cemeteries attached to church houses. Kneeler benches at a bedside. Set-apart spaces where the Spirit was honored as the power of the congregation.

As long as the United States participated in legalized slavery, the traditions of Black worshippers taken together formed a special, set-apart, sacred space that brought spirit, song, and sustenance to the freedom movement. Protest was sustained by a diverse network of faith-rooted institutions and individuals who supported the liberation and humanizing of Black people. Abolitionists in the eighteenth and nineteenth centuries were constantly combatting the biblical argument for slavery, both by outright confrontation and public protest and by subversive tactics, leveraging, and protest by other means.

In many ways, the Black church was the center of the mid-century Civil Rights Movement. Widespread political education, shared inspiration for strategy and resistance practices, direct-action training, and staging for protests all occurred within the walls of Black churches. Even the early movement leaders were ministers and faith-rooted organizers: Fannie Lou Hamer. Ralph Abernathy. Medgar Evers. Pauli Murray.

Even today, movement organizers stay rooted in faith. Since 2016, Black Voters Matter has been one of the most effective Black political power organizations in the South. Co-founder LaTosha Brown is a Christian woman who leads an inclusive organization powered mostly by Black women. The Highlander

Research and Education Center, where many SCLC leaders received training, is also the space where current faith leaders connect with movement organizations and receive training for various forms of resistance to racial injustice. Faith is not foreign to protest people.

We have been here before.

We have everything we need to build a place where we can be ourselves without explaining ourselves. And that place should be bigger than a house of worship; it should be everywhere that God lives. That is the end of our protest and demand. It is the reason for our petition and our proclaiming. It's the reason we demand repentance and the reason we resist any powers that refuse the practice.

## PART 3: PROTEST AND THE PEOPLE OF GOD

When I realized the Holy Spirit was calling me into the movement for Black liberation, I sought the wisdom of God in every way. I prayed and fasted. I talked to mentors, trusted teachers, and friends who had been involved in movement for justice and change. I read the words of Jesus, and I read many Bible stories. Rather, I read the story of the Bible anew. Years before, when I was in seminary, I was trained to connect the activities of God to a story of covenants. That story became more clear to me when I read these covenants as God's actions for the liberation of God's creation. God's interactions with nature and humanity in the beginning are all through a covenant of Creation. God's promise in Noah's story is a covenant not to destroy the world but to renew it. When I think of the different promises of God that are revealed in covenants to God's people, I see a divine attribute of resistance to the common definition of power. The Lord made a covenant with David that his offspring would never be without mercy. Even though God promised to both protect and correct David's line, God made it plain that even in the midst of future failures, "my mercy shall not depart from your seed" (2 Sam. 7:15).

God promises power to stand up to oppression no matter what oppressors do. And this is just as strong as God's promise of presence and peace to go before us and abide with us through all that we endure.

At the intersection of God's command to "be still and watch the Lord deliver" and the righteous movement of shouting down walls of oppression and violence is a spiritual practice of protesting the power structures of our day.

This is exactly what Jesus showed up to do, and exactly what Jesus gave us the power to do in the Lord's name.


The more I participated in protest, the more I sensed my need for spiritual practice as preparation for a very specific type of spiritual warfare associated with it. Christians from evangelical backgrounds often asked about how my piety was supported by protesting. As I reviewed God's covenant faithfulness in the story of scripture, I also recognized a boldness that God's people have inherited directly from our heavenly parentage. God is not only our Creator and Redeemer; God is also the power behind our worth and our work, because we are made to be stewards of God's image and witnesses of God's power and love. Each of us is a beneficiary of the righteous and disruptive attributes of God.

In fact, throughout the story of the Bible, we see divine direct action through protest in the forms of proclaiming, petition, repentance, and renewal.

> In the beginning, God created heaven and earth. And the earth was without form, and there was a great void.
>
> GENESIS 1:1–2 (My own direct translation.
> Gotta use those Ancient Hebrew
> classes for something!)

The very first act of the Creator God in the history of time was a disruption of formlessness. By calling forth light in the midst of darkness, God protested the darkness and chaos that were the identifying features of the earth's void. God changed and set the shape of the earth. The Spirit moved over the waters that soon began to teem with life. God filled the earth with life and light. It looked completely different than it was described in Genesis 1:1–2. God changed the face of the place where humanity would live.

Genesis 1–3 shows us that the origin story of people is connected intricately with the divine. God did not merely provide peace, flourishing, and structure in the midst of chaos; God placed a picture of himself on the planet.

Humans were made in the image of God, and the fullness of the gospel story is that God indwells humans. The creation story tells us that we were made to have agency over all the things God made. The testimony of creation is that an all-powerful God willed a void to be filled with immense creativity. Then God gave the whole world into the hands and imaginations, the wills and the responsibilities, of a created thing. A group of God's creations that would make or break the earth by trying to co-create in the same way the Creator did.

In movement meetings, I witnessed and learned a creativity that I attribute to this same participation with the divine. I learned the saying "Low ego means high impact." This encourages humility and humanity. Malcolm X once wrote, "Don't be in a hurry to condemn because someone doesn't do what you do or think as you think, or as fast. There was a time when you didn't know what you know today."

And it is true that we also did not bring ourselves to where we are today. Jesus taught, "You are reaping what you did not sow." By proclaiming the humility of humanity in the story of our origins, God's creation plan planted the importance of protest long before time would know its own need for the same. It is a protest that proclaims the same virtue as the movement's call: low ego, high impact.

Creator God protested humanity's own overblown sense of grandeur by showing that even the God who made all things knows how to collaborate and share visions.

For the people of God, no person, no system, no idea, and no regime can claim authority over the identity and value of anything created. Once God has proclaimed something good—or exceedingly good—we must call it worthy.

The Birth of Jesus: Mary's Song of Praise
My soul magnifies the Lord,

and my spirit rejoices in God my Savior,
for he has looked with favor on the lowliness of
    his servant.
Surely, from now on, all generations will call me
    blessed;
for the Mighty One has done great things for me,
and holy is his name.
His mercy is for those who fear him
from generation to generation.
He has shown strength with his arm;
he has scattered the proud in the thoughts of their
    hearts.
He has brought down the powerful from their
    thrones
and lifted up the lowly;
he has filled the hungry with good things
and sent the rich away empty.
He has helped his servant Israel
in remembrance of his mercy,
according to the promise he made to our ancestors,
to Abraham and to his descendants forever.

Luke 1:46–55

In the same way that God created the world out of chaos, God sent Jesus into the world to rescue humans from the chaos we created. In creation, God proclaimed that humans were instilled with value; in the story of Jesus's redeeming work, God was reclaiming the dignity humans had stolen from one another. Between these two forces, Mary's is a story that strikes as most unusual. Were one to judge from a position of privilege, she would be an unlikely candidate for mother of God. But in God's economy of human value, showing favor to Mary is the righteous way to redeem humanity—and all creation—from the systemic corruption that hinders low ego, and thus prevents high impact.

This systemic corruption has plagued our world almost since it began. In scripture, from the exodus through the exile, the story of God's people progressed through resistance to the powers of their day.

In the book of Exodus, Egyptian midwives led by Shiphrah and Puah were commanded by Pharaoh to kill Hebrew children born male. But they refused. They marked their objection by recognizing two important things: one, they knew that they were needed in the positions they were serving in; and two, they knew that subversive protest would be the only way. That is, they knew they would have to lie to Pharaoh about what they were doing; they knew that their protest could not be overt or out loud.

By doing and believing what they knew to be right, not what the system forced upon them, these two midwives lived into their true vocation. When they protested injustice, children were saved, futures were built, and a baby who would grow into a most honored prophet would be born. Their protest reclaimed their purpose.

Shiphrah and Puah's resistance has been a lesson for protesting ever since their story first appeared in the Old Testament.

This is the earliest Bible story of God bringing a deliverer into the world. And God was not finished there.

When the Lord stepped into history again to deliver God's people from oppression, another woman of humble background was an integral part of the picture. Theologians often discuss the humble, willing participation of Mary in the gospel story as a picture of redeeming Eve's glory, which was lost when she made the historic decision to eat from the forbidden tree. But I see the *boldness* of Mary as a *reclaiming* of the glory that Eve was created with. I see Mary's *meekness* as a protest of the presumption that strength is egocentric. And I see Mary's prophetic worship as a reclaiming of meekness as boldness. God blesses Mary's meekness with a boldness as strong as the Holy Ghost that has brought the baby boy Jesus into her womb. From the same womb where Jesus grows, the Spirit of the Lord brings forth an anthem of praise for those who have been wandering in the waiting for the Savior, and a word of warning to those who will see Jesus as a threat.

This is God's protest against the powers of that day. In the tradition of the midwives, there is subversion through the foremothers in Jesus's lineage. Tamar, Rahab, and Ruth are all pictures of "unlikely" matriarchs. But all their stories represent divine tenacity and the meekness that is often matched with God's boldness to produce a word and a way for the people of God to press on.

Mary's song is a prophecy of God's coming to reclaim power from every ruler or person in authority who presumed power was theirs alone. For people in liberation movements, reclaiming space and time is how we process our stories of redemption. We take up space and speak aloud in the halls of local governments that have attempted to take our voices away from us. We show the boldness of meekness when we hold silent sit-ins and lay-ins as police try to threaten us with mass arrest for "disturbing the peace."

We make noise in the tradition of Mary's praise: We remind the hungry poor that their material conditions must change, as we are here to send the rich away hungry. We rejoice with our cousins and remind one another that all our liberation movements are linked, each of us is pregnant with a passion for salvation, and much like Mary's and Elizabeth's, our readiness leaps within us when we fellowship. The picture of Mary as determined is a movement mood that I have learned to read as consistent with the picture of Mary as meek. In both vignettes, she stands humbly prepared to receive what the Lord has proclaimed. And she is humbled to the power of playing her part for cosmic redemption, to literally committing her body as a bearer of the peace that only justice can produce.

## PART 4: REPENTANCE IS RESISTANCE

The Black church in the United States was destined to be a place where Black movement thrived. The ministry of doing justice is part of the gospel that we first preached to ourselves and one another. The story of scripture shows that the people of God are built for radicalism, which simply means getting at the root. And the root of God's creation is liberation. The root of humanity's hunger is the freedom to be fully human. The root of God's redemption plan is to insult the powers that assault God's good creation. And the protest imparted to God's people is a call for every beneficiary of those powers to repent.

For me, protest is a spiritual practice of proclaiming and reclaiming, petitioning, repenting, and resisting. The more I participated in protest for the sake of building power with Black people, the more I felt it prepared me for the ministry of preaching that the people's power was built in by God, not bestowed by the supremacy of one person over another. Resisting the narrative of anti-Blackness that is woven into the fabric of America means repenting of my own failure to participate in or contribute to God's celebration of the creation that has been named good.

So the last shall be first, and the first shall be last.

MATTHEW 20:16

The people of God are protest people. From the beginning, God's actions moved the margins to the center. Humans are last and greatest in God's creation order. And God chooses these last created beings to be image-bearers and stewards of the earth. Jesus is the word of God, equal in power to the Creator. Called the King of Kings, but He comes to earth as a baby, born in a humble town far removed from any palace. His family's story is one of survival amid massacre, oppression, and occupation. He is a progeny of protest.

Moreover, Jesus instructs through protest parables; he heals and ministers in defiance of the traditions of the church. The Lord behaves as if this radical behavior ought to be normalized. And in the end of the gospel story that is exactly what he proves—when the Lord brings the renewal of all things, in the greatest act of protest and power-shift that creation has seen since its beginning: it is the last who shall be first. Our strivings to preach the joy of this dynamic today might seem radical, but I believe that they are ordinary, and they are holy.

## CLOSING

All the Black people in us have been here before. And God is taking us to places we have never seen.

From the day that I was born in a segregated space to the day that I heard a Black boy lost his life for his Blackness, it was clear to me that the practice of protest was part of what preserved me and is central to the story of Blackness writ large—over against the global enterprise of white supremacy. Blackness itself is protest.

Once we realized that we were a threat to the very system of policing, that we were the monsters they feared at night, none of us would ever be the same.

The police were taking the lives of our children, our play cousins, our neighbors, with impunity. I learned about the common notion among police forces that controlling people's bodies was needed—in the name of justice, public safety, and law and order. Our lives are now lived as demands of justice for their lives. We are here right now for all our siblings who deserved to arrive at this day. For all our neighbors and loved ones whose spirits are wrapped up in the Holy Spirit that indwells us, we carry them with us.

Every breath is a protest that reminds the powers of our day that we deserve to be alive.

Michael Brown, Jr., deserved life. Vonderrit Myers, Jr., deserved thriving. Trayvon Martin deserved. Amadou Diallo. George Jackson. Fred Hampton. Aiyana Stanley-Jones. None of their shed blood atoned for the sins of the United States. We must not forget these thefts. And while protesting is how we show the penitence that the country should feel, it is also the way that we connect their lives to the shared futures they should be living among us. It is the way that we demand change for our people and the way that we remember we don't want to lose any more of our people at all.

We do justice to their memories when demanding honor for their lives. Michael Brown, Jr.'s life was no sacrifice for all the sins that take place on this land.

Still, if we had the chance to bring Mike Brown back to life and give up all the movements that have happened since we lost him, what would we do?

We who have been awakened by his being put to violent sleep. Do we deserve to dance when our brother has died?

Would we bring him back if it meant that we'd have to close our eyes?

I protest by proclaiming, repenting, and confessing my need for the Savior, who soothes such strong tensions in my soul. I do not believe in human sacrifice, for my awareness or anyone else's. I do not believe in the shedding of anyone's blood but Jesus's, which can bring about healing and the removal of sins. There is no reality in which Michael Brown, Jr., had to die so that God could open my eyes.

The movement for Black liberation is where I find my political home, and the place where I see my whole story welcomed. It is the place where my Blackness in feminine form, lived out in the United States, is the story I am encouraged to tell. Blackness is the lens I use to apply my theology, the way I know God. And it is the lens I use to both emotionally and practically engage with everything God made. Including myself, including my story. The movement that embraces protest gave me the personal meaning that was missing from my ministry. It reminded me that my liberation is linked to the freedoms of all those we fight for. Movement ministry reminded me that God built us to be protest people, to fearlessly protest in every place that the Spirit has been before, so that we can trust in the Lord as he leads us on a journey to places we can only imagine.

> somebody / anybody
> sing a black girl's song
> bring her out
> to know herself
> to know you
> but sing her rhythms
> carin/ struggle/ hard times
> sing her song of life
> she's been dead so long
> closed in silence so long
> she doesn't know the sound
> of her own voice
> her infinite beauty

NTOZAKE SHANGE, *for colored girls who have considered suicide when the rainbow is enuf*

# Decolonized Discipleship

## By Ekemini Uwan

SISTAS, GOD GOT JOKES!

The irony of all ironies is that I originally wrote this essay, "Decolonized Discipleship," years ago because an "urban" white evangelical organization reached out and requested that I write something about discipleship for a magazine they were producing. They said I had the liberty to approach the topic of discipleship from any angle I chose.

I considered the racial dynamics of the target audience—namely, the white male evangelical pastor and founder of the organization, whose ministry is comprised of "urban" (read: Black and Brown) young adults whose ages range from eighteen to about thirty, who were on fire for Jesus. Having spoken at their national conference twice, I felt that I had enough knowledge about the racial makeup and optics of the organization to be able to speak prophetically, effectively, and practically to its founder and to its Black constituency. After praying about the opportunity, I agreed to write the essay.

Now, if you know anything about white evangelical organizations, or white organizations in general, then I'm sure you can predict what happened next. And if you can't, then I'll make it plain: I submitted the essay, and in return I was paid for my labor by—and given additional bonuses of—racism, paternalism, misogynoir, and erasure. This escalated to the point where the *founder* decided to call me to share his consternation. He explained why he would not publish the article he had commissioned me to write. As I recall, in his milquetoast response he prattled off words about "wrestling with the content" and being "uncomfortable with posting the essay." I knew what time it was, because the racist train is never late. I got my bag and disembarked, with an air of sorrow for my Black siblings left in that colony, because the leadership clearly lacked courage. And where cowardice resides, love cannot abide.

Truth-telling is an act of love, and love is an act of spiritual warfare in a world built on lies and the express hatred of Black lives. In the prescient words of Saint Toni Morrison in *Beloved*, Baby Suggs commanded her people, declaring, "In this here place, we flesh; flesh that weeps, laughs; flesh that dances on bare feet in grass. Love it. Love it hard. Yonder they do not love your flesh. They despise it. They don't love your eyes; they'd just as soon pick em out. No more do they love the skin on your back. Yonder they flay it. And O my people they do not love your hands. Those they only use, tie, bind, chop off and leave empty. Love your hands! Love them. Raise them up and kiss them. Touch others with them, pat them together, stroke them on your face 'cause they don't love that either. *You* got to love it, *you!*"

This is doubly true when Black people find themselves trapped in a colony like the one described above, which reminds

me of the words of Frantz Fanon's *The Wretched of the Earth*.
"The Church in the colonies is the white people's church, the
foreigner's church. She does not call the native to God's ways
but to the ways of the white man, of the master, or the oppressor. And as you know, in this matter many are called but few
chosen."[1] Although Fanon's anticolonial body of work was
written in the twentieth century and in the Algerian colonial
context, his words resonate in the twenty-first century, particularly with regard to the white evangelical, mainline, progressive,
and multiethnic church contexts of America.

In recent years, the discourse about decolonizing the faith
has become more pervasive and enigmatic, as it has come to
mean different things to different people. Some have come to
believe that Christianity is "the white man's religion," so they've
discarded the faith completely. For others, due to the ways that
the American church has been steeped in white supremacy,
there can be an overcorrection where scripture, Christian piety,
and traditional doctrines about the atonement, the exclusivity
of Christ, and hell, among other doctrines, are attributed to
white supremacy instead of to the Eastern Christian faith.

From my vantage point, much of the modern movement
toward decolonization of the faith began as a trauma response
to racism, white supremacy, white nationalism, misogyny, spiritual abuse, and sexual abuse, among a host of other sinful practices that ought not be in the church. The culmination of all the
above was embodied in the forty-fifth president of the United
States of America, who had white evangelicals to thank for his
election, as 81 percent of them voted for him to be president.
Under that white-supremacist regime, the body politic experi-

enced collective cultural trauma due to the various ways the former president used white supremacy to marginalize, dehumanize, and exclude people of color. What's more, the unwavering support he enjoyed from white evangelicals caused people—Black, non-Black people of color, and white—to leave white evangelical churches in droves, and some went to white progressive churches. Some of those who made this move adopted the title "exvangelical." Others opted to leave the church completely, while still others left the faith altogether.

It is a lamentable fact that the church was the primary vehicle through which colonization spread on the African continent and beyond. In the United States, and within this trend toward decolonization, I've observed an interesting reality at work. This schism is a family feud between white evangelicals and white progressives. A lot of the exvangelicals who fled white evangelical churches for white progressive spaces are family with those they left behind. They grew up together, went to vacation Bible school together, went to youth-group camps together; these are their people. Essentially, exvangelicals left their families behind.

So, what of the Black people in these white spaces, evangelical and progressive alike? I envision them as a guest invited over for Thanksgiving at a friend's family's house. At first, you might be hesitant to accept the invitation because you're weighing the cost of being the lone Black person at a white Thanksgiving gathering, and you know their mac ain't gon' hit like your mama's; but you accept the invitation and are even grateful for it because you can't make it to your family function for Thanksgiving, and it beats being alone on a holiday.

As you pass the mac, a family squabble ensues when one of the relatives proudly boasts about how they Made America Great Again in the voting booth. You're the only Black person at this Thanksgiving turkey tussle, so you don't have anyone to exchange that awkward glance with as the family business continues to be laid out like a side dish on the table. You scurry off with a to-go plate in hand. The following day, as you survey your leftovers, you realize that *you* are the leftover, as you're now smack dab in the middle of a racial trauma sandwich due to the strays you caught at the Thanksgiving turkey tussle last night.

A hot mess dot com.

This is what I imagine it is like for Black people—and non-Black people of color, for that matter—in either white church space. White evangelicalism and white progressivism are the same beast with different teeth. One might be more cunning than the other, but ultimately, a lateral move from one colony to the next will not protect you, because the beast of white supremacy is ever ready to devour you whole.

Keeping the focus of decolonization discourse exclusively on Black Christians in white evangelical and white progressive spaces would be a miscalculation on my part. Given the ubiquity of white supremacy in this nation—and the church's role in perpetuating it in the past and present—it would be foolish to think that Black Christians in Black churches are immune to the ways that coloniality—that is, the enduring legacy of colonialism—shows up in the Black church. Black Christians are in all of the aforementioned church spaces, so I would be remiss if I did not include the Black church in my analysis.

As I mentioned earlier, decolonization within the church and the faith has come to mean different things to different people, so I might as well add my own understanding to the linguistic milieu.

My presupposition is that the faith is not colonized, and neither are the scriptures. It is the *reception* of the faith that has been colonized. Meaning that there are white-supremacist, sexist, misogynistic, and legalistic additives to the faith that dim the beauty of the gospel, which is why I posit that disentangling the faith from white supremacy is a fruitful endeavor. This requires that the disciple discern the difference between specifically white-supremacist additives, like racist interpretations of Genesis 9 that have been used to justify Black dehumanization and chattel slavery, and more generally sinful additives to the faith such as sexist and misogynistic interpretations of Eve's role in the Fall in Genesis 3, which are used to subjugate women. There is too much beauty in the gospel to allow these death-dealing interpretations of scripture to flourish; and there is too much beauty in the gospel to subject it to the erroneous claim that it is the "white man's religion." Contrary to popular belief, everything isn't white supremacy. And when we attribute *everything* about this beautiful, Eastern Christian faith to white supremacy and whiteness, we inadvertently give the glory to whiteness. Not to God.

And I will not give whiteness the glory. Ever.

I believe this analysis, which disentangles the Christian faith from white supremacy, ought to be sourced from the scriptures, as well as within the community of intergenerational saints, who have gone further down the road than us.

They are our forerunners in the faith, after all. Yet if we ignore these saints and refuse to confront the presence of colonialism in our churches, people will continue to leave in droves. If I'm being honest, I've become increasingly concerned with the way that our people are leaving the faith and thereby throwing the proverbial baby out with the bathwater due to legitimate racial trauma, hypocrisy, church hurt, and spiritual abuse. The time has come and is long overdue for the church to implement *decolonized discipleship:* exhorting Black Christians to hold on to and contend for the faith that was once and for all delivered to us from the apostles and our ancestors by continuing the long-held Black tradition of disentangling the faith from white supremacy.

Decolonized discipleship is not new praxis. Africans have been in the Christian faith for ages. In her article "Christian Imperialism and the Transatlantic Slave Trade," the late Dr. Katie Geneva Cannon quotes Mercy Amba Oduyoye[2] as saying, "Christianity has been present on the African continent for almost as long as people considered themselves followers of Jesus Christ." Cannon goes on to say, "The scholarship and teachings of theologians based in urban North Africa such as Origen, Athanasius, Tertullian, and Augustine shaped Christian thought and practice." I'd also add sub-Saharan African forerunner of the faith and theologian King Nzinga Mbemba, also referred to as "The Apostle of Kongo." And this was long before those ships of terror—named *Hope, Happy Adventure, Perseverance, Grace,* and *Providence*—docked in the Port of Calabar, confining my people to chains, converting them to cargo, commodifying them as chattel in the Americas.

Africans believed in Jesus Christ of Nazareth, the brown-skinned Palestinian Jewish God-man; and they carried that faith with them to their final destinations. Those who were left behind were subject to colonization and Christian imperialism. My grandmother still has the wallet-size photo of white Jesus given to her by the white missionaries who insisted that her family change their traditional Ibibio surname to an English name, which is how, at birth, my mother was given a non-Nigerian first and last name. Colonization does not live in theory; its impact is tangible and generational. These enslaved Africans who survived the Middle Passage—who became members of the African diaspora—became African Americans, or Black. These Black Christians carried on the tradition of disentangling white supremacy from Christianity at hush harbors, which became the cradle of the Black church, born out of resistance to the slaveholding theology of the slavers. As the kids say, "We ain't new to this; we true to this."

Cannon says of author Modupe Labode, who wrote "Christianity: Missionaries in Africa," "She contends that as important as missions and missionaries are to Christianity we should not confuse the history of Christian missions, or the history of missionaries, with the history of Christianity on the African continent."[3] It is true that Jesus Christ our Lord commanded us, saying, "Go therefore and make disciples of all nations, baptizing them in the name of the Father and of the Son and of the Holy Spirit, teaching them to observe all that I have commanded you" (Matt. 28:18–19). But the questions intruding

upon us are these: What kinds of disciples are being made? Do
the minds and the lives of these disciples reflect a baptism of
faith in the marginalized brown-skinned Palestinian Jewish
God-man, Jesus Christ, who was bludgeoned and hung naked
on that rugged cross at Calvary? Or does their baptism reflect
faith in a capitalist white Jesus? There are grave consequences
for worshipping the latter, who is no more than an idol (Exod.
20:3–4), and discipling Black people to do the same.

## WHAT IS COLONIZATION?

Colonization is a violent process whereby colonialist settlers in-
vade land in order to dispossess and plunder the indigenous
people through rape, genocide, and other egregious acts of violence. Those who survive are oppressed, conscripted to second-
class citizenship, and forced to labor on their own land due to
the implementation of systemic racism.

Another aspect of colonization, germane to our discussion
here, requires the degradation of the natives' culture, language,
customs, and personhood. "In the colonial context, the settler
ends his work of breaking in the native when the latter admits
loudly and intelligibly the supremacy of the white man's values."[4] Consequently, the minds of the oppressed become colonized to such a degree that they internalize this colonialist
white-supremacist ideology and begin to loathe themselves,
their culture, and their traditions, simply because these are
theirs. Colonization is inherently violent. Those who were not
felled by genocide are left to discover that a psychological war
began waging in their minds at the very moment the settlers'

footsteps marked the sanguine soil of their native land. This is the psyche of the colonized mind: always at war within itself.

## COLONIZED DISCIPLESHIP

Where it concerns Black believers discipled in white conservative and white progressive churches, the minds of these disciples can bear an uncanny resemblance to the colonial mindset of native inhabitants whose land has been colonized. Not unlike the colonized natives, Black disciples are trained, implicitly and explicitly, to disdain their own culture, traditions, and appearance. Implicitly, they are taught that only white male theologians—be it conservative Americans or progressive German scholars—have cornered the market on epistemology or "solid theology," because those are the only theologians read, quoted, or truly taken seriously. Theology derived from such white male scholars—irrespective of the theological poles they are committed to—is rendered normative. Explicitly, Black disciples are told that their exuberant worship is too emotional. Their style of dress too loud. The music they choose to listen to is unredeemable. Their fluent command of African American Vernacular English is unrefined and simple. Their bodies are only valuable insofar as they can be tokenized, fetishized, and objectified. Black Christians' embodied Blackness is treated like something to be *managed*, not delighted in.

Black women in particular bear the brunt of this last message, finding themselves located on a continuum of objectification, vacillating between hypervisibility and invisibility. Hypervisibility maps onto Black women with regard to the commodification of their bodies and stereotypes about hypersexuality, mannerisms, speech, and the infamous "angry Black woman" trope. These false notions that fuel the hypervisibility that Black women experience also create the precondition for *in*visibility, which is a form of exile. Black women in their embodied Blackness are rendered invisible precisely because they are *too* visible within their white evangelical, white progressive, or multiethnic church contexts. This is because they do not fit the mold of the arbitrary standard of white femininity, and because their faith—like their Blackness—is embodied. It's expressive, exuberant, and vocal. They are perceived only in the fictitious characterizations projected onto them regarding their personhood.

I wish I could say that Black women are exempt from this experience in Black churches, but regardless of the denomination—or non-denominational context—of the Black church a sista finds herself in, she too can experience hypervisibility. Especially if a sista has a voluptuous build, the ushers stay ready to wrap sista-girl up with "modesty cloths" in every size like she is Lazarus resurrecting from the grave, drawing unnecessary attention to her and heaping shame onto her and her body. In an effort to invisibilize her, she is now hypervisible due to a narrow and harmful interpretation of biblical modesty.

Not only have I seen this dynamic unfold right before my eyes, I've experienced it. Several years back, I was attending a church where my then pastor, a Black male, wrongly interpreted the story of Samson and Delilah. As he preached from the pulpit, he put the onus of Samson's faithlessness on Delilah. But apparently that wasn't enough. He went on to cite one of the most misogynistic lyrics from Bell Biv DeVoe's "Poison," exclaiming, "You can't trust a big butt and a smile!"

From the pulpit.

In one swift line, he objectified every Black woman and girl in the church. Discipled everyone in the congregation into this misogynistic form of colonized discipleship. Tutored the men in misogynoir by giving them a crash course on how to objectify Black women—meanwhile teaching the women to internalize such wicked objectification and misogyny.

Every Black woman and Black girl was made hypervisible for the sake of a cheap laugh, at the expense of their humanity and personhood. Around me, everyone in the pews laughed, but that cut me straight to the heart. I left that day with internal bleeding. I suspect I wasn't alone.

Conversely, invisibility manifests itself in the lives of Black women in white evangelical and multiethnic churches through the onslaught of biblical manhood and womanhood teachings. These teachings are extrabiblical and center white middle- and upper-class norms, communicating to male singles that they should look for, desire, and pursue a marriage partner who embodies the characteristics of a "biblical woman." Translation: white femininity and subservience. As a consequence of this legalistic teaching, Black women are implicitly taught to assimilate and aspire toward whiteness. Black women within white and multiethnic church spaces are systematically eliminated from the marriageability pool, rendered invisible to their Black and non-Black male counterparts because they do not fit the white, middle-class profile of a "biblical woman." Black men often aspire for ascendency in these spaces, and one way they are advised to do so is by marrying a "biblical" (read: white) woman. Doing so requires that they jettison their Black female counterparts in their quest for proximity to whiteness. In doing so, they sacrifice Black women on the altar of their quest for white validation and elevation (translation: tokenization) in these churches.

A colonized mind is a telltale sign that the Black disciple has been indoctrinated with a false theology that derives from the empire instead of from the Kingdom of God. Empire theology is focused on the temporal, without regard for eternal things, which are unseen. It only serves the interest of the powerful, maintains the status quo, and perpetuates the demonic narrative of white superiority over and against those in the margins.

Empire theology prances around like an angel of light. It cloaks itself with a domesticated gospel, one that is comfortable—so comfortable, in fact, that there is no *actual* need for self-sacrifice and liberation. But inwardly it is a ravenous wolf. It requires nothing of its propagators, yet demands everything of those on the margins, to whom the theology is given. It ensures that the first remains the first and that the last remains the *least*.

In contrast, Kingdom theology is governed by an inverse inertia that holds eternity in view, where the last is first (Matt. 20:16), the poor in spirit and in the world are heirs of the Kingdom (Matt. 5:3; James 2:5), and everyone, regardless of status, is to look out for the interest of others (Phil. 2:4), love their neighbors as themselves (Matt. 22:37–39), and love God in both soul and body through the indwelling of the Holy Spirit that empowers sons and daughters of the Kingdom to kill sin (Matt. 22:37; Rom. 8:13; 12:1). Consider Esther, who had a choice to make: would she continue to "pass" by concealing her ethnic Jewish identity in order to reap the earthly benefits of proximity to the empire and the king of said empire, or would she forsake it all, risking her very life to reveal her ethnic Jewish identity, in order to save her people from the impending genocide? Through God's providence and Esther's brave act of solidarity with her people over and against the empire, the trajectory of redemptive history continued unabated. Scripture is replete with people like Moses, Rahab, Daniel, and others who aligned themselves with Kingdom instead of empire, making way for the King of Kings, Jesus Christ's advent, and the inauguration of His Kingdom.

## WHAT IS DECOLONIZATION?

"Decolonization is the meeting of two forces, opposed to each other by their very nature . . . 'the last shall be first and the first last.' Decolonization is the putting into practice of this sentence" (Fanon 36, 37). Like colonization, decolonization involves two processes at work simultaneously: The first is decolonization of the mind, which starts by calling the colonial situation into question. The second process is when the natives actively turn the colonial structure on its head, so that the once-colonized natives gain their independence.

Decolonization of the mind is not achieved through osmosis. It does not occur organically, and it is not passive. Decolonization is always active and intentional and requires resistance against the colonial structure of subjugation. Colonization—like every other sin—does not remit with time; it is a wicked and all-consuming force that is only stopped when decolonization efforts meet colonization with equal force.

Colonization, as mentioned previously, is a violent process, and its opposite, decolonization, is equally violent. The minds of the natives are colonized when they internalize their oppression, become self-hating, believe they are inferior to the colonizer, and assent to their colonization, viewing it as a virtue instead of seeing it as a vice fashioned in the depths of hell. Deep, introspective soul work is required for someone to come to terms with the reality of how they have been colonized—discipled into believing that white theology, white doctrine, white ways are higher than those of their own people.

It takes work to admit this.

It takes work to undo this.

It takes work to uproot this.

## DECOLONIZED DISCIPLESHIP

If white supremacy is a global project—which it is—then America is a white-supremacist nation—which it is. As a function of this reality, this means that we, Black people and non-Black people of color, have all had our minds colonized to varying degrees. Through our educational systems, whether they be private, public, or homeschooling; through media, doctrine, and iconography in churches; we have all absorbed a message of disdain for our melanin, bodies, and culture.

On the subject of iconography, white Jesus isn't confined to white churches; white Jesus holds court in some Black churches and other nonwhite church spaces, too.

I will never forget when, a couple of years ago, I was invited to give a lecture at a conference held at a historic Black church in Chicago. I was there to speak about reparations in connection with my people, the Ibibio people, who were stolen and trafficked in the transatlantic slave trade. Just as I was about to take the pulpit and start my lecture, I saw a life-size painting of white Jesus with a receding hairline. (That was a fascinating detail! I couldn't unsee it, and now I'm making y'all see it, too.) The theological dissonance in that moment hit me at breakneck speed. Theological violence has a way of doing that. Not only is white Jesus an idol; it's also a "controlling image," if I may be so bold as to borrow Patricia Hill Collins's terminology from *Black Feminist Thought*. Collins writes, "These controlling images are designed to make racism, sexism, poverty, and other forms of social injustice appear to be natural, normal, and inevitable parts of everyday life."[5] Although Collins coined this term to detail the ways that stereotypes like Mammy and Sapphire are used to justify Black women's subordination, I find Collins's *controlling image* concept applicable to white Jesus, as *this* controlling image has been used to justify slavery, colonialism, Christian imperialism, and a host of other wicked enterprises.

This is why disentangling white supremacy from the faith should be an essential part of discipleship. It's high time for the church to dismantle this relic of white supremacy: white Jesus.

It is an idol.

It is a myth.

It is violent.

It is a weapon.

This weapon has been used to oppress Black people globally, and it will burn in hell, as all idols will. The church ought to get a head start by ridding itself of this controlling image.

But before embarking on this mission, it is imperative that we examine the events that led us to the decision to decolonize.

For Black Christians, it is too often trauma connected to racism, patriarchy, and spiritual and sexual abuse that leads us to recognize the need to decolonize the faith. Quiet as it's kept, the Black church has yet to have a reckoning on sexual abuse. But the time is coming, and it will come when God's justice is made manifest on behalf of sexual assault survivors. Not only in the *by-and-by* but in the *now-and-now*. The silence of the church—Black, white, or otherwise—regarding these particular traumas doesn't mean the trauma doesn't exist. The silence only exacerbates the impact of the trauma on the traumatized, and even ensures that others will be victimized, too, due to the absence of accountability, church discipline, and consequences.

We must attend to this trauma through therapy. Trauma is intrusive, obstructive, and all-consuming; depending on what kind of trauma you are dealing with, it can warp your view of God and the faith altogether. Trauma is so loud that it can impair our ability to discern truth from lies, which prevents us from disentangling white supremacy from the faith. I cannot stress this enough, because some people are decolonizing their faith to the point that they are decolonizing their way out of the faith. Some Black Christians leave the faith altogether because of the white spaces they worshipped in instead of returning to—or entering—the Black church.

To be clear, no church on this side of glory is perfect. The church is being sanctified as all believers are, individually and collectively.

But at the very least, your dignity and humanity as a Black

person will never be despised in the Black church. And for those who don't consider entering (or even reentering) the Black church, this is something to take to your prayer closet. Because this matters a great deal.

Perhaps some think that departing the white church—be it progressive or conservative—requires a total departure from the faith. When they do that, they unwittingly reveal their belief that white Christians have a corner market on Christianity. They are telling on themselves: they cannot imagine a faith apart from whiteness. White supremacy has stolen so much from our people, but we cannot let it steal Jesus, too!

Second, we can begin to decolonize our discipleship by remembering that Christianity is an Eastern religion, and the faith was shaped by African theologians. There is power in reclamation. The scriptures were not written by white male authors, and there are no white people in the Bible. Therefore, our decolonization efforts should be run through the sieve of God's Word so that we are decolonizing based on God's revelation to us—and through the Holy Spirit, who speaks to us through God's Word—to ensure we are not decolonizing in a way that is *right in our own eyes,* exclusively. Boundaries protect what is sacred, and our faith in Jesus is sacred. Christianity is not a Burger King drive-thru; you can't "have it your way." Our faith was never meant to be "just me and Jesus," which is a colonized Western approach to the Christian faith. We would do well to remember that there are older saints who have been running for Jesus much longer than we have, and they too have experienced their own share of trauma in- and outside of church spaces. Reading the Word in community with these saints—who can impart insight and wisdom on the text and about our traumatic experiences we are healing from—is a gift that we ought not take for granted.

We should clothe ourselves with a posture of humility as we seek to disentangle the faith from white supremacy, and we should be intentional about learning church history and how the gospel took root in Africa, Asia, and the Middle East. Grievously, it is a little-known fact that the Ethiopian church was the impetus for the Protestant Reformation.[6] The professor and bishop Dr. David Daniels writes, "Located in Africa—beyond the orbit of the Roman Catholic Church—this first Christian kingdom, according to Luther, served as an older, wiser, black sibling to the white Christian kingdoms of Europe. In a sense, the Church of Ethiopia was the 'dream' for Luther, a true forerunner of Protestantism." We must read Bible commentaries, books, articles, and theology written by women and men who are natives and descendants of Africa and the Middle East, which are the historical settings of the Bible. We must also sit at the feet of our Indigenous, Asian, Palestinian, and Latin American siblings[7], so that we can learn how the gospel is expressed within their respective cultural contexts. Doing so enables us to lay hold of the global nature of the church, which will remain out of reach so long as the colonial mindset persists.

Third, we need to evaluate whether the theology we subscribe to in our churches derives from the kingdom or the empire. Here are a few questions to ask yourself:

Does this theology call me to a deep love for God that causes me to pursue holiness and radical love for my neighbor?

Does this theology benefit the privileged at the expense of the marginalized?

Is this theology good news for everyone, regardless of their racial and socioeconomic status?

Does this theology cause me to look in the mirror and marvel at God's handiwork instead of despising my reflection?

When I close my eyes and picture Jesus, do I see a white man or a brown-skinned Palestinian man?

Your answers to these questions will indicate whether you have been indoctrinated by kingdom or empire theology.

Additionally, for Black Christians in white evangelical, white progressive, or multiethnic church spaces, I'm not here to pull your Black card or even question your Blackness, because I know that these conversations sometimes devolve into such demeaning discourse. There are over a billion Black people in the world, so there are over a billion ways to be Black. With that said, I think it is worthwhile to undertake the project of self-examination to determine why you are committed to these church spaces. Ask yourselves the following questions:

Do I think the ice is colder at white churches than it is at Black churches?

Is my faith in Jesus Christ, or is it in whiteness?

Why and how did I begin to attend these churches in the first place?

"Money talks," but in white spaces, money's got a megaphone, so was it the money that motivated me?

If your answer to one of the questions above is "yes," then as hard as it might be, you have to own your own voluntary captivity to whiteness. There are a host of reasons why your answer might be "yes," but you can't get free until you admit your culpability.


If we take colonization and decolonization out of the realm of sociology for a moment and think about them in a theological sense, we realize we have all been colonized by sin, without exception, because sin is a no-limit soldier. It knows no boundaries or laws; it keeps going and going, because its ultimate goal is to kill you. In Genesis 3:1 and 4–5 we see Satan, the chief colonizer, deceive our first parents, Adam and Eve, causing them to question what God said to them about the tree of the knowledge of good and evil. Like a human colonizer who causes the colonized to question their worth and dignity. Instead of Adam and Eve acting in obedience to God by taking dominion over the serpent (Gen. 1:26–28), they sealed their colonization and ours when they ate of the tree of the knowledge of good and evil, plunging us all into sin, death, and misery.

When we think about the eternal consequences of our transgressions (Rom. 6:23), we see that colonization by sin is violent indeed. Decolonization is equally violent, and that violence was visited upon the body of Jesus Christ, who—of His own volition—laid down His life so that we would no longer be colonized by sin. Every laceration, welt, contusion, and gash from the crown of thorns embedded on His head was endured by Jesus for our salvation—or our decolonization, if you will. The Holy Spirit continues the work of decolonization within us by empowering us to kill indwelling sin as we are renewing our minds and being conformed to the image of Christ.

By analogy, we must account for white supremacy in our discipleship efforts, so that Black Christians are cared for in body and soul. Recognizing that they are embodied souls whose lives were purchased by the finished work of our embodied Savior, Jesus Christ. We are not Gnostics. A disembodied savior is no savior at all. In the words of the African theologian Athanasius, "What is not assumed is not redeemed."

Our physiques matter because Jesus Christ united humanity with His divinity.

Our bodies matter.

Our hair matters.

Our complexion matters.

Our facial features matter.

Our bodies and souls reflect the image of the embodied one, who is interceding for us now.

Christianity predates white supremacy, and it will outlast it.

Thanks be to God!

# Forgiveness

## By Christina Edmondson

"Black women are so bitter."

"I think you have a forgiveness problem."

Ever heard these statements directed at you or someone else? Maybe in pop culture, maybe on Twitter, or maybe at times it was your own internal voice accusing you. Everyone seems to have an opinion on how Black women should forgive.

Forgiveness has to be one of the most complicated and difficult elements of applied Christianity. Yes, the faith is to be applied to our lives, thoughts, money, bodies, etc. It is confusing and humbling to determine what the application of forgiveness looks like, even with the necessary empowerment of the Holy Spirit to make it so.

We might intellectually know that forgiveness, grace, and reconciliation are at the epicenter of the gospel. But the *application* of forgiveness is often resisted, misunderstood, and certainly manipulated. It becomes important for believers, then, to continually answer the questions: What is forgiveness? Whom, and under what conditions, are we to forgive and be forgiven by? And practically speaking, *how* do we forgive? In other words, when it is all said and done, how do we know we have forgiven? To explore these questions, we must first consider how to apologize—and what happens if an apology or repentance due to us never comes.

A couple years back, I posted a comment on social media about some persistent element of racism in America. I honestly don't remember the event that prompted this—there are too many—but I shared my observation of the performance and persistence of racism. The post was reposted by others and eventually received a variety of comments. I am not likely to engage beyond a minute in comments, whether positive or negative, but one left me shaking my head. A white pastor weighed in—not to engage the statement or the injustice it referenced but instead to opine about my "mean and angry ways." "Christina is just an angry person."

Yes, I had been *angry-Black-womaned*—another version of the scarlet letter assigned by men of social privilege as a means of control. One of the fruits of illegitimate social power is an awareness of one's undeservedness. So social control becomes a necessary and rotten fruit of faux supremacy because it's inherently untrue and fragile. Name-calling, gaslighting, stonewalling, and even violence are on the agenda of unacknowledged male privilege.

I must admit, I read this pastor's words out loud in the voice of a preschool-age boy saying, "She is shhhooo mean. A big ole meanie!" I am mean and angry? Come on, man. I began to rant out loud about all the ways that my post was actually gracious. I followed up with the mental gymnastics about his obvious

insecurity, deflection, and unfitness for leadership. I fully diagnosed this man as a bona fide fool and reason #1,429,195 that
white evangelicalism lacks moral credibility. I completed this
mental image with his full defrocking and removal from leadership. Tired from all of this, I dusted off my virtual sandals and
kept it moving.

Or so I thought. The expenditure of all that mental energy
was evidence that his words had struck a chord.

"Stereotype threat" is a term coined and studied by social psy-
chologist Claude Steele and others. Steele describes this physiological phenomenon as the bodily response to the fear of
confirming a negative stereotype about one of our social groups.
It is both a physiological and a behavioral response that creates
an additional layer of stress to whatever already stressful thing we
are engaging in. It impacts our performance because we begin to
manage our image, whether through avoidance or overcompen-
sation. Because of racism and sexism, being a Black woman requires extra psychological and emotional work, dispensing energy
that could be used for the business of creating, collaborating, and
loving. I spend a fair amount of time teaching students and leaders about how this concept impacts performance, and how to
continually release ourselves and our organizations of it.

The layered stereotypes, anxieties, and burdens of being a
Black Christian woman steadily tap on our shoulders before
adding another brick. Yet we are told to respond with a smile.
In some cases, we are asked to *literally* smile. Maybe one of the
only benefits of the pandemic's necessary masking require-
ments was that it reduced the likelihood of supervisors and cat-
callers asking us to smile or gesture for their ease.

All of this makes me think about Christian singer Canton

Jones's hilarious 2008 music video for the song "Stay Saved."
Jones walks through a host of scenarios that challenge his
Christian witness, from being cut in front of at the movies to
being completely disrespected in a fast-food line.

> Gotta stay prayed up 'cause people will test you. . . . Even
> though I'm hot as fire, I'm gon' love you anyway.

That's Jones's way of mentally psyching himself up to deal
with the foolishness of fools. The everyday everyday. In Black-
church-woman parlance it might be "I am too blessed to be
stressed" as we reach for our blood pressure pills. In Black political rhetoric it might be the words of Shirley Chisholm, "I am
unbought and unbossed"—now remixed with the millennial
flourish that they are also "unbothered." These mantras have a
real or assumed function, or they wouldn't be around. They help
us to cope in the moment, but none have the power to sustain
us in the smog of misogynoir.

The racial caste system has specific and tailored burdens for
groups. This isn't oppression Olympics; this is the reality of our
country's caste system. American racism and colorism mythol-
ogize and cement the lie that Black and Indigenous women are
inherently deviant, criminal, and invisible. Therefore, though
painful, it's not hard to intellectually understand the prevalence
of ingroup- and externally-inflicted suffering experienced by
Black and Indigenous women. Dehumanization creates manifold consequences, including the minimizing of pain. White
supremacy doesn't believe in victims. The high tolerance of others and, too often, ourselves for the burdens, rejection, and
abuses of Black women is costly.

The more socially marginalized identities one has—be it Black, female, transgender, poor, or disabled, for example—the greater the risk of harm and lack of earthly justice. This should not even be a controversial statement. That is one aspect of Kimberlé Crenshaw's theory of intersectionality, confirmed and further advanced by others. This is a concept that Christians can see worked out frequently in the scripture as we read descriptions of compounding identities like the Samaritan woman, the rich young male ruler, and the Syrian widow. Donald Trump was elected president (albeit through dubious means) because of his compounding identities like male, old, wealthy, tall, and very white. That conflation, along with his dog-whistling and bullhorning antics, signaled to some that he was their representative—and maybe even more important, that he wasn't my representative. "We want Saul." "We want Barabbas." The strategy of selecting bad leaders to oppress others by using stereotyped compounding identities is a centuries-old practice.

The way that our compounding identities increase our social vulnerability and limit justice is a recipe for bitterness that will cause us to break. The bitterness will break and break others. It is in this backdrop that the socially vulnerable now hear Christ's words to Peter—and wonder if He is talking to us, too:

Then came Peter to him, and said, "Lord, how often shall my brother sin against me, and I forgive him? Till seven times?"

Jesus saith unto him, "I say not unto thee 'Until seven times' but 'Until seventy times seven.'"

MATTHEW 18:21–22

When Jesus gets prideful male leaders all the way together, I'm like the Black teen boys in that infamous viral gif hyping up "their boy" after winning a freestyle battle. "Yeah, son!!"

You know how we do as we listen to a pointed sermon and think, "I wish *such and such* was here to hear this. Mmmm, *they* really need this word." The impulse to fixate on specks to avoid removing beams is real. Yet, the correction from Christ is an expression of grace even to those bullied by the sins of the world. Sin against us does not negate sin within us, and Christ has a response of grace and justice that we desperately need. Everybody, even the socially marginalized, is told to "go and sin no more."

There is so much in the exchange from Matthew 18 that fascinates me. Peter, the one who would soon deny Christ three times, buckling as he is called out by a socially marginalized girl, wants Jesus to clarify the limits of forgiveness. Jesus, God in the flesh, responds by drawing our attention indirectly to what we ask and need of Him: continued intercessory forgiveness. For He—Emmanuel—is the one who came to give us grace in a world condemned.

Jesus's response to Peter is respectful, because Jesus is not our homeboy but our Savior. But His response is also absolutely over-the-top. I notice that's something that Jesus does repeatedly, whenever we play perfect or independent and try to get out of entrusting ourselves to Him and loving our neighbor. *Oh, I see, you have obeyed all the law, rich young ruler. Okay, so sell everything and give it away. Look, now you are walking away sad.*

In reading from the Christina Standard Version (CSV), Jesus says: "Peter, you think you are really doing something by following the cultural religious norms on forgiveness. It's not seven but seventy times seven, son. I am calling you to live as forgiving people because you have been forgiven more than you can even comprehend. That is what seventy times seven means. It is encompassing. It oozes. It is fully complete and comprehensive. It's not what we do but rather who we are. We are forgiving. Chainless and free to love, we cancel moral debts and surrender debtors to the God of justice."

Seventy times seven does not represent a literal number to be tallied, but rather a way of being.

Live as a forgiving person.

Live forgiven and repentantly day to day.

But is the God of justice telling us to *just forgive*? Is the God who hates sin telling us to *just let it go*—all the pain, suffering, destruction, and continuous abuse? Is the God who fiercely loves and protects His children saying, *Just move on*?

We are all invested in this call to forgiveness for deeply personal reasons. I am certain that someone has indeed sinned against you. Someone has sinned grievously against someone we love deeply. Peter knew what it meant to be sinned against as well. We are not getting through this journey called life without having that experience many times over, resulting in varying degrees of pain.

I can still see them. A grown man rocking back and forth in a ball in my office recounting his only mother figure's sexually and physically abusive actions. A teenager's sweet voice describing the unspeakable. A little girl recounting the sound of the keys jingling late at night, and knowing that soon she'd need to hide from her mother's abusive boyfriend—and also knowing she'd be found by him. Humans have greatly sinned against other humans. The sadistic ritual of the lynching tree in America stands as one among many reminders of our capacity to pretend that others are not human. Dismissal after dismissal, abuse upon abuse, and denial on top of denial chips away at our fortitude, like Jenga blocks being removed one at a time until we come crashing down.

Have you ever worked as a telemarketer or, worse yet, a bill collector? Call after call, you are avoided, blamed, cussed out, lied to. But every once in a while, a debt is actually paid. You are blown away that the debt is legitimately paid in full, completely acknowledged—and the person at the end says something like "Thank you for your patience and bringing this to my attention." You sit back, thinking, "Am I being punked?" The feeling of having someone sincerely apologize and offer to make repairs is amazing. You feel seen and relieved. Especially because, like Mother Fannie, you are sick and tired of being sick and tired. Nothing is more fatiguing than sin, our own and the sin against us. So you sit with that relief.

When people acknowledge their debts to us, we are able to live onward with a bit more hope. Maybe even enough to call the next person on the list, or to say, "Forget about it; we're good." We might even find ourselves open to self-examination about what we owe others—this time, looking inward at the ways we have hurt others and not only outward at how others have harmed us. Certainly we, too, have a rap sheet. Intentionally or unintentionally, we have harmed others, sometimes even as a result of our own pain.

This brings to mind the Lord's Prayer: "Forgive us our debts, as we forgive our debtors."

But here's the thing: some of us live as perpetual debt collectors. In fairness, we don't all have the same amounts and types of suffering, in history and in personal experience. But emotional debt collecting can be a full-time job, with overtime and a night shift. When we are consumed by collecting even legitimate debts, the process of seeking acknowldgment and awaiting repair eats up the time we could give to other things. We carry around the unpaid invoices, and they crowd our purses. So many invoices that they weigh down our book bags. Erykah told us we gonna hurt our backs dragging all them bags like that.

When we make our willingness to heal dependent on the system or person who has harmed us, we are cooking up a recipe for lasting pain. Think about that for a minute. I am going to give myself the gift of restoration, care, therapy, and relationships only *after* the wrongdoer does right by me? My goodness. The wrongdoer is skipping along or maybe dead and in the grave while we are making repeated attempts to get water from a rock.

Don't get me wrong, it is vital to acknowledge pain. It really matters. Without it, we won't be able to heal those wounds.

But that acknowledgment, surprisingly, does not need to come only from the wrongdoer, who in some cases has no credibility. Our own acknowledgment and flat-footed rejection of agreement with those who have harmed us is just as important.

We know that young children who experience abuse are positively impacted by the validation of just one trustworthy adult who says, "I believe you," responds empathetically, and makes gestures of justice—even if the child is unable to fully grasp it. That positive impact has ripple effects into the child's physical, emotional, and relational health going forward, even well into adulthood.

In the 1990s, epidemiologists and clinicians conducted research to better understand the social and emotional foundations of our public health problems. This led to the beginning of the Adverse Childhood Experiences (ACES) project, a still-growing body of research that encompasses divorce, parental violence, sexual abuse, and mental illness. ACES doesn't just study individual children situated in a single generation but investigates multigenerational impact on children by studying groups like the descendants of the Holocaust or Great Migration. Their research in neuroscience and epigenetics shows us that the past makes a claim on the present in our DNA. This impacts health outcomes throughout the life cycle and is a root cause of many adult health issues. This is yet another reason to add to the list of why African Americans rightfully warrant reparations that address economic, health, relational, and education disparities today.

The trauma of my ancestors lives in my body today. I only need to walk by a mirror to be reminded of the sexual subjugation of Black women. I am not aware of any ancestor in the last hundred years who married cross-racially or had biracial children, and yet my DNA claims to be a quarter European.

Several years back, after exclusively breastfeeding my youngest child, I developed a breast injury that I had never experienced or even heard of. I thought it was strange, unique—until my doctor told me that he had seen this kind of development among wet nurses in Africa. In that moment, I was teleported back to the reality of the Black woman's body as a means of capital through suffering: the assaults by white slaveholders, forced breeding with enslaved men, and mass production of breastmilk—often to care first for white children. This is why body autonomy is crucial for Black women, even beyond white-centric labels of pro-life and pro-choice. To value life from the womb to the tomb in no way requires the devaluing of the bodies that carry children. Any call for such a truncated morality or outrage is driven by partisan politics and empowered by polarization, to no one's good. I need no lectures—nor would my ancestors—on the consequences of others claiming dibs on the reproductive health of generations of Black women.

Telling people to let go of the past without honoring its consequences in the present calls to mind the words of an abuser dodging accountability through manipulation. This is important for us to remember. Forgiving doesn't mean forgetting, lest we walk right back into an abuser's trap. We dare not agree with the sin done against us for the appearance of kindness or tolerance. For that path leads to conscious retraumatization.

Even if we know the system or an institution is trash, pursuing justice is worthwhile. We must avoid covering up or minimizing hurt, because it will come back for us and our children and our children's children.

Can I say something?

Telling the truth about sin and pursuing repair are not in conflict with justice. Christianity is a confessional faith. We open up our mouths, which reveal the matter within our hearts and speak the truth. We confess to Christ as Lord, but that does not end our confession. We are not a one-and-done confessional people. We confess privately and communally as a gift of grace. Our confession is a gift to ourselves, freeing us from self-deception, but it is also a gift to those we have wronged or overlooked.

Here's the truth: forgiveness, healing, and justice are not in competition, but rather, interrelated. They fuel, inform, and prop one another up, almost like a three-legged stool. Our forgiveness looks like trusting God to collect the payment so that we can be free to heal and enjoy and do justice, unpolluted by bitterness. In forgiveness, we are freed to not be defined by our suffering or a wrongdoer's emotional fingerprints on us. Lawyer and civil rights activist Bryan Stevenson often reminds us that we are more than the worst thing we have done. I'd add that we are so much more than the worst thing ever done to us.

There are both external and internal narratives that plague the Black Christian woman. Ours is a pain often minimized, ignored, or pathologized, laden with heavy doses of internalized religious guilt about what to do with our traumas, hurts, and perpetrators. Some of us break under the burden and throw it all away. So when Black Christian women live congruently, expressing through words, art, worship, and emotions the disappointments of misogynoir, they are often labeled as being too extra, too dramatic, too *anything*, and are coached and taught to push past their pain. Maybe you have heard praises of how strong you are—not to empower you but to pacify you so you don't seek out real reparation. We are prompted to move past our pain by those who hate our voices and, even more, the truthful words coming through them.

But what if being a "good Christian" includes calling out and calling forth? When we call to repentance those who have hurt us, we model dignity, hopefulness, and the steps to real repair— even as we are being healed by Christ. Have you felt like the walking wounded lately? Imagine the beauty of resting in God's promised healing power.

Forgiveness is the canceling of debts. A legitimate debt that we are due is taken off the table or emotional ledger. We are able to look at the debtor in our mind's eye and say: "I want for you to experience the grace of justice, correction, and transformation." We hand the debtor or the situation over to God to ultimately reckon our debt. It is hard for us to embrace the truth that God will fight our battles when we think we have the strength or calling to do it ourselves.

> Therefore, since we are surrounded by such a great cloud of witnesses, let us throw off everything that hinders and the sin that so easily entangles. And let us run with perseverance the race marked out for us.
>
> HEBREWS 21:1

All sin entangles and snares. All sin is ultimately against God, mocking the Father's holy throne. This is a theme we see communicated in the Psalms repeatedly by King David. David knew about grievous sin. His debts were high; many were humanly irreparable. He had many humans to make things right with and knew that appeasing the justified wrath of God was impossible apart from grace. The prophet Nathan replied, "The Lord has taken away your sin. You are not going to die."

God takes sin against you and me personally. We are made in the image of God; every pain we have experienced God knows, not just intellectually but intimately. Christ Himself knows what it means to be slandered, publicly humiliated, and disbelieved. Yet, in His divine wisdom, which knows beginning from end, He cries out, "Forgive them, for they know not what they do." There is only one who is guiltless among us, and He extends His presence to us by the power of the Spirit. It's the same power that raised Him from the dead, rested on Stephen the deacon at his stoning, and fueled the courage of martyrs like Perpetua and Felicity.

We can entrust even our most wicked abusers over to Christ. Better in His hands than in our minds. The one who has the power to bring justice rolling down like waters, righteousness like an ever-flowing stream (Amos 5:24), and the moral authority to even exact revenge (Rom. 12:19).

Maybe at this point your mind is recounting a debt someone owes you, big or small. Maybe it's an abusive or cold parent, a former homegirl, an ex who abandoned you, a disappointing leader, or even God. That's right: if we are honest, the most painful no's and experiences of suffering in our lives often leave us silently or openly accusing the Creator.

*Why did you let this happen?*

*How could you?*

While in no way do I believe that God, who is holy, holy, holy, has sinned against me, I know personally what it means to see that God, who has all power, has allowed the unallowable. I am convinced that theodicy—the attempt to make sense of God in suffering—causes more departures from the faith than anything else.

When we don't understand God in suffering, when we doubt the Divine's love for us, we respond reactively—from rebellious tantrums of sin to believing that we are no longer God's child. However, not even our feelings can separate us from the love of God. This might seem laughable or even enraging to us who have truly suffered. But in the midst of suffering, sometimes all we have is a promise from God. I know a promise does not seem sustaining or satisfying, but it is a promise spoken by the one who spoke the world into existence. The promise is that every tear will be redeemed, all injustice will be made right and full, complete healing will come, and our eternal life will look back on this vapor of a life and understand it all.

Selah.


*Imagine and long with me. And mindfully breathe deeply. This exercise is not a one-and-done practice. This is an invitation to breathe this continually over ourselves, over our hurts.*

*Can you see yourself lighter, freer, with extra room to love and breathe, without the weight of unforgiveness in your pockets?*

*Seen by self and others as wiser, softer, not harder—yet not needing to pretend wrong isn't wrong. But rather embracing that we are more than what wronged us. No longer needing to see the world through our traumatized lens. Just this thought makes things brighter, more vivid. Even if it's hard to conceive, would you want to forgive?*

*After paying the high cost of wanting to forgive and taking the steps to do so, we reap more discernment and greater peace, becoming more like Christ.*

*No need to be loyal to replaying the wrong. It can pass by, like a helium balloon.*

*Visualizing the process of ultimately entrusting the wrong and the wrongdoer to Christ, even when we pursue earthly justice while doing so. Take the hurt in your heart and mind, and place it in your hand. Walk toward Christ so that your yoke can be exchanged, giving the heavy and laborious to God. And receive your portion—it is light. And it is no longer yours to carry alone.*

*Without having to haul alone those heavy, dead bones, where shall you journey next?*

# PART II

# Love

EKEMINI: Whew! We went to the deep end on life. We didn't give the sistas an on-ramp or nothin' as is our custom at the table. What we talkin' about next, y'all? I need a break from life. 'Cause life be lifin'.

CHRISTINA: We might as well rip the Band-Aid off and go ahead and talk about love!

EKEMINI *(in a Tina Turner voice):* What's love got to do with it?

MICHELLE & CHRISTINA: *(\*cackle\* \*cackle\* \*snort\*)*

EKEMINI: Remember when they used to talk about "it's raining men"? It's a dry and barren land. Is God gonna make a man?

CHRISTINA: God gon' have to make a man outta dirt. Not just a man, a whole army.

EKEMINI: Jesus be a matchmaker!

MICHELLE: Welp! Here we go!

# Hidden in Plain Sight

## A SINGLE BLACK WOMAN'S MANIFESTO

## By Ekemini Uwan

MUCH HAS BEEN SAID ON the subject of single Black women, our marriageability rates, and the abysmal dating pool available to us. You might even say *too* much has been said about all this. There is no shortage of people within and outside our community telling us that our standards are too high, and how we need to be "high-value women" or settle for whoever shows us a modicum of attention.

And if that weren't enough, it seems like mainstream media can't get enough of this subject, either. In the early 2000s, there was a flood of exposés on all the major U.S. news outlets about the "Single Black Female," which often focused on the question "Why can't successful Black women find a man?" Much of the reporting devolved into paternalism, false assertions about Black pathology, and overworn stereotypes about "the strong Black independent woman." Not unlike a frog cut open during a middle school science experiment, Black women were prodded, poked, sliced, and examined like specimens as their interior lives were dissected under the microscope of America's paternalism.

To add insult to injury, Black male TV personalities with no legitimate expertise or educational credentials on this sociological issue were brought in to give their "expert advice" on why single Black women can't get a man. Unsurprisingly, their expert advice amounted to nothing more than grade-A gaslighting. We are the reason we are single. Our standards are too low. No, they're actually too high. We talk too much. No, we don't talk enough. Men are fixers, not talkers. Chivalry is dead. Chivalry is back. Men need sex. But wait ninety days to have sex. Don't have sex too soon. Don't have sex at all.

These "relationship experts" are double-minded and unstable in all their ways.

They sold their books. The news outlets made out like bandits, while Black women were left holding the bag.

I was in my mid to late twenties when this media frenzy and obsession with Black women's marital status was all the rage. You couldn't escape it: on TV, at church, on the radio—these conversations were happening everywhere. Everyone saying more or less the same thing: successful single Black women can't find a man because [insert any misogynistic trope here]. After it's all said and done, our singleness is our fault. I listened to and read this information, yet even then I knew that the narrative was off. But at that time, I was unbothered. Although I was among the single Black women represented in the reports, I wasn't pressed at the time, because I was significantly younger than the Black women profiled in these news stories. So I used my youth to shield myself from the data and subpar reporting, choosing instead to dwell in the tents of theory, thinking, "This won't happen to me." Sistas, the temptation for denial was real!

But as the seasoned saints at my old church used to say, "Just keep on living, baby!" And live I did, as I am now in my late thirties—the same age as the Black women featured in those news reports. Thankfully, my proximity to the single Black thirtysomething women at my church had cut my delusions of theoretical tent-dwelling off at the pass. These women were my mentors in the faith. I saw how the statistics and structural realities mapped onto their lives in real time, and it was a heavy load for them to bear. Brilliant, bright Black women with full-time careers and 401(k)s who battled cancer, housing insecurity, and systemic racism, and who had to carry these burdens alone. I could not in good conscience allow them to bear it by themselves, any more than I could live in a delusional reality banking on exceptionalism as my escape hatch.

No, I was a single Black woman in my twenties, and I am still single in my late thirties. I've been reluctant to contribute to the cacophony of opinions about Black women and singleness. I do not want my life and ministry to be defined by my relationship status, which is why I talk about my singleness only sparingly. And honestly, it's traumatic. Yet I recognize that I am my sister's keeper; and in the same way that I shared the burdens of my single Black mentors in the faith, I won't allow my sistas at the table now to bear this alone. Me being the lifelong single Black woman at *Truth's Table,* my lot has been cast and necessity has been laid upon me to thread the needle on this sensitive subject. Above all else, this is an issue that's salient for the sistas at the table: on every season of *Truth's Table,* this is the topic we are most frequently asked to discuss.

Having said that, I am the expert on my own experience—
not your mama's and your cousin's, too—nobody else's but my
own. As such, I share my story of singleness merely as a vignette
of what it's like to be a Black woman ensnared by structural
realities designed to destroy the Black family. My story is in no
way representative of the dating experiences of other Black
women; it is uniquely my own. I recognize that not everyone
desires marriage. And even for those who want to be married, I
recognize that marriage is not the end all, be all—it's not for
me, either. But I am speaking to those who do desire marriage
and are baffled by the fact that they remain unmarried. Which
is why I share this part of my narrative: in hopes that in its
extremity—and it is extreme—other Black women might find
some semblance of resonance within my story. When I wrote
about my experience as a lifelong single years ago, I received
countless messages from many Black women and others outside of that demographic who identified with my story. Nevertheless, I still maintain that my story is an outlier when
compared to the dating experiences of other single Black
women. Still, it's instructive, as my story serves as a site where
the structural mechanisms of mass incarceration, colorism, and
desirability map onto me and other Black women whose dating
experiences track with Black heteronormative dating experiences.

This is my story, this is my song: I am a thirtysomething
single Black woman, and I have never been in a dating relationship. I've never had a boyfriend. I've never brought anyone
home to meet my family. I've never even been pursued or sought
after.

In my early twenties, people thought my singleness was endearing. In my late twenties, endearment gave way to bewilderment. As I entered my early thirties, bewilderment morphed into mystification. And in my midthirties, mystification produced shame. In my late thirties, shame has transformed into anger.

Honestly, I'm not sure how it happened. It's not like I've been passively waiting around for it—I don't subscribe to an eisegetical interpretation of Proverbs 18:22: "He who finds a wife finds what is good and receives favor from the Lord." Nor do I subscribe to the way this verse is falsely preached as if it's biblical law that keeps women waiting on men while simultaneously restricting their agency, rendering them passive in their love lives. While this verse is certainly true, when proverbs like this one are misapplied, people can be harmed.

There is an abundance of grace and liberty for women to express interest in a man and initiate if we choose to do so. When I was younger, I rarely, if ever, took the lead in dating situations—though there was this one time when I dared to defy my natural inclination by expressing my feelings for a guy I found attractive, only for it to be a failure of colossal proportions . . . but I digress. Now that I'm older and healed from that particular experience of rejection, I've since learned to *shoot my shot:* if I'm attracted and interested in a man and sense that the feeling is mutual, I'll initiate. Still, that's not my standard approach in my interactions with men whom I'm attracted to, as I prefer for the men to communicate their attraction. It's just the way I'm wired.

My perpetual state of singleness is an enigma. It is not for lack of trying; I'm certainly not a hermit. I travel, work out, take in festivals, enjoy concerts, and attend academic lectures to satisfy my intellectual curiosity. I participated in the early iteration of online dating back when online dating was viewed as weird and suspect. eHarmony, match.com, Blackpeoplemeet.com. I was even on Black Planet. Y'all remember Black Planet?

I'm true to this, y'all!

When dating apps became the norm, I moved with the times and downloaded a few of those apps on my phone, where they remain at the time of writing this, because I'm still single. Now is as good a time as any to say that dating apps are a special kind of hell all their own, and I would not wish them on my worst enemy. But I continue to walk through the valley of the shadow of ratchetness and check them a few times a week as an act of faith. There are times when, in the name of self-care, I will delete all the dating apps for at least six months to protect my peace and sanity. And when I feel like I have the emotional latitude, I reenter the dating app ghetto, pressing X on profile names like "All About the Benjamins" and "Pure Trauma."

Despite online dating, dating apps, and my friends' well-intentioned matchmaking attempts, these efforts have only ever resulted in "situationships." Surely you know what situation-ships are—and if you don't, perhaps you've unwittingly experienced one. Situationships are those faux relationships that revolve on an axis of gray, refusing to be black or white, constrained by an unspoken mutual attraction and enmeshed with all the anxiety and heartbreak that comes with a relationship. Yet after enduring situationships in the typical four-to-six-month installments—and in some cases, even a year—heartbreak and sorrow, even without the "girlfriend" title, were the only evidence that something had transpired each time.

Make it make sense: either our singleness is our fault or it ain't. 'Cause you're not gonna tell me I haven't put in the work.

I posit that Black women who desire to be married yet find themselves single are not more broken than anyone else on the dating market. And I categorically reject the idea that our single status is due to some pathological phenomenon within the Black community, as researchers, journalists, and even some Black churches have suggested. Rather, Black women are ensnared by interlocking structures that render them single for far longer than they intend, with fewer intraracial dating options.

To the Black church that I love, we must see this for the structural injustice that it is. But first it must eschew the gaslighting it too often directs toward single Black women, with or without children. *You just need to be content; you just need to trust God more; you can't live as a girlfriend and expect to be a wife.* Meeting a structural issue with trite potshots aimed at single Black women who are persevering despite forces out of their control is cruel.

I don't believe that cruelty is the point when it comes to the Black church. I love the Black church. That is where I got saved and that is where I remain, which is why I'm challenging the Black church to come up higher on this issue. In many ways, I think much of the finger-pointing, victim-blaming, and personal attacks leveled at single Black women by some Black churches is due to an obliviousness about the gargantuan size and scope of the relentless assault against the Black family.

The Black church knows that the Black family has been under attack since time immemorial. Now it's time for the Black church to connect the dots between our congregations teeming with single Black women and the two single Black men in our pews. We must make these granular connections in order to respond with the comprehensive force needed to combat this mammoth justice issue, because the situation is dire. White-supremacist structures of domination are highly imaginative and adaptive, which is how white power is sustained. It started with chattel slavery and morphed into several different mechanisms of domination designed to destroy the Black family: the war on drugs, racist welfare policies, and mass incarceration, to name a few. If we view the milquetoast response of the Black church as a microcosm, it mirrors the response of the Black community at large; for it is a significant justice issue, and we are missing it.

Within my own family, aunts and uncles are perplexed as to why the cousins and I are single. It's not even a familial pressure; at this point, they know something's up. They'll share their questions, and I'll talk to them about the systemic factors that feed into the interpersonal. The lightbulb clicks for them, and they'll ask what they can do to help. I tell them we need the aunties to start an intercessory prayer line, 'cause if God don't do it, it won't get done. Dr. Barbara Thomas-Reddick taught us!

When I read Dianne M. Stewart's *Black Women, Black Love: America's War on African American Marriage,* I felt seen in her descriptions of the systemic forces working against us. Stewart lays out the issue masterfully when she says, "Most heterosexual Black women in America today, whether parenting offspring or not, are single by circumstance, not by choice." Stewart continues, "The trouble is not with Black women failing to value marriage; it is the shrinking demographic of those whom Black women want to marry. . . . In some cases Black women lack dating prospects within their socioeconomic group, and in other cases they don't have any dating prospects *at all*!" She characterizes Black women's lack of opportunities for love and marriage with Black men as "the nation's most hidden and thus neglected civil rights issue to date."

For example, the 2010 U.S. Census revealed that in 2009, 71 percent of Black women in America were unmarried. Of that group, 71 percent of Black women between the ages of twenty-five and twenty-nine and 54 percent of those between the ages of thirty and thirty-four had *never* been married.[1] This is by design, for there are over four hundred years' worth of receipts that attest to Black love as a contested site in this nation.

To use Stewart's language, the "war on African American marriage" continues apace.

This war began when West Africans were stolen from their land, kin, spouses, indigenous culture, and everything they ever knew, and were bound in chains, trafficked through the Middle Passage, brought here, and conscripted to life under chattel slavery. The war continued on plantations, where the foundations of colorism in the United States were laid. And the war raged on during the postemancipation era, which ushered in the terror of lynchings of over four thousand Black men—and women, like Mary Turner, who was pregnant at the time of her lynching. Her fate and her child's and, in turn, her Black family's were tethered to that gruesome death.

In response to the racial terror of these lynchings, Black people fled the South in what became known as the Great Migration. In search of greener pastures and more employment opportunities, they moved up north and out west, roughly from

1916–1970—only to be met with discriminatory welfare policy practices that became apparent beginning in the mid-twentieth century. These policies prohibited Black love by keeping Black women's love lives under surveillance. Stewart writes, "In order to qualify for welfare, mothers had to be single and unemployed with underage children to support. If a recipient developed a romantic relationship with a man or got married, her male consort or husband had to assume full financial responsibility for her and her children's care and well-being; thus, she would no longer qualify for public assistance." In other words, these welfare policies sealed countless Black women to a fate of singlehood.

In the eighties, Reagan's draconian "war on drugs" laid the foundation for what is perhaps the most trenchant weapon against Black love in modern-day history: mass incarceration. According to Stewart, "In 1980 143,000 Black men were incarcerated. By 2008 that number climbed to 846,000." Stewart goes on to say, "When we add the numbers of Black males locked away in jail cells to those serving prison sentences, our nation's carceral facilities actually house nearly 1 million Black men today." Seemingly overnight, nearly one million Black men disappeared into public and private prisons all over this country, depleting the Black marriageability pool and leaving a deleterious impact on the Black family in its wake. This issue is the sleeping giant in our community because it has taken us unaware. The mass depletion of the heterosexual Black marriage market—and the speed at which it occurred—will reverberate for generations to come.

For all the noise about singleness and dating—all the blog posts, advice columns, think pieces, and YouTube videos—we rarely reckon with this sleeping giant. Instead, we get platitudes and verses thrown at us. Sometimes singleness is spoken of as if it's a chronic condition in need of a cure or a gift that most Christians don't want. Often it is framed as suffering. Others speak of it with contempt or with an eventual resignation that this will always be their lot.

Yet the assumption underlying most of these conversations about singleness and dating is that the intended audience has been in a relationship or is dating on a regular basis and just hasn't yet met their spouse. But there is one perspective I have yet to read, and it's that of a person who is perpetually single, like me.

Without a doubt, there are structural realities that have contributed to my singleness, like mass incarceration. "There are approximately 100 unimprisoned Black women to 91 unimprisoned Black men," according to Stewart. Ta-Nehisi Coates shares a litany of harrowing statistics in *The Atlantic* ("The Black Family in the Age of Mass Incarceration"): "In 2000, one in 10 black males between the ages of 20 and 40 was incarcerated—10 times the rate of their white peers. In 2010, a third of all black male high-school dropouts between the ages of 20 and 39 were imprisoned, compared with only 13 percent of their white peers." Coates also writes, "One in four black men born since the late 1970s has spent time in prison." In other words, in the year 2000, as I was entering college—one of the most viable ways to meet a suitable marriage partner—my Black male peers were entering cages all over this nation.

Additionally, colorism is an intraracial dynamic that has played a role in my singleness. Researchers have found that dark-skinned Black women like me are less likely to be married than our light-skinned counterparts. Dark-skinned Black women are also dis-proportionately impacted by the depletion of the Black male marriage pool. This point is underscored by Darrick Hamilton, Arthur H. Goldsmith, and William Darity, Jr., in "Shedding 'Light' on Marriage: The Influence of Skin Shade on Marriage for Black Females." They found that 55 percent of light-skinned Black women had been married, compared with only 23 percent of their dark-skinned counterparts.

My particular experience of singleness is categorically differ-ent from that of someone who has had a relationship that fiz-zled, or who found love and lost it. Still, I've experienced the fizzling without the courtesy of a clear relationship status. To put it bluntly, I've been ghosted more times than I can count or even care to recall.

For those who don't know, ghosting is a pervasive modern dating phenomenon whereby the person you have an estab-lished connection with, have gone on dates with, and have been corresponding with on a daily or consistent basis, without warning or explanation, stops talking to you via all modes: phone call, text messages, FaceTime, social media, email, mes-sages in bottles, and carrier pigeon. I'm being facetious about the latter two mediums, because humor blunts the trauma.

In my view, ghosting is a cowardly act that lacks integrity and care for the other person. At best it's careless, and at worse, it's dehumanizing. When someone is ghosted, they are literally and functionally treated as if they do not exist and are rendered invisible. There is a real person on the other side of ghosting. It is cowardly, dishonorable, and loveless. Ghosting ought not be the modus operandi of Christians, who are bound to the second greatest commandment that Jesus gave us, which is to love our neighbor as ourselves. The people we choose to date are our neighbors, too, and if we say we are Christians, then it's incumbent upon us to choose courage over cowardice. Courage is a prerequisite for love, and love is the most excellent way. Walk in it. Stop ghosting people.

This is different from the suffering that attends a failed relationship. I don't want to minimize that experience, for joy is joy and pain is pain. Nevertheless, there is another dimension of heartbreak that comes into view when one is seen but not sought after. I call it *rejection through forcible abstention*,[2] which is to say there is a rejection that stems from never being chosen, or from choosing to initiate but never having the one chosen reciprocate your desire.

While I'm on the subject of desirability, let me state for the record that desirability is a scam. If I had a dime for every time I heard, "But you're so pretty! I don't believe that you've never had a boyfriend!" I could pay off my student loan debt and all the student loans of the sistas at the table! By generally accepted Black girl beauty standards, I am considered attractive. I'm tall, dark (although, controlling for colorism, this is typically a disadvantage; more on this in the colorism chapter), and fit. I work out religiously because I'm determined to combat the weathering effects of white supremacy on my body.

All that to say, I'm what people would classify as desirable. However, this was not always so. The world around me taught me that beauty did not belong to me. Beauty was something I saw in music videos—back when music videos mattered. Beauty was something reserved for the video girls, light-skinned women with "good hair." Now, this was in the early 2000s, before the natural hair movement—so don't throw stones at me;

these were the rules of beauty, and I followed them as a rule of life. I wish I could tell you that I did not internalize the messages of undesirability, but that's simply not true. Especially as a dark-skinned Black girl turned Black woman who was born and raised and lived my entire twenties in California.

It wasn't until I moved to Philadelphia for graduate studies that this began to change. My physicality remained the same, but my mentality about my appearance started shifting. In Philadelphia, I found that a broader Black beauty standard existed—one that included Black women who are tall, dark, and fit like me. But in California and on the West Coast, these same traits rendered me invisible and excluded, especially due to my complexion.

Beauty standards are not transnational, which is why my *sweet mother* would often remind me that my gap-toothed smile is a symbol of beauty back in her home country of Nigeria. But in my home country, the United States of America, it is not. Beauty standards are socially, culturally, contextually, and even regionally determined, which is why I am considered beautiful in Philadelphia and undesirable or ugly in Los Angeles.

Lastly, beauty standards do change with time. On the fickle field of beauty, the goal posts stay moving. I've observed how the mobility of desirability has expanded to include Black women who look like me. Still, this doesn't negate my assertion that desirability is a scam. As human beings, we gravitate toward beauty; we create beautiful things in the world. And that's a good thing. *However,* the way we commodify, compare, manipulate beauty? The way we contort and control beauty, creating structures of beauty that idolize some and malign others? A scam.

Beauty or lack thereof does not determine if an individual will or won't be married. I think we know this intuitively, but due to our socialization, we continue to deceive ourselves into thinking that if we enhance, lighten, tighten, lift, *then* we will be desirable and partnered.

In her book *Thick,* Tressie McMillan Cottom writes, "Women's desire for beauty is a powerful weapon for exploitation. Even if the desire is natural, in that it is rational and also subconsciously coercive, open wanting against a backdrop of predatory constructs of cross-gender interactions is dangerous for women."

Desirability is a scam, and the Black male relationship hustlers (there are Black female relationship hustlers, too) who comprise the YouTube-and-Instagram-relationship industrial complex know this full well. I won't dignify their shameless hustle by naming them, but if you know, you know. They prey on Black women's genuine desire for marriage by telling them if they diet, defy the aging process, dress sexy (but not too sexy), and act like a wife before becoming a wife (whatever that means), they will achieve a higher level of desirability and inevitably land a husband.

But desirability is no match for the structural realities Black women contend with on a daily basis. Desirability's arms are too short to box with the enduring legacy of chattel slavery, which resulted in colorism, mass incarceration, and beauty hierarchies. Furthermore, desirability or lack thereof are not necessarily predictors of who will or won't get married because marriage markets are fundamentally inequitable—and doubly so for Black women. There are countless beautiful Black women you may know personally or in Hollywood who have never been married and may never get married, regardless of whether they desire it or not.

For my part, I do desire marriage. However, the school of undesirability taught me that desirability is a depreciating investment. The returns are marginal at best. I told y'all desirability is a scam. Now, because I came into awareness of my beauty at a very late stage in life—sometime between twenty-nine and thirty-two, if I had to put a number on it—I've never had the blessing—or the curse—of viewing my beauty as a site of my worth. And so I divested from the desirability industrial complex and invested in my mind and my spiritual growth: reading the Word, reading books, developing my own political education, and cultivating my inner beauty and other traits that are not subject to time, chance, and systems of hierarchy.

If there was an upside to the absence of a legitimate relationship, perhaps it's that I came to realize that there is abundant life outside of the male gaze, and that there is more to life than beauty, because desirability is not an appreciating investment. If you want to make yourself look good for you, by all means do so. That's how I live: I express myself through the way I dress, with bold prints, jewelry, and shoes. When I look good, I feel good. But if you're doing it to pull a man, you're making a bad investment, sis. Let's be honest: the way patriarchy is set up, a good portion of our male counterparts are hardly coming close to the desirability structural standards set by society, because they don't have to. Black heterosexual men are given a disproportionate amount of leverage because their dating pool is teeming with a bevy of Black women and non-Black women to choose from, and they are keenly aware of this. I suspect this explains the incessant relationship discourse on Black Twitter, which typically devolves into a zero-sum game: Black men lord their options over Black women, and Black women clap back saying they don't need a man because they have their own financial resources.

Desirability is a scam.

What shall we say to this constellation of oppression—mass incarceration, colorism, the desirability pyramid scheme, and the multitude of other weapons that got us here? Conventional wisdom may say that "nice girls finish last," but here's what happens when the finish line never comes into view: shame arrives in its stead.

In his book *Shame Interrupted,* Edward T. Welch defines shame as "the deep sense that you are unacceptable because of something you did, something done to you, or something associated with you. You feel exposed and humiliated." Later in the book, he explicates the nature of shame, saying, "You can do a fine job of heaping shame on yourself. All it takes is a tradition of demeaning, critical words from the right person. All it takes is *nothing* from the right person. No interest in you, no words spoken to you, no love. If you are treated as if you do not exist, you will feel shame."

For a long while in my experience of singleness, rejection and shame were my teachers. They worked in tandem, turning me inward and tutoring me with interrogating lies. Worth? I have received nothing; therefore, I am nothing. Desirability? I am not pretty; that's why guys don't pursue me. Adequacy? No matter what I do, it's never enough. I don't measure up. *Shame.*

It took years of prayer, meditation on God's word, discipleship, ongoing therapy, and a deeper understanding of the gospel of Jesus Christ to graciously pull the wickedly stubborn root of shame and rejection from my heart. Even now, there is still some scar tissue. Shame's dastardly lessons from the past haunt me sporadically. How can they not? After all, the Gospel doesn't inoculate us from the pain we experience in this fallen world. In fact, it is promised to us that, by virtue of our union with Christ, we will suffer to some degree (Phil. 1:29).

Believe me when I say that I am deeply acquainted with suffering, to the point that I've almost got a PhD in it. In the words of the prophetess Mary J. Blige, "If you looked at my life and see what I see," you'd know that the school of hard knocks raised me. So I understand that we will suffer in this life. I also know that God's Word says, in Isaiah 54:17, "No weapon formed against you shall prosper." But these weapons formed against *us* feel like they are prospering, and I need to know: why do Black women suffer to the greatest degree?

In her book *In My Grandmother's House: Black Women, Faith, and the Stories We Inherit,* Yolanda Pierce punctuates my query with a piercing question of her own as she masterfully lays out the plight of Black women. Pierce asks,

Does God love Black women? Statistics reveal the crushing inequality that marks Black women's lives in the United States. More than one-quarter live in poverty, a rate more than double that of their white counterparts. Black babies face double the risk of dying before their first birthdays as white babies do, and Black women are two to three times more likely to die from pregnancy-related causes than white women. Black women are significantly more likely to be the sole wage earner in their households; to never marry at all; to suffer divorce; or to be widowed young. Black women, even the most educated, struggle with housing insecurities at high rates and significant wage disparities. Black women are incarcerated at twice the rate of other women and face higher rates of death from treatable and preventable diseases. Despite pursuing post-secondary education at the highest rates in the nation, becoming entrepreneurs and business owners in unprecedented numbers finally breaking through corporate, ecclesial, and academic glass ceilings, Black women still face unemployment, poverty, disease, and loneliness. Black women are still paid sixty-two cents on every dollar that a white man makes.

The receipts abound. These are questions that need answers. When I first began writing about singleness years ago, shame was the only emotion that I could name at the time. But as I've grown older and had more time to analyze my relationship status, dating experiences, and the collective single status of this sorority of single Black women that many of us did not pledge but were hazed into, shame has transformed—or progressed— into anger.

If I may be so bold, I'd name this particular kind of anger *righteous*. Shame is so insidious, and it turns us inward. I don't want to presume that there isn't some vestige of shame that still lingers within. So I think it best to unpack both the shame and the righteous anger that I feel. I began with shame, since that's an emotion that I've known for a longer period of time. Its ubiquity is instructive, as it is a site of resonance for many of the sistas at our table.

The shame I once felt (and that might still be lingering) has been eclipsed by the righteous anger I feel. Yes, I'm angry, and *righteously* so. To hell with *stereotype threat* about *controlling images* like "Sapphire," and forget the "angry Black woman" tropes. In the words of the sage Solange Knowles, I got a lot to be mad about. So don't ask me why I'm mad. Ask yourself why you aren't.

I'm often reluctant to claim righteous anger, because I'm aware of my own capacity for sin, which can impede my ability to rightly assess issues. Anger is not a sin; it is a valid emotion. However, anger—even when it is legitimate—can be an all-consuming emotion that springs up within us when we are wronged or if we perceive that we have been wronged. If that anger is not harnessed and channeled in productive ways, it can be self-centered, misdirected, retaliatory, and in extreme cases, it can be deadly.

But righteous anger is generative. It rises up within us when we see that justice is denied, delayed, perverted, or suppressed. Where shame turns us inward, collapsing us into ourselves, righteous anger turns us outward toward our neighbor, our community, fighting against systems of injustice. Righteous anger is a fire burning deep inside our bones. And when it comes to the unjust and systematic depletion of the intraracial marriage pool for Black women, I am confident that my anger is righteous.

Consider Matthew 21:12–13:

Jesus entered the temple courts and drove out all who were buying and selling there. He overturned the tables of the money-changers and the benches of those selling doves. "It is written," he said to them, "'My house will be called a house of prayer,' but you are making it 'a den of robbers.'"

Now, Jesus is God, and God is holy. Therefore, it's redundant to call Jesus's anger righteous, because He is *altogether* righteous. So I'll forgo the "righteous" qualifier when talking about Jesus. Upon entering the temple, Christ sees the money changers and merchants taking advantage of the poor. At the time, worship required sacrifice, so people would purchase animal sacrifices in order to worship God in the temple. Knowing this, the merchants hiked up the prices, extorting money from the poor, which obstructed the people's means of prayer and worship.

Christ was outraged. And out of His anger, Christ forcefully puts a stop to this injustice.

He begins to quote Isaiah 56:7, emphasizing that God's temple is a house of prayer for all nations, where the burnt offerings and sacrifices of the gentiles will also be accepted. It's no coincidence that this verse in Isaiah comes from a chapter about salvation for the gentiles. Yet the money changers and merchants had erected in the temple a system of injustice through extortion and ethnocentrism. When Jesus turned over the tables of the money changers and merchants, He was resisting that system. It was an act of restoration to reclaim the temple as a house of prayer for all nations. Righteous anger can be restorative.

When I think about the convergence of shame and anger, I'm reminded of Hagar, the Egyptian slave of Sarai who became the second wife of Abram, and whose story is recorded in Genesis 16:1–16. She knew both emotions all too well. Sarai and Abram, who grew impatient with God's promise that they would have a child, used Hagar as a means to an end by forcing her to marry Abram in order to conceive a child for them. As if that abuse weren't enough, Sarai began to torment Hagar. The weight proved too much for Hagar to bear, and when she discovered she was pregnant, Hagar was furious and began to despise Sarai. Sista Hagar had a right to be mad.

It's important to name the nature of her mistreatment, because euphemisms veil the suffering that Hagar endured. It's crucial that we examine the interiority of Hagar's life and her lived experience as a slave. We always want to pay close attention to the most marginalized person in the text.

I believe in calling a thing a thing, so I will lift up a few verses from this passage for closer examination.

Verse 3: "So after Abram had been living in Canaan for ten years, Sarai, his wife, took her Egyptian slave Hagar and gave her to her husband to be his wife." In her desperation, Sarai *saw* Hagar, she *took* Hagar, and she *gave* Hagar to Abram. Sarai objectified, exploited, used, and abused Hagar by forcing her to marry Abram. There are entire books written about the ways women are complicit in the oppression of other women.

Verse 4: "He slept with Hagar, and she conceived. When she knew she was pregnant, she began to despise her mistress." This is a significant act that is often missed in this text. Now, it must be said plainly that this was not a consensual sexual act; it was rape, because Hagar was a slave. This is what I mean by examining the interiority of Hagar's life. The power dynamics must be accounted for. Her agency was restricted, and she *could not* consent to sex, because of her status as a slave, which was changed to "wife" via forced marriage.

It's an unfortunate reality, but rape can and does occur within the covenant of marriage. People get uncomfortable when you expose the egregious sins of the patriarchs and matriarchs. But we don't need to absolve them, nor can we cover their sins; God did that through the sacrifice of His Son, Jesus Christ. The matriarchs and patriarchs were saved by faith and in hope of the One to come, Jesus Christ. We must see them in the fullness of their humanity—the good, the bad, and the ugly—so that we know beyond a shadow of a doubt that the grace of God and forgiveness given to them is extended to us as well. Sin is ugly, but grace is scandalous. We are not more gracious than God.

But God's grace does not negate consequences.

After being left in the merciless grip of Sarai, Hagar did the only thing she knew to do: she escaped. Renita J. Weems says this in her article "Do You See What I See? Diversity in Interpretation": "We know only too well the kinds of violence the Egyptian woman must have been forced to endure: beatings, verbal insults, ridicule, strenuous work, degrading tasks and the like. For to be under the power of a resentful woman can be a dangerous thing." After enduring this violence, Hagar, a sexual assault survivor, escaped her abusers with a belly full of life—though certain she was running to her own death and that of her unborn child.

Lo and behold, a Divine plot twist awaited Hagar in the wilderness, where she was met by the angel of the Lord. This is poetic justice, as this is the first time that "the angel of the Lord" appears in the Bible. Oftentimes, these appearances are thought to be the appearance of God in physical form, which is called a "theophany." God chose to reveal Himself in this way for the first time to Hagar, an Egyptian slave, an African woman, and our ancestor.

God binds Himself to the oppressed.

In their interaction, the angel affirmed God's love for Hagar, expressed in this promise: "I will increase your descendants so much that they will be too numerous to count" (Gen. 16:10). And then the angel instructed Hagar to return to the house of bondage.

Truthfully, I struggle with this part. Every time I read it, I exclaim, "*Why,* Lord? Why would you send Hagar back to the site of oppression? You're the God of liberation, deliverance, and justice! That's who you are!" According to Delores S. Williams in her book *Sisters in the Wilderness,* by sending Hagar back to Abram and Sarai, God is giving her a "survival strategy." Williams says, "God apparently wants Hagar to secure her and her child's well-being by using the resources Abram has to offer." Hagar could not do that in the desert. God works through ordinary means.

As I wrestled with this verse in particular in light of where we have come from as a people, what we have been through, and where we are now, it became clear to me that Hagar stands as representative for Black women, which might also explain why her narrative resonates with so many of us. Hagar escaped into the wilderness, where she was sure to die, for she had no practical means of survival as an enslaved pregnant woman on the run. But it was there that she had her divine encounter with

God in the wilderness. The very site of death became a site of liberation and life for Hagar. Only God can do that.

Don't tell me what God *can't* do.

After receiving this precious promise from the Lord, in jubilee, liberation, and in holy boldness, Hagar named God. "She gave this name to the Lord who spoke to her: 'You are the God who sees me,' for she said, 'I have now seen the One who sees me.'" (Gen. 16:13). After reading this, and the passage as a whole, the earlier questions bear repeating:

Why do Black women suffer to the greatest degree?

Does God love Black women?

And now: Does God see Black women? Has God given *us* survival strategies, too?

Dr. Pierce brings these questions to life when she says,

And yet Black women are among the most faithful and religious Americans by any measure. We attend church more frequently than people of any other race and more frequently than Black men. We pray more, give more, and serve more. We open the doors of the church, clean the bathrooms, and then close the doors of the church. With membership that is on average 85 percent female, Black churches across the nation rely on our tithes and offerings to literally keep the lights on. We consistently indicate that faith is the most important aspect guiding decisions in our daily lives. So how can we reconcile the stark contrast between Black women's material existence and our demonstrated love for God and faithfulness to God's people? I have never doubted, not even once, that the Black women in my life truly love God with all their might. I have sometimes doubted, however, whether God loves these faithful Black women in return. Even accepting the theological tenet that it rains on the just and unjust, that bad things happen to good people, I could not understand why such a disproportionate share of suffering seemed to be the lot of Black women. Why did it appear that the more faithful a Black woman was in her service to God, the more she suffered?

Why do Black women suffer to the greatest degree? Honestly, I don't have the answer to my own question. This question is one of theodicy: how can God be good in the face of evil? Theodicy is a question that theologians have been wrestling with for centuries, so I'm embracing my finitude by exercising theological humility in saying: I don't know. I don't know why we suffer in all the ways we do as Black women. What I have come to learn during this faith journey is that our "why" questions to God are soul cries for which there exist no satisfactory answers on this side of heaven. I realize that even that answer is insufficient, but it's truer to the human experience than trite platitudes about "God giving his toughest battles to his strongest soldiers," or however the saying goes.

Does God love Black women? Does God see Black women? Has God given survival strategies to Black women? Undoubtedly, yes—and it is Hagar, our ancestor, who provides incontrovertible evidence that Black women are loved by God, seen by God, and equipped with survival strategies to continue our sojourning.

As I stated earlier, I see Hagar as a representative for Black women. Because of this, I marvel that the first recorded appearance of the angel of the Lord is in this encounter with Hagar. At this point in history, covenant promises were given to the Israelites. But Hagar was an Egyptian, and an enslaved woman at that. Still, God remembered Hagar, heard her cries, pursued her, and called her by her name. Hagar's cause was not disregarded nor forgotten by God. God took her shame and anger and unbowed her head by blessing her with honor and a promise. The Lord is the lifter of Hagar's head; and as she is our representative, God sees us, remembers us, and lifts our heads, too.

Just as Hagar had to return to the house of bondage for a time, with a belly full of life and promise, Jesus leaves us with a promise of His return and the indwelling of the Holy Spirit as we contend with the structures of domination against us. We are reminded daily by our social media timelines and the evening news that we live in "this present-evil age" (Gal. 1:4). And so, we find ourselves living in the tension of the already and the not-yet. In other words, Christ's Kingdom has been inaugurated by Christ's coming and finished work on the cross; but the full manifestation of the Kingdom of God has not come and will not come in its fullness until Christ's return. However, since the Kingdom of God has broken into this present evil age, we are to seek justice and expose evil systems of oppression, bringing them from the realm of darkness into the light of Truth.

Bible study's over, y'all. Respectfully. So, what is we gon' do?

The far-reaching tentacles of oppression via the transatlantic slave trade, chattel slavery, racial terror in the form of lynching, the "war on drugs," racist welfare policies, mass incarceration, colorism, and beauty hierarchies have depleted the Black male marriage market, leaving heterosexual Black women who desire marriage single for far longer than they intend. It is one thing for a Black woman to *choose* singleness—which is her prerogative; not everyone desires marriage. It is another thing entirely to desire marriage and to have your agency with regard to your marital status stripped away from you due to mechanisms of oppressions that have been in motion for hundreds of years. Part of what it means to be fully human is to exercise our God-given agency. When this is restricted, injustice is afoot.

Again I say: what is we gon' do?

One of the ways we contend with this injustice is by utilizing the survival strategies God has given to us through the Gospel, His word, and the church.

The Black church has always been on the forefront of civil rights issues. Undoubtedly, it is a bulwark against injustice. This particular justice issue, however, seems to have taken the Black church unawares. As Dianne M. Stewart says, "Black women's lack of options for meaningful love and partnership with Black men is the nation's most hidden and thus neglected civil rights issue to date." I don't believe that the entire onus of this falls on the Black church exclusively. But I do think there are some viable paths forward.

It is much easier to diagnose a problem than to provide solutions, but I offer some interventions that can provide support to single Black women who want and need it in lieu of marriage.

While Black women are one of the most educated groups in the country, it is no secret that we are saddled with student loan debt, housing insecurity, and wage discrimination; we make sixty-two cents for every dollar a white man makes. We are ensnared by anti-Black racism, sexism, and misogynoir, all of which have a negative impact on our health.

Since this is the case, I have often thought of single Black women as the modern-day widows. In the Bible, widows were often marginalized, oppressed, and disregarded because their livelihood and value were connected to their spouse. Without their husband, they were conscripted to a life of poverty apart from divine intervention (2 Kings 4:17). Scripture is replete with instructions to care for the widow, defend the widow, visit the widow, and care for the widow. Even in the early church, we see that widows were neglected in the distribution of food (Acts 6:1).

Although women's lives and livelihoods are no longer bound to their marital status, I consider us modern-day widows because as single Black women, we are especially vulnerable to and impacted by the oppressive systems described above. As such, where possible and needed, I believe the church requires a more expansive use of the benevolent fund, which is typically reserved for the widows, single mothers, the bereaved, struggling college students, and the "sick and shut-in." But this also needs to include single Black women, our modern-day widows. By God's grace, we're the ones who keep the doors of the church open with our tithes, offerings, and service to the church. At what point do the material conditions of single Black women get acknowledged and met by the church? When do we reap what we've sown?

Real talk, this is not transactional. I love the church—I'm not trying to creep on a come-up.

But this is about a *particularly* critical injustice that must be dealt with *particularly*.

Another intervention that can help single Black women is cooperative living spaces that are built by Black churches, where single Black women can opt to live in community with other Black women who may or may not have the kinship networks that serve to provide housing and communal support. The women would pay rent at just below market rates, and they'd have the built-in community of other single Black women on whom they can rely for grocery runs, transportation needs, and a friend to accompany them to doctor's appointments. As people are being diagnosed with life-altering diseases at younger ages, a trusted and safe community is critical for cancer diagnoses and other health crises. Even in the more mundane tasks, like digging out our car after a snowstorm, or dealing with a furry rodent who makes an unexpected appearance in our living quarters during the winter months, it would be a great relief to know we can rely on someone within the cooperative living space to help with those ordinary nuisances.

Lastly, due to the scope of the depletion of the Black marriage market in the United States, we need a pan-African response. It's imperative for Black churches, African churches, and Caribbean churches to come together to dialogue and dream together about some tangible ways to support the single Black women in their congregations.

Last time I checked, we are not God and can't create Black men out of the dust. What we *can* do is take a global approach to this issue. My suggestion? A pan-African dating service or app. This would offer options either for Black women in the United States who are interested in moving out of the country for love—and because America is off the chain—or for Black men abroad who are interested in moving to the United States.

This would also give options domestically for those who are interested in dating within the Black diaspora, but exclusively within the United States. For those who want to get in their *90 Day Fiancé* bag, they'd also have the option to stay in the United States while searching for bae abroad. With "approximately 100 unimprisoned Black women to 91 unimprisoned Black men," as it stands, for single Black women like me who desire to be married, the reality is that not everyone who shares that desire will have it fulfilled apart from a pan-African response and God's will.

As for me, by God's grace, shame no longer defines this area of my life as it has in the past. A beautifully redemptive combination of age and God's means of grace has helped me arrive at the realization that God has an immense calling on my life that reaches far beyond my marital status. Yet this doesn't necessarily preclude marriage.

I've come to hold all things loosely—including the good things I desire. As I get older, I realize that this unrequited desire may never be filled. But I arrive at this conclusion with a peace that surpasses all human understanding and an inner resolve wrought by the Holy Spirit.

I know that God promises to be "a sun and shield; the Lord bestows favor and honor" (Ps. 84:11). God did that for Hagar, so I know He will continue to do that for me. "No good thing will he withhold from those who walk uprightly" (ibid.). I'm learning that what God hasn't given to me is not necessary. Marriage is not food and water; I will not die without it. But it would be nice to laugh with and love someone and have that love reciprocated in this cold, hard world. Yes, this hope deferred would make this heart sick, leaving an indelible soul wound (Prov. 13:12). And yes, my lived experience, and that of other single Black women, did not happen naturally by osmosis; it was systematically engineered before we came to be. Yet none of these things minimize my desire for marriage—specifically, for Black love. As I ponder this aloud to the Lord, I consider the Black love He *has* given me:

In friendships.

In the local church.

In mentors.

In my family.

Black love is a survival strategy in a country hell-bent on destroying it with each successive generation. When you see a Black woman marry a Black man in this present day and time, know that you are witnessing a miracle, and God is still in the miracle-working business. I was formed and fashioned in the depths of thick, deep, and rich Black love that my mother and father had for each other. Their Black love is etched in my soul in such a way that even if I never become a partaker of Black marriage, I cherish the fact that I've come to know it tangentially by recognizing Black love for the miracle that it is. May we all behold this miracle. And may we work toward the manifestation of this miracle for the single Black women who desire Black love.

# Divorce

## By Michelle Higgins

Now unto the One who is able to keep you from falling; the One who has the power to present you faultless before the presence of God's glory—with exceeding great joy. To God be glory and honor, dominion, and power, now and forevermore. Amen.

JUDE 24–25

I WAS MARRIED IN 2007; I filed for divorce in 2018. The in-between time was ministry, mothering, and making music amid a mutually manufactured mess.

I left my husband in my heart—and in my behavior—about a month before I was able to physically move my body to tell my family and my children.

People ask me all the time, *If you just had to get out of this marriage, why wait and plan and deliberate for a month after knowing for sure you wanted to go?* I don't mind the question, no matter how condescending and challenging it might seem. I count it as an opportunity to tell my story. If they want me to answer for every person who has ever left their partner, I cannot supply that. I have ended my long-term career of playing God.

But if, on the other hand, they want me to answer for *myself,* if they want the answer that describes *my* thoughts and actions, *my* spiritual and emotional state, then I tell them exactly that: my story. And I simply ask them to listen.

So pull up a chair and have a listen.

## PART 1: WHO IS ABLE TO KEEP YOU FROM FALLING?

When we got married, we made a plan: He'd hustle so I could get through grad school without needing to work full time. And then I'd hustle so that he could launch his business.

So in 2009, we moved to St. Louis, Missouri—my hometown—so I could pursue a Master's in Divinity, the degree that clergy people are often required by denominations to complete for ordination. During my four years in seminary, I gave birth to our two children. After I graduated in 2013, I served as a music director and worship leader for two churches, led a community choir, and co-founded two racial justice organizations. By 2017, I was planting the St. Louis office of a national initiative to interrupt predatory cash bail. Throughout all of this, I remained committed to supporting my husband's dreams as he had been committed to mine. I thought that was the formula for health in marriage.

Our busy, fast-paced lifestyle did not come without challenges, which increased along with our calendar conflicts in the three years following my graduation from seminary. While my husband launched his business and I worked three jobs, we leaned on my family to care for our children and on our community to keep us updated on any needs that we could help meet. We mistakenly mistook marital health for ministry involvement. Because few people in our church cared about social justice issues, our outward work and service were constant. We did not hold ourselves and one another accountable to the same ethics by which we served others. We loved our neighbors more than we loved one another and ourselves.

We began to argue about never having time to process emotional struggles, often after hosting parties or meetings. He felt that I was always creating space for mentoring and leadership development, but not for developing our relationship. When my husband felt a dive in his emotions, he told me that I had the power to make him feel relevant, but I was not giving myself emotionally to the marriage in the same way that I had served logistically. He wondered if my ministry and movement work was more exciting to me than our relationship. He told me that I clearly did not want to talk about our problems. He was not entirely incorrect. Whenever he wanted to talk about our problems, I could not look him in the eyes. This is because we often could not have a reasonable discussion without first exchanging words of discouragement. He told me that I must think that meal prep and calendar planning can count as intimacy. He told me that I was only pretending to support launching his business. That I really only worked multiple jobs so I could impress people by paying for expensive dinners and get-togethers. So I could buy stylish clothes. I understand why he would make those statements, but the words were hurtful, and I did not feel invited to converse when he spoke them. Within hours, he would apologize for all the depressing things he said to me. Each time I'd tell him, "No worries."

And I was not lying. I was not worried. I thought that his behavior was tense because we were in a really busy time in our lives. I knew that his actions were in direct reaction to my inaction. I knew I was to blame for so much of what was happening.

I didn't worry, because I thought, "Can't nothing hurt me!" As the old song says, *I been lied on, cheated, talked about and mistreated.* I been rebuked and scorned, been talked about soon as I was born. In the moment, I felt confident that I would overcome every mean word and harsh statement. So I let arguments slide, and I covered the hurts with a happy face and more hours of work. I created distance when he or I slipped into discouraging speech patterns or actions. I would make sure our family had evenings and weekends full of outings, hosting parties, and other social plans. I agreed to every speaking engagement, paid or not. On days when I knew that my husband would be at home, I spent afternoons at my church office after picking up the kids from school.

We were very much visibly together. Our relationship appeared to be strong and joyous, and a few people said we looked like we were in love. I was not worried, and I did not think I needed to be.

But I should have been worried. After ten years in a marriage of "making it by faking it," we ended up breaking it.


On a foggy February morning, I was preparing to leave the house for a road trip, to lead worship at a conference a few hours away. The bedrooms in our apartment were close to each other. The children were in their bedroom getting ready for school as I packed my things in my suitcase in the bedroom beside theirs. My husband began confronting me about our half life. He said that if I cared about him half as much as I cared about ministry and movement work, he'd be the happiest man on the planet—but he was the opposite. "You're making me miserable," he raised his voice through an attempted whisper.

Before I could respond, I heard my worship team arrive outside to pick me up. We were running late, so I decided I didn't have time for this mood that morning. I turned to leave the room, and I saw my children holding hands with each other, staring at me. This was the first time they'd heard an argument in our house. You could see it on their faces. This was the first time they watched my countenance fade. All of my "I got this" attitude suddenly disappeared as I watched them look at me, then look at him, then turn and look at me. They wanted to know what I was going to do. And I knew whatever I did next, it would teach them what love is.

In an instant, I went from feeling bulletproof, armored against our issues, to worrying my children would think that our relationship was any kind of example of real love. They'd just witnessed harsh words that they had never heard before—a puncture in the lovey-dovey façade we'd been displaying for them. When it was just me and their father alone in a room, I could tend to my wounds on my own. But when this confrontation happened in their presence, with no warning, my worry went from zero to a hundred and I realized one thing: my children would suffer from us wounding each other. So, right in that moment, in front of our kids, I tried to manage just how wounded I felt. I spoke some words in what I prayed was a hopeful and apologetic tone, though I now wonder if it came across as dismissive and rushed or condescending. I promised my husband that we would talk as soon as I got home from the conference. I turned and reminded our kids to call and say goodnight and send me pictures. I told them to listen to their dad. I kissed all three of them, we prayed together, and I left the house. I wept the whole road trip, and at the conference, when I wasn't preaching or singing, I was sick to my stomach and fatigued. My team went out to dinner and movies, had fellowship, and encouraged one another. They worried about me and cared for me so well. Back at my house, when they'd arrived to pick me up, they'd heard some of the words exchanged. During the weekend they did not pry, but it was clear to me that they wondered if I was okay from their general "how are yous" paired with concerned glances. But I didn't know what to say.

A few weeks after that trip, I made plain to my husband that I had covered up my feelings about all the mutual disrespect that plagued our marriage. I was guilty of allowing him to think I was okay when I was not okay. I was allowing myself to be mistreated, and I admitted that I deceived him and everyone around us by pretending that our lives were happy.

From day to day, I told him, I was not sure if we showed signs of rot or resilience, because we so perfectly performed in spite of our problems. But I did not feel mutual respect and encouragement in our marriage, and I had to face the fact that he felt used. But I did not feel humanized in our marriage, and he had made clear that he felt used.

"The truth is this," I told him, "you need to talk to me like my daddy is in the room. We need to talk to each other like our Father is in the room. We have never done this." All our discouraging words had brought weakness where we should have shared strength. They brought fear of failure instead of fortitude

by faith. I believed him when he said that I make him miserable. No one deserves to be stuck in such a life.

My children and I moved in with my parents, who also live
in St. Louis.

My husband told people I'd left him and taken our children
with me. This news did not upset me. I know that my departure
was a weight and a shock to him. I felt a massive sympathy and
sadness about departing in a way that he felt was extremely
abrupt and unkind. I was silent and did not communicate for
weeks. I had no other options in considering my well-being.

For all those years I'd spent wrestling with blame, for all
those years I'd spent covering up his suspicions and my pain, I
was now paying the price. For too long, I deceived the people I
loved—including my husband—into believing that we were in
a healthy marriage. I deceived myself by telling my heart, mind,
and body that I was okay. I told myself that I could carry all the
issues in my marriage and my life, and even my husband's life.
And I thought that I could, in part because I did. I was convinced that I was able to keep us from falling.

When the word got around at church that I was leaving my
husband, the gossip mill took no time. People began confronting me in the church bathroom and over Facebook, asking me,
"Who had an affair?" And "Who hit who?" This particular community of Christians interprets divorce as forbidden by God,
except in the case of adultery or physical violence. So the only
way that my church could support me ending my marriage
would be if I was in one of these situations. Church leadership
asked what was so overwhelming, what was driving me to need
to be apart from this man. I suppose nothing I offered was grave
enough, because I was told that divorce is serious, and the lead-

ers of the church weren't certain that I was taking this situation seriously. I was told that because I was the worship director, my presence in leadership at church would cause too much confusion, and I ought to think about a sabbatical, for my health. Meanwhile my husband felt attacked and abandoned by people who he claimed sided with me and therefore hated him. He began searching for a different church home.

I agreed to step down from church ministry for a few months. The leaders of my church encouraged the congregation to pray for my family, and not to judge us or gossip about us. I was still able to travel and speak at conferences, as I was still assisting in paying for day-to-day expenses—for both my husband and my children. I was also trying to maintain rapport as a ministry leader, despite growing gossip among church families—and Christians I didn't even know.

But all this was eating away at my confidence and my already fragile peace. I answered a dozen questions a day for people I felt responsible to, whether or not I trusted them. I chose to visit different churches where I was not known as a leader—or anybody, really—and connected with fellow church ministry friends whose places of worship I wouldn't normally be able to visit on a Sunday morning. This looked more like me crying in the back of different sanctuaries and less like a grand tour of Sunday morning visitations.

This circus of self-explanation exhausted me. After several weeks of this, some church leaders arranged to interview me. They needed to decide whether I was to undergo church discipline for my decision to stop living with my husband.

For the interview, five of us met at the edge of a small office in the church building. I sat with my head bowed, arms folded and legs crossed tight as they could, in a small chair. I was asked to give a timeline of when exactly I felt the marriage fall apart. They spoke softly and sadly but encouraged me to be as honest and detailed as I was able. I felt interrogated. I wasn't sure how to answer that question, since I couldn't be sure that I ever had a marriage that was at all put together. I had only doubt that I could satisfy a group of men that I was not being rash or reactionary in my decision to end my marriage.

In the weeks following the interview, I did away with the secrecy of my decision to separate from and divorce my husband. I did not make any public statements, but I was not in hiding at my parents' house, and I told my children that their father and I would not be living together and someday would not be married. My church leaders connected me with a trusted church minister for direct pastoral care, and they offered my husband the same. Over the next few months, I felt resigned to the social and spiritual atmosphere of a Q & A session.

Friends and faith leaders from communities who uphold a complementarian view of marriage visited with me in my home. They spoke of how careful I needed to be about explaining why I wanted to get a divorce now, but never sought support or help with the problems in my marriage. They agreed that any gossip was wrong but insisted that my time away from leading worship was for my benefit. I expressed my understanding at how sudden and complicated my decision might seem.

For many of my visitors-turned-interviewers, it seemed that none of the issues I described were considered problems in marriage. I spoke of our arguments, our shared feelings of disconnection, the lack of understanding we left unmanaged that led to ever decreasing respect. I felt that I was simply not allowed to say, "This marriage is over." It was not good enough to say that I was just done playing superwoman. I was worn out from failing to seek help or share my burdens. I felt that I'd be judged as having no good reasons for wanting out of the marriage. I could not say, "This is what's best for my health," and be supported in my choice. I told them that my husband was miserable and we were both wounded from years of verbal volatility. They said that misery is not a reason to end a marriage. Most folks told me they were very sorry to hear that all of these things piled up. "But it sounds more like he needs to be admonished."

One Saturday morning in July, a few church leaders from different congregations came to visit with me informally. It was my wedding anniversary, and I was sick with shame and finding it hard to function. Conversation drifted to the divorce, as was usual by that time. When I shared that my marriage did not provide safety, someone said, "But you have said that he has not hit you." Correct, I said, that had not happened. And none of them agreed that I was unsafe.

I was again completely confused, deflated, and so deeply forlorn I could not lift my head to look at any person or object in the room. Nobody asked me, "Well, what do you mean?" No one in that room encouraged me to describe my view of safety in a relationship. I wanted to paint a picture of the impact of reassuring words in contrast to discouraging words. One type of speech brings life; the other one ends it. I saw myself describing every little wound that my husband and I had caused each other over the years, until finally the wounds were our only witnesses. I wanted to ask how two people who have done such damage to each other can truly keep each other safe.

I heard stories about how "we all say cruel things in anger sometimes. Everybody does it. Nobody means it."

One person looked at me, held my hand, and said, "Anyone who says they have never called someone worthless just because they're mad, come on."

*Jesus Christ of Nazareth,* I prayed in my mind as their words wrecked me. "Be careful, little mouth, what you say" rang the voice of every Sunday-school teacher and children's choir leader I ever knew. My Blackness was burning within me. My whole soul and body wanted to ask, "*Are y'all really trying to tell me that as long as you apologize, offensive words are* meaningless?" Instead, I phrased it in the form of a statement.

"When words flow from the heart," I told them, "even in the height of emotion, even in our anger, we are giving insight into what we truly believe. We are still being honest. We are still wielding a two-edged sword." There would be no more conversation after this. No one said it; everyone felt it. Every person in the room was speaking from their own baggage rack of bias. One brought a smooth suede satchel of newly learned seminary smarts, another a weathered leather briefcase filled with decades of depreciation and guilt. Mine was a three-piece set with a matching diaper bag, overstuffed with sensitivity to and suspicion of every word. We sat in our corners and convinced ourselves that each of the other people needed help, but we were right, and we would wait for them to come around.

Visitation from my evangelical friends continued, yes. But not community.

"I cannot be a good wife under the weight of causing and carrying so many years of unaddressed pain," I told many church leaders and friends. "Yes you can," they responded. "You can do all things with Jesus strengthening you."

Friends and mentors said that both my husband and I needed to get help, and that my husband and I certainly needed to be apart for a while. But unless I could prove physical abuse, we should only seek temporary separation.

In the view of my church community, it would be unbiblical to divorce.


## PART 2: "AND PRESENT YOU FAULTLESS"

In the evangelical church community, my divorce was talked about more widely than among the few congregations I had personal history with. A pastor at an entirely different church was known to have said, "I saw that coming; she's never at home," speaking openly about my pending divorce at a church event in the presence of people who knew me and were being pastored by him. This church had previously invited me to teach their ministry leaders about social justice and faith-rooted witness.

I won't narrate every second of the new kind of pain that I felt. What I will say is this: for months, I carried the sting of indifference from a church "community" who knew nothing about the true story of my marriage and cared more about my marital status than my own self. I spent those months trying to be happy for the sake of my children, sitting on my parents' bed weeping, sitting in my bathroom crying. (I met one of my now-dear friends, Stephanie, in a grocery store just after I was crying.) I was shedding tears in so many spaces I was almost laughing, thinking, *I have become a Lifetime movie.*

But it wasn't just faith leaders and gossip-prone pastors who made it hard. Even the presence of God in some of my church relationships felt forced and awkward. God's people talked of God only to enforce the command to stay married. Church members took me to lunch, brunch, and coffee, they FaceTimed and texted—all just to tell me, "I will not be able to talk to you for a while. I need time to process what you have done." In this moment I would like to say that I had learned my lesson about honesty and awareness of my wounds. But I reverted to the famous words "That's fine. It's okay," and I am sure I knew that I was not speaking truthfully, but I didn't have the strength to say more. And I did not have the time to do anything more. I did not know what could be done about these reactions anyway. Is anyone built to bear the weight of wondering how to comfort friends through your own distress?

In that season of upheaval, I was hungry, desperate even, for friendships with people who would humanize me. But I learned that I would not discover the fullness of that welcome at my church.

An old neighbor kindly asked me to explain my actions in light of a scripture that said, "What God has brought together let no one tear asunder." I was told more than once that people were praying that I would not choose a path "God would hate." People would tell me these things earnestly, but these "encouragements" only stung me more. Somehow the Bible became a force for keeping me in a marriage that was destroying me.

I stopped trying to root out the gossip. I confessed that I was constantly obsessing over my own reputation. I had spent almost ten years trying to control every outcome and strategize for every scenario. Deep down, I wasn't really upset by the fact that my husband treated me like a god, because I was trying to live like one.

The truth is, though, playing God was killing me.

This might be a good time to mention that the leadership and staff of my church community was at the time mostly comprised of white and conservative church folks who upheld the cultural perspective of complementarianism as the best way to interpret relationships between men and women. This view centers the belief that in marriage and spiritual relationships, women are meant to submit to men.

Long before my marriage or divorce, this belief already made no space for me. As a Black woman who worked outside of the house, the only thing I had in common with the average complementarian woman was a white husband.

Complementarian readings of scripture highlight marriage as a symbol God uses to show Jesus's love for the church. God uses the position of husband and the position of wife as analogous to Jesus and His followers. The popular doctrine attached to this symbolism is that, since God uses it, marriage becomes the place where two people experience God's love the most. Thus, it felt to me that it is not possible for a Christian who is not married to experience the deepest realities of Jesus's love for the church. I have a lot of questions for complementarianism.

But in 2013, after graduating from seminary, I was invited to share my perspectives on biblical manhood and womanhood, and I wanted to brush up on the different viewpoints—which I rarely thought about. One of my former professors directed me to resources on a popular white evangelical website, noting that the issue was centered in the "Marriage, Divorce, and Remarriage" section. The page described broken marriages as a "chaos," a reality stemming from the sins of Adam and Eve. I remember looking for guidance and support for women undergoing divorce, but the only information I found presumed infidelity and abandonment as the causes.

I noticed that none of the teachings came from women. This worried me. But I realized that this lack of representation matched the website founder's view of women not being built to teach the Bible to men. The more I read, the more I was able to name the truth of my experience of the complementarian view: the husband assumes the position of God, and the wife takes the position of worshipper. As I scrolled through this information, I was shocked. I longed to find some room for women in this understanding of marriage. And I longed for the presence of God. God who covers, God who rescues us from the pit. God who promises to restore all things. God who says, "Cast your cares on me." I longed for the God who says, "I care for you." Suffice it to say, complementarianism was not a worldview that brought me nearer to that God. This worldview that misuses the words of the Bible misses the God of the Bible entirely.

Complementarianism is a type of legalism that makes God as fragile as the people that Jesus was sent to save. When Christians berated me, dismissed me, gossiped about me, it was as if their picture of God's love could be marred by the failure of my marriage. But few people gave a second thought or concern to my remaining in a marriage that constantly failed to testify of God's power and love. After I spent almost a year in this season of strangeness and *caucacius* Christian confusion, I was yet determined to seek wisdom and welcome from the people of God. But I knew that real words of life could not be spoken under a worldview where women are silenced.

I resolved to seek out the wisdom of the wisest people I knew: the people who made me. I sought the womanist-rooted, maternal theology of the Black church. No time stood between me and my spiritual home. I preach, sing, and lead worship in the tradition of the Black Pentecostal church. I served in different pulpits for the Pastoral Fellowship of St. Louis. I was invited to licensure and ordination through my uncle's church, Peace Tabernacle. I was director of the St. Louis City Mass Choir. In spite of those things, I convinced myself that there was no room for me to be vulnerable in the presence of my people. I thought that I would be ashamed and anxious once I began to tell the truth—about my complicity in my failed marriage; my presumptuousness in pretending that the Black superwoman was real, and that she was me.

Instead, I was surprised—and deeply convicted—by the kindness I received.

I talked to my extended family first. My sister and I met up with my cousins once a month as part of a family support circle, and I immediately realized I'd had everything I needed all along. I stopped avoiding phone calls from my sisters Ekemini and Christina, my co-hosts, before whom I longed to maintain some ideal image. The Holy Spirit moved through these people, bringing a swift comfort and even a shared sadness—which enveloped me in community. My mentor since the Ferguson Uprisings, Rev. Karen Anderson, an AME pastor, told me, "God hates divorce because God is empathy. God hates the pain that you are going through, the pain that you were caused, and the pain that you believe you caused. God will never hate you or your husband. In fact, God is forgiving you both in ways that you might never be able to forgive each other."

During my separation, before my divorce was finalized, I lost speaking engagements and had invitations canceled because hosts or venues considered divorce a controversy. There were a few exceptions. Rev. Alexis Carter Thomas, a pastor at a Baptist church at the time, was the most brilliant of those beautiful exceptions. Alexis became a peer-mentor for me. She introduced me to the leader of the DivorceCare ministry at her church. (And right here, dear reader, dear sister, I ask you to recall any resource on divorce from white evangelical blogs that say only chaos is possible in the experience of divorce.)

Now I want you to turn to the sister sitting next to you, turn to your neighbor, and say "Neighbor! Sister! The word is care—not chaos but care."

Alexis pastored me. She checked in with me every week and prayed for me as I shed many tears. She reminded me that my longing to show love to my children was from the Lord. When we were having dinner together one evening after I had spoken at her church, I reminded her that this was an invitation I feared my divorce proceedings would cause me to lose. But sitting quietly alone with me, she didn't hesitate, and I am not sure she needed much time to think (in part because she is a genius). She preached a simple truth to me that gave me so much life: "God does not want you to perish."

So many people saved my life. My co-hosts, my cousins, Rev. Carter Thomas, Rev. Anderson, my uncles and aunts, my parents and sisters. More than anything, I was protected and supported by Black women of faith. In the months after my divorce was finalized, I experienced what should have been a more difficult loss. Evangelical Christians who tolerated my separation found my divorce unbearable. Queer and straight women surrounded me, raised money, offered their homes and childcare assistance. One of my fiercest comrades in the movement had the power to create a stable job for me in an organization she founded, so that I could slow my hustle and concentrate on my healing and my children. Black women became not only my truest confidants but the people who prayed for me with everything they had and everything they were. My sister friends sang me to sleep and reminded me to take showers. They celebrated my birthday when I didn't feel like it. They sent me voice memos of psalms and prayers, and hit that FaceTime over and over until I finally answered. When I was running out of hope that I could function as a single mother and still bear witness to God's grace and power as a member and minister of a church, Black women prayed for, encouraged, and admonished me. Black women saved my life. Black women heard me, held me, and did not give up on me. The people that made me did not let me go.

## PART 3: A PEOPLE IN NEED OF GOD'S GLORY

A 2018 CDC report put the national divorce rate at three people per thousand, which is a more than 50 percent decrease from the average in 2000. The divorce rate for women is almost five points higher than the national average. My heart is hurt by these facts, and I feel that sometimes in our efforts to fight divorce rates among Christians, we ignore the causes. I wonder if we are so busy fighting divorce that we forget to define, live, learn, and lead in love, which has an impact on how we disciple people about marriage. Most every married person (happy, surviving, or miserable) will probably say that they don't want or need "picture perfect," but many married, engaged, and divorced people would discuss the levels of loving that conflate protecting our people with hiding our pains.

History, culture, and spiritual heritage demand a distinction between the special and the covert. When partners in a loving agreement are not equipped to call for help without shame or fear of retaliation, then a relationship that is meant to be sacred becomes more secretive in the face of strife. Because the churches that I served so elevated marriage to be a picture of the divine, people who struggled in marriage were less likely to identify their problems as urgent, choosing instead to hide or minimize them. Surviving in marriage was seen as success. Many years meant much health. Decades equaled devotion. Faith leaders hold meetings, write curriculums, and set protocols about church members seeking divorce, but there is little ongoing discipleship for people considering marriage, living happily in marriage, or settling into merely manageable marriages. Jesus said that the greatest commandment is two: love the Lord your God with everything that you are, and love your neighbor as you love yourself. By now you know my emotional biases and can see my sensitivities on the surface—I believe that words of life, earnestly spoken, are crucial to saving relationships from death. And I believe that famous quote from Ida B. Wells applies to justice in many forms: "If you want to right wrongs, you must shine the light of truth on them." The church in the United States needs strategies for clinging to God's greatest commandments as a baseline for everyday communication and everyday life. The fruit of this work might just be the honest, hopeful determination that causes committed relationships to thrive.

I have seen the critical need for honest speech and relational support play out in real time. Across the churches, organizations, and denominations I have served, I have seen women who are ministry leaders plan outings to drink and trash-talk their spouses as a means of surviving the commitment they believed God was forcing them to uphold. The same women who proudly post anniversary pictures on social media will freely refer to their husbands as babies and idiots; as freakish, hideous, and useless. I have listened to women complain that they are pressured to have sex too soon after they had a baby. I have heard pastors' wives talk about the mechanics of getting just drunk enough to "lie down and take it" when they got home but not so drunk that they would not be able to drive. This was all part of the complementarian culture that confused me and cast me out. These women were miserable, but they thought they were supposed to be. They were not in loving marriages, but "that's just how it is sometimes." They did not view their trash-talk survival strategy as sinful slander, but had no problem naming the evils of divorce.

This is unaddressed violence that has been labeled as holiness. It is a failure of an entire worldview that confuses sacrifice and abuse. I believe that some of these women were being vicious and malicious. I believe that some of them were being abused, but all of them were being honest about one thing: the church has a serious problem.

In 2018, I helped to launch a campaign amplifying the stories of women and girls who suffered violence and from their faith communities received retaliation or neglect instead of support. The campaign, #SilenceIsNotSpiritual, fights violence against Black women and other women of color, with a specific focus on encouraging churches to refuse to cover up, be complicit in, or outright condone actions of violence against women.

More than challenging churches to listen to and support women who are bold enough to come forward to share their experiences, we designed this campaign to respond to the #MeToo movement by confessing that churches are systems in need of restructuring.

Many churches elevate marriage as an unspoken requirement for earning respect and participating in vocational leadership while at the same time ignoring red flags, poor health, and abuse in people's actual marriages. My hope, in telling my story, is that church families will protect the people who experience abuse, and learn how to identify situations that cause people to become abusive. Church families host financial-literacy classes and foster-care info sessions. I have seen daycare centers and private schools attached to churches. What if the call by survivor communities for churches to become trauma-informed is not a trend but a much-needed change? In recent years, I've seen faith communities become more willing to address bullying, addiction, body shame, and other social issues, but when it comes to sexual violence and intimate-partner strife, we are secretive and silent. This is not the spiritual practice that God has given us. The Lord wants us to bring everything out of hiding, so that we can see God's truth heal and work through us in the marvelous light.

Doing this requires us to take seriously the stories of emotional and spiritual abuse. It means uprooting the historical practices and church polity that make people feel unsafe. We need to listen to our sisters who share their stories, then invest in accountability structures that protect survivors and prevent predators. We need to respond to the impact of pulpit-powered toxic masculinity on people of all genders. We don't need another wake-up call. We are being activated by a generation of people calling all of us to fight the presumption of health by marriage, and to transform environments of low accountability, fear of failure, and fragility in the face of necessary reform.

# PART 4: THE JOURNEY TO EXCEEDING GREAT JOY

Now unto the One who is able to keep you from falling; the One who has the power to present you faultless before the presence of God's glory—with exceeding great joy. To God be glory and honor, dominion, and power, now and forevermore. Amen.

JUDE 24, 25

"You have to keep us together."

What I once took as a compliment from my husband now falls on me with the weight of a wall collapsing after I have tried to hold it up, brick by crumbling brick, for over a decade. In the years since my divorce, I have felt crushed under the weight of my own outsize expectations that were reinforced by an image of Black women as savior figures who never needed to be saved. But I have been saved, by a Savior who is not fragile to failure, mine or others. I have been saved by a real Savior, one whose word reminds me that God has designed me for dignity, not destruction. I have been saved by a God who reminds me that there is only one true God.

By God's grace and years of intensive therapy, divorce freed me from being "The One" who could keep my husband from falling. Divorce forced both of us to get serious and repent about a marriage that was meant to bring life but only brought us closer to emotional death. I might never know marriage again; I might never recover a full friendship with my former husband and now co-parent; but I am determined to open my hands and leave the future to God.

My divorce made me face and renew my commitment to living like Jesus.

There is no replacing Jesus as the true bridegroom and husband of every person in the church. That experience of Jesus's love is not limited to people who have found marriage.

Men and women who get married do not play the role of Jesus and church. The Bible says that we are all Christ's brides. This might be the key component that causes strain in patriarchal and complementarian marriages. When a man believes he must feel like God, it becomes his wife's responsibility to worship him, and in turn, his responsibility is to guide and correct her worship. This builds a heresy, not a home.

My divorce taught me the seriousness of marriage, motherhood, and ministry. Healing after my divorce was a work of the Spirit through the people. Both platonic and romantic relationships have renewed my belief that there is beauty in marriage, that it can reflect the love of God—just as any relationship can.

For instance, God's love and glory can be evident in a relationship story that has many chapters. They needn't all be romantic. A caterpillar marriage becomes a butterfly divorce, and this transformation brings more than a change in flight and function. In my case, it brings a new identity I never thought possible. My ex-husband and I both assumed that marriage would be our butterfly. But our relationship was repaired by cocooning our romance and shedding it like a weight that prevented us from our true functions. Divorce was on the healing path for both of us. I have been more honest, understanding, anger free, and trauma conscious since going through divorce, and my ex-husband has shared with my family that he is doing similar work. But I am not encouraged to make that statement in every space. There is little room for care teams in the culture that gave us chaos theory.

Still, I do have a positive view of marriage. One of my favorite things to do as a minister now is to perform weddings and speak about a couple's dependence on God for their value, and about leaning on each other as a picture of God's love for them.

I pass no judgment on people who have judged me. I am joined to the One who is able to keep me from falling, the One who is able to present me faultless, with exceeding great joy.

My conscience ain't ever been so clear.

# I's Married Now

## CHRISTIAN MARRIAGE FOR GROWN BLACK WOMEN

## By Christina Edmondson

> The practice of love offers no place of safety. We risk
> loss, hurt, pain. We risk being acted upon by forces
> outside our control.
>
> BELL HOOKS, *All About Love: New Visions*

*DEARLY BELOVED, WE ARE GATHERED here today in the sight of
God to join this man and this woman in holy matrimony. Not to be
entered into lightly, holy matrimony should be entered into solemnly
and with reverence and honor. Into this holy agreement these two
people come together to be joined. If any person here can show cause
why these two people should not be joined in holy matrimony, speak
now or forever hold your peace.*

For most Westerners, these words or some approximation of
them represent the entrance into holy matrimony. Ironically,
although Bible verses are commonly lifted at Christian-friendly
weddings, scripture itself does not offer us ancient marital vows.
As one who believes the Christian faith is more about princi-
ples than prescriptions, I appreciate God's gracious liberty as
we construct marriage ceremonies while also acknowledging
that marriage is confusing—and often subject to the whims of
interpretation by those with social power.

In the mid-1500s, Thomas Cranmer wrote the original Early

Modern English version of what is above. We can and ought to debate the more controversial elements of Cranmer's vows, especially requesting obedience of women and not men. However, I am in agreement with his early sentences that marriage ought to be entered into with weighty sobriety and deep respect put me in agreement with that part of the English protestant man's words.

## MARRIAGE IS NO JOKE

My name is Christina, and here are my receipts: I've been married for twenty-plus years. I'm married to a pastor—allegedly they are hard people to be married to (some more so than others, I imagine). I'm the child of a fifty-year marriage. I have a PhD in psychology, which makes some people think I can hold a relationship together because of that alone (which isn't true).

And you know what that makes me qualified to talk about?

*My* experience in marriage.

Welcome to my musings on matrimony. Some of these I've shared among adolescents and college girls, girlfriend chats, late-night chats with my husband, academic research, conversations with recently divorced friends, and premarital counseling sessions with engaged couples.

The tales of hopes and horrors from widows, divorcees, singles, and long-term married folks are abundant. I've seen marriages so strong that they are pillars of not only their families but by extension their churches and communities. I've known singles deeply fulfilled and content in their singleness. Yet I've also witnessed and ministered among marriages so toxic, abusive, and destructive that they seem straight out of a Lifetime movie. Or a Tyler Perry movie, filled with large doses of disrespect, flat-out abuse, entitled infidelity, cover-ups, and unlimited Christian catchphrases from grossly unhelpful clergy members. I've cried with young and old widows and widowers alike experiencing the pain of having a spouse snatched from their grasp. Their hearts weren't just broken but crushed, moving from aching to ashes. Finally, so many Black women singles, not by choice, are frustrated, lonely, angry, and losing hope.

Yup, it's hard out here. It is hard out here for everybody.

## REALITY CHECK

Within marriage, the hardness of life itself brings its own perpetual weightiness to both partners. The partners' love, communication, and fidelity must bear up under weights that often have nothing to do with the marriage itself. Layoffs at work. The dementia of an aging parent. Church scandals. The disability of a beloved child. An unprecedented pandemic. Unexpected cancer diagnoses. Plaguing student-loan debt. Housing costs in Los Angeles, New York, Nashville.

The list goes on.

I've seen the way these painful things weigh on marriages. I've lived and am still living some of these, too. And because marriages mature and change just like an individual person, I've seen the way marriages unravel in the face of these difficulties. On the flip side, I've seen marriages strengthen over time, too. Sometimes, the hardness of life refines a marriage. When a marriage strengthens amid the internal and external storms of life, the partnership isn't just a gift to two lonely hearts but is a communal blessing.

Everyone benefits from strong marriages. Marriages that are built on mutual submission. Compassion. Companionship. Responsibility. Delight. Children, churches, society, and obviously each member of the coupleship benefit. What strong marriages represent is something stable and assured in a world that is covenant-breaking, topsy-turvy, and dysfunctional. And in a hyperindividualistic, white-supremacist culture, Black Christian marriages are a necessary countercultural act of grace.

Talking about marriage and the need for healthy marriages can feel like a Republican talking point designed to avoid attending to the exploitative and rampant injustices of this nation. To be clear, the answer to systemic racism is not Black marriage. But strong Black families are a form of resistance. White supremacy certainly has a field day in dismantling Black love, love for self, and love for each other. When your cultural history includes familial ties ripped apart, force-bred for profit, and dehumanized, marriage remains powerful and important. We all need family. And while family in the Black community is broad and inclusive out of necessity and compassion, to jettison Black marriage as unnecessary, simply because of the real forces working against it, is to enter an agreement with the destructive forces. I won't be agreeing with the devil anytime soon.

I will be the first person to tell you that people don't need marriage to be full, whole, and complete. And when one recognizes that marriage is not for them, that is indeed a gift. Marriage is not for everyone. But I also have no hesitation in saying that while we don't individually need to be married, societies need marriages. Until Christ returns, the metaphor of marriage preaches the gospel. Consequently, marriages like those of Priscilla and Aquila or Hosea and Gomer testify to and point to the covenant-keeping God.

Whether Martin and Coretta, Frederick and Anna, or Big Momma and Granddaddy, it is a sight to experience couples who strengthen and sharpen each other and hold each other down. Holy Bonnie and Clydes, Barack and Michelles, Ossie and Rubys who fan each other's flames of talent and gifts. In our misogynistic, male-centric culture, we swoon at images of men simply doing basic household tasks and publicly calling their wives smart, not just beautiful. Thanks be to God that we can demand more from both parties when it comes to marriage.

Black folks need strong marriages. But the strength of a marriage is not conjured through some magic spell or formula.

No amount of relationship coaching, Proverbs-31-womaning, withholding, or complementarian pandering will produce a healthy relationship. No amount of rereading *Act Like a Lady, Think Like a Man* and *Men Are from Mars, Women Are from Venus* will exempt us from the work required in relationships.

Love between humans is inherently uncertain, so we grasp for systems, laws, formulas, and reassurances that things will work out. We often want a love that feels easy and effortless, but this desire must not tempt us into an autopilot approach to loving others.

There's no way around it: Love takes hard work. Love involves uncertainty. Even the hard work doesn't guarantee anything, but there is no healthy marriage without it.

# A WORD ON LOVE

Love is a natural need, but we don't love well naturally. We must *learn* how to love. We must learn how to direct our love so it aligns with what the God of love calls us to and through. We must love as Christ does: vulnerably yet fiercely.

Behind every couple who appears to have an easy love is a strong scaffolding, for which the assembly manual will rarely appear on social media.

Love is powerful, and threatening to the wicked.

For hundreds of years, social forces have worked to pull apart Black love. The pages of history reveal torn covenants. If you listen close, you can hear the echoes of Hagar Blackmore's heart breaking as she is snatched away from her husband and nursing infant in 1669. She was robbed of her husband and family, as documented in *Love of Freedom* by Catherine Adams and Elizabeth H. Pleck. Even before stepping foot on American soil, Hagar experienced the kind of white-supremacist covenant breaking that tore people and families apart.

In the white-supremacist system, marriage can function as a deep comfort. At its best, marriage *humanizes*. Animals may mate and breed, but people *love*. People grow and build. But there are centuries of receipts revealing the ways Black women have been robbed of this option to contribute to their own homes and families. Later, in the twentieth century, we see and hear white feminists' well-documented disdain for being labeled only as wives and homemakers. But so many Black women—then and now—are robbed even of the option of marriage.

This only amplifies the cruelty of those who attempt to lec-

ture Black people about the importance of marriage and moth-
erhood. There is no *Leave It to Beaver* mythology for us, as the
Black woman's body is used for profit. Like mules, Hagar
Blackmore and my own African ancestors were brought to
America to be physically exploited—seen and not heard, used
and used up. The pain and desperation of the Hagar of the Old
Testament coming down through them and following their Af-
rican daughters into America.

I have been thinking about the Black family for a while, y'all.

During my final year in college, I was tasked with complet-
ing a senior project. I opted to write on perceptions of the marriageability of Black men. I was a sociology major with an
emphasis in race, class, and gender, at an HBCU known for
Black marriages—both in research and in practice. To research
for my project, I read no shortage of articles describing Black
family dynamics during U.S. slavery and perused qualitative
material describing the realities facing modern-day Black
women. I also interviewed Black women firsthand, including
my mother's friends. With my novice research, I gleaned the
kinds of historical narratives and pop-culture clamor that had
gone into the idea that there were "no good Black men." As a
consequence of such conjured and real stories, the sex-ratio
theory was at work. Basically, that means that when heterosexual men are outnumbered and able to select from a wider pool
of women, they are less likely to select in deeply committed
ways. They have the luxury of looking for "the one" while passing over dozens. Conversely, the theory posits that women select in more tedious ways when they are the minority.

Crudely put, one group goes for quality and the other goes for quantity.

I remember going to clubs where "ladies get in free." This practice ensured that men would show up—and they did. All kinds of men showed up, to be clear. And in college, when I was an undergraduate student, I remember hearing Black men on campus confess that *knowing* they would be outnumbered by the beautiful Black women on the yard solidified their decision to attend. These were Black men who liked Black women, at least aesthetically. The admissions-and-recruitment department wisely loaded mailers with images of smiling Black women.

Today, I hear horror stories of singles ministries and mixers that are basically single Black women support groups. There are no large crowds of Black heterosexual single men heading to the club or the university to find "Lisa from Queens." Beautiful, single, and smart Black women are not a draw, especially when Black men have been told implicitly there is something else to desire, so why settle and put a ring on it.

We ought to pay close attention to the challenges and dynamics that arise even in the dating desert. For these offer a sober foreshadowing of the challenges of marriage.

Christian marriage requires mutual submission, with a lived commitment to love and respect. When people hear the passage in Ephesians 5, we often hear it in terms of what the *other* is called to do in marriage for *us*. For example, a man might read the scripture and only absorb what wives are called to do, and vice versa. But Paul directs his writing at the readers, calling them out by name: Hey, husbands, this is just for you; hey wives, this is just for you. He's saying, *This is what you, reader, are supposed to do.* In our already sexist and imbalanced society, this can pose yet another burden on women, who might strive to make themselves more lovable and to meet the standards of respect set forth by their husbands (who are nonetheless sinners). The verses in this scripture can too quickly become admonitions to obedience as opposed to the laws of love they were intended to be.

Can you imagine what it means to really sign on to this idea? Some of us await proof of loyalty and compassion, needing verifiable receipts from the other before offering our mutuality. But add to that the internal anxiety of knowing that, in this world, you are in a constant fog of misogynoir—or in the case of Black men, being the face of the guilty and inferior.

The caste system seeks to raise Black men into a model of manhood that is fiercely controlling of Black women. Consequently, Black heterosexual partners too often find ourselves looking to each other for social validation and comfort, to attend to a gaping and constantly picked wound. Both partners are the walking wounded, sometimes walking toward or away from one another, demanding validation from one another— a validation to compensate for the social stratification that created our gaping wounds.

Black men, comforted by the lie of patriarchal privilege yet traumatized by anti-Blackness, implicitly and explicitly demand that Black women act like a stereotype of a white woman for them. Black Christian men might find themselves parroting the rhetoric of white male patriarchy, contributing to the misogyny and gaslighting directed at the women they claim they love and are called to lead.

Marriage is hard enough.

Marriages that *stand* are truly an act of grace.

I am a Black woman who has been married for over two decades to a Black man.

The reality of this sentence is an act of resistance in a nation that dehumanizes Black people, undermines Black love for profit, and pits Black men and women against one another in their struggle for equity. It has been articulated as rare, but surprisingly, most Black women I know in my age range—forty and up—are indeed married or have been married to Black men. This is what I see today. But without intentionality and intervention to protect Black love, I don't know if I will be able to say this ten years from now.

I also recognize that my marriage is a privilege. While I believe it is a blessing, a strong marriage should not be a sociological privilege or rarity. Due to mass incarceration and Black women having higher educational attainment currently than Black men, Black women are the least likely to marry. Too often, the most renaissanced of men long to be ahead of their wives in some tangible way; in our capitalistic world, that means income or professional status. Women with darker skin tones are further marginalized because of the socialization of white supremacy nationally and globally. Colorism among Black people echoes back to the slave block. There we see the roots of our insecurities and caricatures regarding skin color preferences. And the way we overcompensate through colorist preferences. These preferences too often reveal implicit biases and even sexual stereotypes. For example, it is true that there are economic and sociological advantages to having lighter skin—especially in white environments. Yet when it comes to men, even a marginalized characteristic like having darker skin can favor men in-group, making them appear more masculine and powerful, possessing more sexual prowess. This is residue from the "Black buck" enslavement caricature. Conversely, this same caricature punishes darker-skinned women, deeming them more masculine or unattractive. As if testosterone and estrogen have skin tones.

We ought to reject all such foolishness.

And we ought to invite the Holy Spirit to scan our preferences and standards of beauty and attractiveness. Without doing so, we risk living out preferences influenced by dehumanizing tropes and stereotypes, instead of delighting in the creativity of God's hand, as shown through our shades, sizes, and textures.

Colorism is trash. But it isn't the only thing getting in the way of Black love. The sociological mechanics against Black marriage are many. Black family therapists like myself know just how jacked up it is. If you wanna learn about this from the brunt of the single person's vantage point, read Ekemini's chapter on singleness.

When I think about my relationship with my beloved husband, these are some things I've learned over the last two decades. We've learned these lessons through tears—sometimes tears of joy, sometimes tears of grief.

1) **Marry someone who wants to be married to you.** That's a two-fold implication: marry someone who wants to be married, and marry someone who wants to be married specifically to you. There shouldn't be even a hint of begging a union to be. Life brings out its own set of insecurities; you

shouldn't be convincing your spouse of your value, or the value of marriage.

2) **Speak clearly and speak kindly.** Familiarity can cause us to become loose with communication. Sometimes the assumptions that come from deep familiarity can produce a cold, unclear dialogue; but it's important for us to be clear and kind. I know this well, because I feel like I know and trust my husband more than any other human. This actually makes me more likely to speak in an unfiltered way. But neither spouse is a receptacle for our prickliest emotions. Keeping it real must also include keeping it loving.

3) **Your marriage isn't a performance, but it is being observed.** Know who your audience is—whether it's God, whether it's your children. Not everyone is invited in to take stock and observe your marriage, but there are people whose voices really matter when it comes to the marriage. Within our family, we care a lot about what our children think about our marriage. While driving to school one morning, I asked my daughter, "What lessons of life and love do you think you're learning from me and Daddy?" I was surprised to hear her say, "Most people I know, their parents don't get along. Their homes are tense. But our home doesn't feel tense. I know that y'all like each other." My husband and I have had the beginnings of some heated conversations in front of our kids—so it's not like she hasn't seen us disagree. I'm grateful, though, that she doesn't believe that disagreement means disintegration."

My parents have been married for nearly fifty years. They were HBCU sweethearts. Both had experienced tremendous loss prior to their marriage. My mother reminisces about growing up in a two-parent home, with a mother who was as strong and stable as an oak tree and a father as warm and hospitable as the chocolate cake he baked each Sunday after church for his family. When she had barely reached adulthood, both parents succumbed to unrelated illnesses. By contrast, my father grew up poor, in a home without heat in the winter, and was raised by a fierce, under-five-foot-tall mother. Today, she is almost a hundred years old and her fortitude, along with help from the family women who surrounded her, lifted her children out of a shack and into lives beyond what she had experienced. Together, with their distinct backgrounds but with shared pain, my parents built an imperfect life together. They are as different as night and day, yet I was convinced of their love for me and their commitment to each other.

One afternoon, when I was a junior or senior in high school, my dad and I were cooking together in the kitchen. He worked at a butcher shop when he was a kid, so he'd coach me through my knife skills. My dad would act out like Julia Child, and I was his protégée. As we were prepping food together, I forget what exactly we were talking about, but I remember he asked me what I thought about something. To which I gave a no-nonsense response. My dad jokingly responded that I was "ruined for marriage" and it was all his fault. I was taken aback.

My guess now is he was reflecting on my sense of independence and my direct communication style, especially with men. From a young age—probably since high school—I haven't felt intimidated by men. I'm not a misandrist; I don't need to make men small in my mind in order to work with them or correct them. I don't experience men as a group with burden, bitterness, or fear. In his dadness, he valued my independence, praised it even. But in his maleness, he could foresee the risk of isolation that could create for me.

I am one of two daughters, a child of a man who would have loved to have a son but didn't. A man who was not raised by his father, who he knew was in the same city, raising another family. Ironically, I would eventually come to know my paternal grandfather as my "grandad," largely through the efforts of my mother, a woman who knew orphanhood and valued family deeply.

I grew up in a family with an all-hands-on-deck approach to creating belonging. It was a full-time job for everyone. Family is everything to us, and marriage is immensely important. No one gets left behind.

With this family background and the resources that come with growing up Black and middle-class, frankly, I was certain that I would get married—so certain that I even communicated this in college to my then-boyfriend, now-husband. "Somebody is going to want to marry me." I chuckle now at my young, foolish pride, but I was taught early on how to spot a marriageable, stable man. I also knew that marriage was work—work I was willing to do. Clearly, I had no idea what that would mean on the inside of marriage. Compatibility and romance are incredibly important, but a pursuit of a corporate good is an entirely different mountain to climb.

I eventually married my HBCU sweetheart, a tradition not completely uncommon at our alma mater—even if it took a decade or so after graduation to make it happen. After all, HBCU homecomings have the capacity to be amazing singles events, with a plethora of well-educated and great-smelling single Black men. Many of these heterosexual men have a preference for Black women and, having been educated alongside them, are well aware that Black women are indeed relational assets.

The truth is, I was surrounded by Black marriages in my parents' largely middle- and working-class friend network in Maryland. When I was growing up, divorce didn't happen often, but when it did, we all felt shockwaves. When my parents' friend, a beautiful and well-educated Black woman, was abandoned by her husband for a white woman, it sent rage through their network.

I was in elementary school at the time, and this was the first time I heard about divorce. It shook me—when other peoples' parents get divorced, you realize *your* parents can get divorced, too.

When I overheard my parents talking about their friends' divorce, it was my first memory of seeing my mother angry and appalled. My father tried to figure out what friendship would or could look like between him and his friend, the husband who left.

Here was the unstated rule I heard: Black men of character and substance have a wife, more than likely a Black wife, and they don't call it quits.

I used to think that I simply fell into being a marriage therapist, but when I reflect on my childhood, this path makes sense. During my training, we often discussed the therapist as holding the hope for the marriage. Couples drained and exhausted by dysfunction arrived at therapy sessions on the brink of goodbye. When I reflect on my own marriage, twenty years in, I realize how critical it is that each partner be committed to the marriage, and to the other's flourishing.

Passion for marriage and passion for a person are not the same.

Ironically and thankfully, I married a man who, like the prophet Zechariah and Dr. Cornel West, described himself as a "prisoner of hope." This bound optimism spills over, to the extent that my realism probably feels like pessimism to him in our life together. At our best, we take turns holding hope for each other.

## NOW SAY IT WITH ME

This I know is true: marriage will not make you whole. Marriage will not save you but rather expose you. Marriage is like going into labor: you can and should prepare, but at the end of the day, you will be surprised—hopefully, more by beauty than by pain. Strong marriages are where ego, unresolved trauma, and unforgiveness go to die. If these things don't die, they'll become cancers that take over the entire body of the marriage. Marriage doesn't solve emotional problems and gaping holes in the long term. It's more likely to hold up a mirror and expose our core issues. That's why, as Black women, single or married, we must never stop doing our own work.

All relationships are transactional. To say that out loud can feel cheap or shallow, but I am holding to it. I actually think it's gracious to not delude ourselves with any other notions but to interrogate the roots of our perceived needs.

What do we seek, expect, demand?

What are we willing to give? What do we honestly have left to give, as the mules of American capitalist patriarchy?

After all, even affection and sacrificial love for a small, precious baby comes with the implicit anticipation of the adult child who will value and validate our parenting. Anything less feels like disrespect or parental failure.

Black women, married or single, we got our work to do. If you don't believe you have a portion to give, feel you have nothing left to give, or are offended by the ask, Christian marriage is not for you. We must continually examine to know what we *actually* want and need out of our spouse, and if it is indeed their burden to carry or fulfill. We must examine our expectations; still, it is reasonable to know what is due to us in a covenant relationship. We are simply due some things as an exercise of love by a husband.

To be candid, I am tired. Tired in a way that necessarily shows up in my relationships, especially my closest ones. This soul tiredness seems common among even slightly socially aware Black women. Perpetual fatigue has its relational costs, even in a good marriage. It is a type of emotional and spiritual hole that needs divine filling, not a husband's opinions or rescue attempts to remedy, but it certainly cannot bear the burden of an abusive or abandoning husband.

Our emotional work requires the skill of a competent therapist. A husband isn't in charge of fixing our core issues, in the same way wives are not treatment centers for husbands.

Reader, our emotional work requires an honest self-dialogue about forgiveness, self-care, and boundaries. A vulnerable self-dialogue, not Twitter as a journal. We all need the privilege of a private place to search and be searched by the power of the Holy Spirit.

## MAKE IT PLAIN

In my opinion, the best of husbands provide support to wives whom they have the maturity and capacity to *delight* in. As a woman raised by a man who wanted sons, I've come to learn that I am a strong cup of coffee and that it's essential that women marry men who delight in their growth and success. Sis, you need a quarterback *and* a cheerleader. The male cheerleader literally holding up the pyramid. Husband-bae is the quarterback who can run the ball if need be and get it done for the team, not just himself. No doubt many contemporary men believe that this is who they are—but without being tested and empowered by the Spirit, they cannot honestly say it is true. We all think of ourselves as further along than we are. I certainly do. I often see marriages tremble beneath the weight of a woman who rises and a man who remains stagnant. But what's really causing those marriages to crumble is the weight of unmet and unspoken expectations—especially expectations fueled by insecurity, void of a fierce commitment to love.

Can you hold me down, or are you just holding me down?

This may sound old-school, but that's what I am. And Christian marriage, in many ways—especially in light of our cultural moment—are old-school. Even the most egalitarian versions of marriage between a Black Christian man and a Black Christian woman are old-school. *Marriage,* at this point, is old-school.

A man who is unable to discern his instability is a recipe for disaster to himself and others. It is unloving and unwise to expect Black men in this racial-trauma-rich and fallen world not to have some issues. With that said, those issues—which we all have—*never* justify disrespect and mistreatment to Black women. Insecure men without self-awareness will hate themselves because they have internalized what they feel are unmet standards of maleness, and will not be able to love a Black woman well. After all, the call to husbands is to love their wives as they love themselves. The biblical assumption is that love flows from love—that external love springs from internal love. 'An insecure man,' immature and entitled even if clothed in arrogance, will not and cannot meet his marital obligation. His wounds make him pathologically selfish—a type of selfishness that really is self-survival and will be shocking to strong Black women who are socialized to care for and about everybody else.

Godly husbands don't have all the answers, because they aren't God. Godly men delight in knowing God is in charge. Godly husbands have the humility to know their leadership or partnership is presence, commitment, and care. While there are men who, for whatever reason, marry women less informed than them theologically and intellectually, Godly men seek to be sharpened. For me, love looks like delight in personhood, acceptance, tenderness, and deep respect between parties. I don't know a Black man or a Black woman in marriage who doesn't need or crave these things from their partner. We get it twisted when we pretend that humans have different fundamental needs.

Unashamedly, because we are fully human sexual beings, we might prefer the man who gives us goosebumps and gets us pregnant at a glance. Pop culture won't teach us how to identify the man who has the love and maturity to hold his wife's hand when the doctor says there is no heartbeat. Ideally, they are the same person, sexy bae and dependable bae—or better yet, dependability and empathy are sexy to us.

While wanting great sex isn't unreasonable, it's also not as romantic or automatic as the movies imply. Everything in marriage can be built or destroyed with an actual partnership.

Let me say that again: a partnership *builds*, but a hierarchy controls and stifles.

Mutually gratifying sex is built through patience and intimacy.

As in sexual intimacy, all things require unity. When two spouses set goals together, when two spouses parent together as one thoughtful voice—these activities require actual skill development and attitude regulation. Again, it takes a partner who can truly hear a Black woman to work together with her. No respect, no building.

A wise woman builds her home (Prov. 14:10). Wisdom builds the systems, structures, schedules, and boundaries for flourishing individually and relationally. Likewise, it is the wise man who learns about his wife in order to love her with specificity and honor God. In the New Testament, husbands are urged "to be considerate as you live with your wives, and treat them with respect as the weaker vessel and as heirs with you of the gracious gift of life, so that nothing will hinder your prayers" (1 Pet. 3:7). No learning, no love.

If we accept even temporarily that relationships are transactional, what does this mean for Black wives' relationships with their husbands? First of all, we are not superwomen. Yes, it is time to cue Karyn White's 1988 hit song. We cannot do all the things in our own strength, nor is it our calling. That's a recipe for martyrdom, illness, pride, or bitterness. In marriage, we are hopefully married to a peer and have committed to seeing our spouse in this way—never as a boy. Any hint of that dynamic reeks of internationalization of white-supremacist beliefs about Black men. Talk about disrespect.

When Black women treat Black men as boys and Black men treat Black women as mules, it is a replay of slavery that should cause us to run and resist. I am a grown-grown Black woman. I personally get the need for respect, yet there is an abundance of messages that women are called to raise their husbands. We marry a peer for one reason: to sharpen each other and grow together. Even under the guise of traditional gender roles, I have seen women strategize ways to manage their immature husbands while pretending publicly that they believe them to be spiritually and emotionally mature—all the while building resentment as they commit to "obeying" a man who lacks wisdom, or whom they don't truly respect. Told to obey, women rightfully resent the absurdity of doing so in God's name and perform compliance with a bitter heart. They will pretend to buy the lie or embrace the legalism of this botched call to obedience.

But is it any wonder that we are unable to sustain what the Spirit has not promised to empower? The Spirit does not empower us to obey laws that we make up, or that are out of step with the actual Lawgiver. That's love.

Scripture calls wives to build and guard. This seems obvious to me as a Black mother. This seems apparent as a Black auntie. This seems clear as a Black wife to a Black man. Why are we building and guarding? Spiritual warfare, y'all. The Bible uses military and construction terms when it speaks of the role of wives in its original languages. "Submission" is an often dreaded and misapplied English translation of the Greek word *hupotassomai*. Too often preached as a green light to unquestioning obedience, *hupotassomai* should make us think more of Beyoncé's "get in formation" than June Cleaver's passivity. Children are called to obey parents, who are called to raise them with discipline and kindness. Wives and husbands are called to get into interconnected formation. To actually practice oneness with an intimate partner requires resisting the darts of the enemy. Scripture often uses the same word, *ezer,* to describe the helping role of a woman as it does to describe the God helping humanity or Israel. Clearly, God is not subservient to humanity, but he does serve us. Simply put, *ezer* doesn't mean just "helper" but "warrior helper." Why do we need a warrior helper in this life? Seriously, have you lived at all? This language of dignity and duty to women was countercultural in ancient times and is countercultural now.

Marriage is challenging. Hear me: a healthy marriage is challenging. A bad marriage is nearly unbearable, like a toxin. Spiritual warfare abounds. We wrestle with spiritual forces, social inequity, unresolved trauma, and the imperfections of our spouses. Again, we don't get formal vows in scripture about marriage, but one verse often comes to mind when I reflect on the marital covenant.

Take a look at Mark 10:4. The people say to Jesus, "Moses permitted a man to write a certificate of divorce and send her away."

"It was because your hearts were hard that Moses wrote you this law," Jesus replied. "But at the beginning of creation, God 'made them male and female.' For this reason, a man will leave his father and mother and be united to his wife, and the two will become one flesh.' So they are no longer two, but one flesh.

Therefore, what God has joined together let no one separate" (Mark 10:5–9).

One hard heart can wreck a marriage. God graciously upholds his covenant with us, even when our spouses do not. God graciously upholds us even when divorce is the only way forward from abuse, infidelity, and abandonment. God graciously upholds his covenant with us even when we are the hardhearted ones. We are invited to entrust ourselves, our spouses, our exes, our spouses we hope for, and our marriages to God. The creation of one flesh is another mystery and miracle performed by God, but it does not surpass the miracle and mystery of Christ's atonement on our behalf. There is a bridegroom who will never fail us, who awaits the word to return for his bride, the church. Whether we are single (by choice or circumstance), married, divorced, or widowed, let us be found awaiting His return.

"So Christ, having been offered once to bear the sins of many, will appear a second time, not to deal with sin but to save those who are eagerly waiting for him" (Heb. 9:28).

*God, grant me the faith to entrust my deep inadequacies, traumas, fears, bitterness, and bashful joys to you. Let me not demand that my spouse meet needs that only you can. Grant me a real partner to build with and love. Let me honor my spouse or my spouse-to-come's humanity and love them through respect in public and private, empathetic care, and peer-to-peer accountability. Protect me in this world that treats me with disregard. Make my home a refuge for all who reside and enter. Amen.*

# Disciplining the Church

## By Christina Edmondson

ALL THEOLOGY IS POLITICAL.

Theology—or, put more simply, God talk—is interconnected with our self-talk, social perspectives, and expectations. The late James H. Cone was spot-on in saying that "what people think about God, Jesus Christ, and the church cannot be separated from their own social and political status in a given society." Our politics, like our theologies, attempt to make meaning of life, and our social positions impact our sense of priority about what warrants meaning-making attention. However, we often have varying definitions and emotional responses to even the word "politics."

Politics, especially in the United States, is caricatured and too often misunderstood. Coming from the Greek word *politika*, "politics" literally means the "affairs of the city" or of a people, and ultimately comprises the practices that enable us to secure position and resources for groups. As humans, we live in groups and are social beings, and politics shapes how we live together. We get what we need or want by politicking. Of course, we can see this on a local or global level, but also in microsystems such as couples, families, companies, and denominations. Politics asks the questions: What needs to be done? How do we get something accomplished? Who is responsible? Who is and isn't resourced? It does not necessarily ask *Is this right or wrong?* but rather *Is this my right or our right?* Therefore, the motives and moral implications of our politics need to be evaluated. Whether by ethics, religion, or some other method, our motivations require an external assessment or judgment, so to speak.

And if each one of us requires an evaluation of motivations, so must communities check themselves, too. After all, organizations, made of people and expressions of power, fall woefully short in honest self-assessment. And so the truth remains: we all use politics to meet our needs. We are all political beings, regardless of our awareness and its moral implications.

There is a thin line, often unseen to us, between politicking by means of *enforcement and control* and politicking through *advocacy and creativity.* We utilize our own set of politics to shape our worlds as we want them to be, to the extent that we have power and influence. But when we politick, we are often living out our own hunger for power. In other words, we use what power we *already* have to gain *more* of it. Additionally, our own theological insecurities can find us most passionate about what we are most uncertain of as we pull for agreement or compliance to substantiate our beliefs. Buy-in from others serves as a beam or a crutch, propping up our most fragile and guarded ideas or convictions.

The church is not immune to the use of politics—nor should

it be, as "politics" is defined as a strategy to govern among groups. Politics are always in play, even and maybe especially among those who see themselves as the "just preach the gospel" crowd. Denying the embedded politicalness of the church makes it no less political. After all, denial itself is a political strategy to control dialogue, image, and culture. The church is a political system. And what we ignore, support, or villainize has internal and external implications for the spiritual and political lives of people. Members, newcomers, and neighbors alike experience the social shaping of the church's politics and practices.

Just as all theologies are political, they are also spiritual. The "God told me" card gets played frequently in our world, even if we say it by using the "love looks like" or "sound doctrine is" cards. The way we see ourselves, our neighbors, and God is spiritually informed and expressed. When it comes to the spiritual dimensions of humans, religion researchers will often measure one's sense of deeper life meaning, values or convictions, sense of transcendence, connection to self, others, or the Divine, and personal growth. Engagement with any level of organized religion—from local places of worship to broader religious traditions—will profoundly impact these dimensions. It's only a matter of whether they impact our spiritual dimensions for our health or our harm.

A well-rehearsed African proverb reminds us that, in the same way it takes a village to raise a child, "it takes the church to raise a saint." This is a quote I have heard my spouse use frequently to bring community responsibility and love to bear on the care of a church member. The business of raising saints is messy and humbling. I call this "church discipline." It's the system or strategy—even the necessary politic—of maturing a body of believers.

## THE POLITICS OF CHURCH DISCIPLINE

Church discipline is just as much a part of the spiritual formation of each saint as it is a political strategy used in micro and macro systems, such as a local congregation or nation. Yet, the concept of church discipline is unfamiliar to or misunderstood by many—or, like politics, is dismissed or minimized, despite the implicit and explicit ways it operates in many churches.

A few years back, I was the target of "correction" gone amok. Simply put, I was at the receiving end of a combination of vitriol and lack of protection. In this particular church, I was hyperseen in ways that led to my being quickly caricatured and underseen—and therefore, my pain went unnoticed and unappreciated.

When we talk about "church hurt," we're usually talking about church leadership being punitive. And don't get me wrong, that played a role in this, but what was more dehumanizing was the fact that the church refused to protect me.

Privilege protects people from the discipline they so desperately need.

At the time, I was a member at a church whose congregation reflected a variety of denominational and theological influences, under the guise of cultural homogeneity. As in many churches, the leadership believed a certain set of things, but the people in the pews ran the gamut when it came to secondary issues. However, at times, the leadership was steered by a small minority of crochety individuals—although I'm sure they saw themselves as principled. This group would nag the church's leaders all the time, bickering about all kinds of things. One day, I became the focus of their attention. Now, I've been giving talks at conferences, churches, and schools for years, and my talks have been publicly available online. Someone in this group caught wind of one of my sermons online and was shocked to see a woman from their church preaching. Remember what I said about being hyperseen and hyperunseen?

This minority group flagged this concern to our church leaders, demanding that they denounce me and my preaching. The leadership did not ultimately denounce me, but they took a middle road that did not protect me—nor did it appease the critics. It lived in a non-conflict space, though all parties felt the impact of this conflict-avoidant leadership. Ultimately, it was an attempt to manage and tamp down the complaining group. Their method was more nonconfrontational appeasement than anything corrective. Nobody is safe under the dynamic of the likable Mister. Rogers, who won't do anything about the mean Mark Driscoll. Sometimes in churches there are people who are not pastors or elders and yet hold enough power to keep the church hostage. These people may never step foot at the pulpit, may never wear a robe, but they operate as the power brokers of the church.

This experience was one of the most overt examples of church power-politics I had personally experienced. Being trained in trauma therapy, I was well acquainted with "church hurt" and the misuse of power through the stories of clients and friends. However, being the direct target of mistreatment as opposed to experiencing suffering vicariously cultivates its own trauma lens.

In previous instances where power was misused against me, people believed that they were protecting the purity of something. Simply put, my being, experience, expertise, questions, or even courage was the contaminant. Anything outside their understanding or cultural experience was a contaminant. Not only did they believe themselves to be pure, they believed they were the keepers of purity. They saw themselves as gatekeepers, crusaders, and leaders. To the extent that they felt unable to move me or change me, they saw themselves as persecuted and mistreated.

In retrospect, neither critic was motivated initially by a love for me, a claim I'm comfortable making in light of their own verbal and written admissions and actions. Come, let us reason together, the scripture says. But how *can* we when the people are gripped by fear, entitlement, and unwillingness to consider a theological perspective—or even a thought—beyond their own?

Not to mention: undoubtedly, misogynoir was in play. The cultural blind spot and conflation of unchecked racism and sexism in these examples were obvious to me and others but likely escaped the conscious awareness of the crusaders/purists/accusers. White supremacy sells a lie that it is the only authority. When Black women know more about any topic, it is doubted or deemed insufficient, and people will call for additional burdens of affirmation. Our cultural narcissism causes us to feel that our culture has no bearing on our understanding or entitlements, while believing others are totally driven by cultural bias. As I write this, I am aware that my lens is shaped by intersecting cultures in ways that I don't have the wisdom to fully discern. I pray that when the assurance of interpretation and intention comes, humility will also come in double measure.

But discernment is woefully absent in these instances of church power gone wrong. In these types of cases, the white males involved see themselves as having biologically and divinely given authority over women. They preach this at the pulpit, and they practice what they preach in this regard. Ironically, they embrace political ideologies steeped in meritocracy while accepting without critique a belief in their own unearned authority—in the world and in the church. If it wasn't so grievous, this contradictory belief system would be laughable. But these individuals have been nurtured by micro- and macrosystems that they reinforce by their rules and their pedagogy—a phenomenon that Willie James Jennings calls an "imperialistic domination obsession."

These people create systems, and then they create theologies to uphold them so they can maintain power.

Such is the imperialist imagination.

Those words may sound harsh or disorienting to some. But if we look closely, we can see all around us self-serving, unrepentant, authoritative dominionists wearing the well-ironed clothing of servant-leaders. Frankly, if we are honest, vulnerable, and released from fear, we can admit that it is nearly impossible to differentiate between them.

## LOVELESS LEADERSHIP

Consider the fear of the Pharaoh in Exodus 1. That fear was similarly the fruit of an imperialistic imagination paired with its cousin: a necessarily fragile self-prescribed divinity. Pharaoh found himself projecting his imagination of dominance onto an oppressed people: "They must think like me." He assumed their motivations to be identical to his; he thought they, too, must want to dominate. This created paranoia—something we see in modern evangelical debates, as heresy hunters ignore their own burning houses of abuse and bigotry to avoid repentance and accountability."

> "Look," he said to his people, "the Israelites have become far too numerous for us. Come, we must deal shrewdly with them or they will become even more numerous and, if war breaks out, will join our enemies, fight against us, and leave the country."
>
> EXODUS 1:9–10

In these verses, Pharaoh is vexed by the belief that others will soon rise up, becoming great in number and power, build alliances, take over, and enact revenge. We also see Pharaoh's ultimate goal: to keep others in the system of stratification for his gain. If this worldly ideology is to remain dominant, an oppressed group must always be identified and controlled. In the oppressor's mind, if it is not the other, then it might become him. If Black Americans or indigenous peoples, for example, receive their rightful reparation, white fear speculates they will then become the oppressor. If women are no longer excluded from positional leadership, male anxiety fears competition and defeat.

When televangelist Pat Robertson warned against critical

race theory in 2021, he appealed to white fear. "Critical race theory wants to take the whip handle and give it to Blacks," he warned and lamented. Robertson is not alone in this white fear of retribution. If you listen closely, you can hear it and see it demonstrated in voting and hiring practices that appear open enough to pacify uprisings while retaining power for whites.

In Exodus 1, Pharaoh feels his vulnerability. And so Pharaoh oppresses, because oppression remains his only perverse hope to hold on to power.

Does this sound familiar? Pharaoh's motive and methods echo throughout history. It is not lost on me that Pharaoh's reasoning was operating when enslaved Africans rose up to fight alongside the British during the Revolutionary War, motivated by the promise of their freedom. During the Great Migration, Ku Klux Klan members stood watch at train stations to intimidate Blacks in the South, fearing they would lose their place at the top of the Jim Crow economic system. Similarly, and painfully, this abuse of politics for control in the church works to ensure that people stay in their place, because the caste system is unwieldy and requires the compliance of the oppressed.

All of us, even "the most disrespected people in America," as Brother Malcolm put it, struggle against our inner dominionists. Scripture shows us multiple instances of the ways in which our earthly social location bring about enormous temptation to maintain unjust power and privileges. Many rich young rulers walk away sad from the grace extended only by the God of the oppressed—both those oppressed by their sins and those suffering from the sins of the world.

How grievous to use the name of the Lord to create a system

to condone domination through paternalism—a breaking of the third commandment. In fear, we subjugate image-bearers and blood-bought and Spirit-gifted humans. And so we must ask ourselves: What does our fear cost us? What does it cost our neighbor? It is easy to call out Pharaoh or, in our present context, haughty white male egos and practices. And it's true that all leaders need great accountability, especially to those they regard as their inferiors. At the same time, we need not deny injustice to open the invitation to search ourselves. When we feel particularly called to tell the truth about the Church, power, government, or history, it becomes easy to exclude ourselves from the truth-sharing journey. But humility is always in order, and it offers a subversive strength.

As we consider humility, we must also consider love. We cannot correct anyone without love and an honest and humble assessment of our own limitations. Our Christian faith guides us to avoid haughtiness, a true punishment to self and others. We are necessarily limited and needy, even as we are fearfully and wonderfully made—not for the sake of performative depravity but to cultivate gratitude, neighbor respect, and God-dependency.

## SACRIFICIAL LEADERSHIP

Together, we can imagine all the reasons for those with limited social power to fear church discipline at the hands of the undisciplined. We are all harmed by leaders who believe that some element of their very personhood equips them to rule others or gives them authority to correct and control without sound reason, love, humility, or biblical integrity. In these cases, and in many of the other examples reported by my clients, Christian and otherwise, over the years, fear and control raged in the powerful undercurrent beneath the actions, gossip, and stubbornness of the accusers and enforcers.

To this day, I've witnessed and studied many instances of church discipline being used as a tool for men to secure social power or authoritative family position, and far fewer cases of it being used to address racism, misogyny, cruelty to children, greed, and manipulative theology. Yet, as destructive as misuses of correction are, I deeply value church discipline as a tool to protect the vulnerable, build communal safety, create a standard for how we treat one another inside and outside the church, and cultivate trust for leadership through godly actions. What I don't value is discipline in the hands of the socially powerful who shape policy to their advantage. Still, lamentable as they are, egregious cases of bullying, manipulation, slander, and control among Christians make me value church discipline even more. It is important for the witness of the Church, but also for the care of the saints, and especially those with less social currency in the family of faith and society.

Too often, true correction and external accountability are not applied to those who misuse power. Decisions about what *is* deemed worthy of correction—and how it is corrected—fall solely in the hands of our leaders. We too often ignore the wisdom of James the Just, selecting the same type of people who lead in worldly systems to lead in ministry (James 2:5–6; 5:1). Modern Protestantism as we know it began with Martin Luther's stand against the indulgences of the Roman Catholic Church. But our modern Protestantism still bears Luther's biases—including his well-documented disdain for the book of James. It is to our shame that the leaders of the world—elevated by privilege instead of obedience, character, good fruit, and good works—are so attractive to us.

We've seen this, right? Leaders who abuse and neglect church discipline. Leaders who are rewarded for ignoring that which we must correct.

These leaders remain in power when our faith communities do not uphold the church discipline required to correct them.

Church discipline that allows everyone to be built up and strengthened is healthy—not just for the congregation but for the leaders, too. It means they are under the same guidelines that strengthen and build us up.

We shouldn't be surprised when ill-equipped leaders don't keep the faith community safe, for discipline is a means of encouragement, correction, and safety.

But listen. This does not diminish the case for love-oriented church discipline; it strengthens it.

Let me repeat that: love-oriented discipline is the key. It is at the heart of discipleship. We have very little credibility apart from the security and sincerity of our love for others. We show our love for God in two ways: personal holiness, because we are learning to love ourselves, and love of neighbor because of love of God. We are called to enact love; after all, it is a verb that points to the God of love. Our correction of others cannot outrun our connection to them.

Can you hear the rebuke? It's the angry and hurting preteen yelling back at his punitive parent or teacher, "You don't know me." *Knowing* someone here means demonstrating an actual connection, care, or bond. When we attempt to correct someone without connection, care, and vulnerability, our correction becomes more like bullying. We might be right to point out an issue in someone's life, but our approach can be wrong. And for the people of God, both motives *and* methods matter. Correcting and coaching people is always limited or strengthened by our lived connection to their stories and experiences. Love is the fountain of our credibility. Our pursuit of knowing someone must come from an agenda of love. We use that knowledge to grow and demonstrate compassion and connection.

This is the heart of discipleship. No discipline, no discipleship.

I've often referred to the local church as the funniest, most inspiring, and unfortunately, most heartbreaking place on earth. At this point in time, the church is a hypocritical, unfinished work.

The church is so broken that it can almost seem audacious for the church to have anything to say. Given our reflection on the brokenness within our church culture, this seems obvious. Yet, the church is *still* called to proclaim and embody the Gospel. She is to be salt and light in the world. Thanks be to God for the promises that reveal what the church will become, and for the glimmers of heaven that we can see now.

When the people of God get it wrong, their lack of repentance reverberates throughout the church and world. However, when we get it right—or rather, when we repent—it's like the triumphant final scene in *The Color Purple*. Can you see it? The rebellious daughter runs back to the country church of her childhood, into the softened arms of her fierce and demanding father.

Shug Avery, the "out there" daughter, is beckoned to the

church altar as the sounds of "God Is Trying to Tell You Something" ring out through the trees and fields. As if being pulled by a supernatural force, she is drawn back, flat-footed, singing and walking more resolutely with each step. There, her father, the fire-and-brimstone preacher, stands robed at the pulpit. They embrace as she says, "See, Daddy? Sinners got soul, too," and we can see two hardened hearts soften through the force of love and reconciliation. Their reconciliation is so powerful that it reverberates through a community and changes the malicious heart of Mister, who uses his hidden savings to right his wicked wrong. Repentance begets repentance. Grace begets grace.

We probably also want to credit the power of great Black gospel music as tears fall from the viewer's eyes. Still, despite its fictive theatrics, the emotions the scene stirs are real. They resonate because we all need a way home. Maybe you are trying to find your way right now. Even in the midst of our spiritual foundness, we can feel very far from home.

Back to Shug. If you pay close attention to that scene, you'll notice a poignant moment when she is stopped dead in her tracks after soulfully belting out the line "Let me tell you something, sister" from "Miss Celie's Blues." You and I often have much to say to ourselves, to others, and even to God. We have much to tell, and too often we are unheard or misquoted. However, like Shug, there are times when we need the Spirit to still us and tell *us* something. This generous act of mercy when God pulls us into a new song—I see this as the goal of church discipline. God says, "Let me tell you something, daughter." The song that God sings over us changes our path and our future.

At its best, church discipline is the practice of encouraging and correcting one another toward love of God and love of neighbor. Its inclusion and practice are an essential mark of a healthy denomination or local church. Simply put, if there is no discipline, there is no love or safety. This concept might seem new to some, but I hope to make the case that it is indeed one of the most neglected and abused practices in the church in America.

Church discipline is a kind of discipleship that pulls us born-again believers from our slumber and realigns us with the moral will of God. God's moral will is always impossible apart from God and the means of grace, but it is ultimately what is best for us. It's important for us to discern the generous grace of God, *and* it's important for us to recognize the deceiving, lulling nature of sin and allow discipline to shake us awake. Off our autopilot. Out of our unhealthy desires. Out of our misdirected loves. Discipline reveals to us what is the most God-honoring direction for us to pursue. Think of church discipline as a map: It directs us toward where we need to go and instructs us on what we need to avoid. It realigns us, recalibrates us, and prompts us to ask and wonder, *How ought we to live? How ought we to love?*

Sadly, many of us associate the act or concept of church discipline with trauma. I bet you can see another scene now. An unmarried pregnant teen is brought to the front of the pseudo-sanctuary for scrutiny while the church as an institution turns a blind eye to its own systemic sin and complicity. The teen is "sat down" and given the scarlet letter. She bears shame because the evidence of premarital sex is growing within her body. Yet no male is rebuked, and nobody considers the power dynamics at play that may have led to this pregnancy. This image reeks of injustice and cruelty.

Early in my counseling training, I worked with a college student who had been groomed and abused by her youth minister. But that is not the way she described her experience initially. One or two sessions in, she asked me about my own faith convictions, even though we were working together at a secular counseling center and had never talked about faith. I was open to stating my faith, as I stand in agreement with feminist psychotherapists who believe that faith disclosure can help patients have insight into the potential biases of their therapists. So when she asked, I responded, "I'm a Christian. I'm a Christian in a way that makes a claim on the way I personally live." I spoke truthfully and concisely; after all, it was her session, not mine. From there, she shared her fears of how she might be seen by the church, and specifically "pastors' wives," going forward.

Why was she so certain of this negative response and perpetual disbelief? She went on to share about being "in a relationship" with her youth pastor. The youth pastor's wife had blamed her for luring her husband into sexual sin. The church folks whispered behind her back that she was "fast." They described him—a thirtysomething-year-old married man who misused his position and power to rape an adolescent girl—as succumbing to temptation, while she was seen as the tempter.

I don't remember all that we talked about that semester, but I do remember saying to her things like . . .

"I believe you."

"I am sorry."

"We, the people of the church, failed you."

"Your youth pastor was wrong and manipulative."

"Your pastor's wife was wrong and cruel."

"Your church is complicit in your abuse. Maybe they wanted to avoid bad press, so they turned on you. That was selfish and evil."

"Hear the words of the Lord regarding you, a child of the church. 'If anyone causes one of these little ones to stumble, it would be better for them to have a large millstone hung around their neck and to be drowned in the depths of the sea.'

"You are one of these little ones."

When the church fails to discipline wicked leaders, it puts itself under the fiercest of public judgment. It becomes the subject of the evening news, reality TV shows, and blog posts. Evangelists are met with resistance because the word on the street is that "you church people are all hypocrites."

I will never forget my client's beautiful face when I'd speak these words aloud. Even as a college student, she looked very young. A part of her was stuck in time at the page holder of her trauma. Her shame led her to resist her parents, who urged her to press charges against her abuser. Her parents were urged by leaders to let it go and were told that their teen daughter shared blame. Involving law enforcement would "ruin this Black man's life," they pleaded. In her mind, if she wasn't *truly* a victim, did she *really* deserve justice or the right to heal? The church's inaction toward justice and action toward wickedness created a deeper wound in her life than the youth pastor's grooming. The entire system was in on it—*it* being the exploitation of an adolescent girl and subsequent cover-up—all because they would not respond to anyone involved in the way that love demanded. Grievously, this ultimately rocked my client's self-image and image of God.

## THE REAL CHURCH RECEIVES CORRECTION

I say this as someone who loves the church: the church warrants ridicule from our neighbors and rebuke from God when it's too busy "straining out gnats and swallowing camels" to face its obvious failings. Straining out gnats instead of holding leaders accountable. Straining out gnats instead of repenting for obvious bigotry. When we avoid repentance, the world puts us on trial, and we find ourselves subject to a form of loveless punishment set to humiliate us and cut us off from redemption—not true, godly discipline. This is what happens when we resist redemptive correction.

A couple of years back on a podcast episode called "Why the Church Matters," I quipped that the United States should not have required a civil war—especially among self-identified Christians from the North and South—to end slavery. Church discipline should have been enough. Slavery and racism in America should have succumbed under the weight of the courageous enactment of church discipline and correction for the sake of justice, grace, and restoration. Think of saints like Charles Spurgeon and others who argued that slaveholders should not be able to take communion until they repented. Communion represents many things, including being in communion with one another—but slaveholders broke communion with the church by deciding to own, sell, and breed those made in the image of God.

Truthfully, there is no guarantee that this act of correction would have ended slavery. However, I am inclined to believe that it would have exposed the false church among the true. It

would have made clear the necessary call for the church to disentangle itself from world empires, lust for power, and domination. Would the church have been persecuted for disentangling
from empire? Yes—and we have no shortage of receipts indict-
ing the violence toward saints and truth tellers who did divest
from empire, chattel slavery, white supremacy, and greed. But
this would have only made it clearer that the persecuted church
in America was indeed the truer church in the land.

Today, we rightly honor Christian abolitionists and freedom
fighters who stood then against racial injustice in Jesus's name.
The reality that white theological heroes like Jonathan Edwards
or George Whitefield would have had no qualms about owning
and selling Harriet Tubman stands as an indictment of the en-
grained, racist wickedness of the white evangelical church tradition. The pollution from this robs the credibility of their
witness at this very hour.

Hear me on this. Thanks be to God that Christians don't
demonstrate their calling from Christ by way of moral perfection, but rather through a life of gratitude, showing repentance,
and love. Born-again believers are committed to striving toward
the high mark of our calling in Jesus Christ as we wrestle against
sins like white supremacy, greed, and self-idolatry.

Many people call themselves Christians, especially in nations where that title offers religious privilege. That's definitely
the case here in the States. But the people are confused. The
principalities are all up in our churches, muddling what it means
to be a Christian. So I ask: will the real Christians please stand
up? And, God, will you let us be among them?

I know I'm not alone when I ask these questions. Historically, no shortage of creeds, confessional statements, and church

covenants have served to reveal what some Christians believe we ought to all believe and stand for, across the ages—sometimes for our good, sometimes for our detriment. The Belgic Confession is one of many historical confessional statements written as a theological response to a cultural or political moment. It was written before North America was colonized. I admire the way this statement distinguishes the true from the false in the face of a society full of governments and systems that claimed to be a part of the church. Here is a short excerpt that I find helpful:

> The true church can be recognized if it has the following marks: The church engages in the pure preaching of the gospel; it makes use of the pure administration of the sacraments as Christ instituted them; it practices church discipline for correcting faults. In short, it governs itself according to the pure Word of God, rejecting all things contrary to it and holding Jesus Christ as the only Head. By these marks one can be assured of recognizing the true church—and no one ought to be separated from it.
>
> Excerpt from the Belgic Confession (1561),
> Article 29: "Marks of the True Church"

The confession goes on to describe the true Christian as one who flees sin, pursues righteousness, and loves God and their neighbor. This true Christian the confession describes is not without weakness, but they fight against it by the Spirit.

The confession contrasts this with the false church, painting a picture of a church without humility—a church greedy for power. It is a church that attempts to speak for God, assigning more authority to its own voice than to the word of God. It is not submissive to God's Word or will. It cherry-picks the Word of God for its own agendas. And it persecutes those who live holy lives according to the Word, and who rebuke it for its faults, greed, and idolatry.

> These two churches
> are easy to recognize
> and thus to distinguish
> from each other.

> Excerpt from the Belgic Confession (1561),
> Article 29: "Marks of the True Church"

Nearly a hundred years before we get the development of race as we know and use it, the Belgic Confession speaks about the political practices of the church within its context. By the way, the Belgic Confession was written in the mid-1500s just before the Dutch would engage in the trafficking and selling of over a half million Africans, which would go on for the next few hundred years. I raise this point to say that our stated convictions are never enough, and that our actions reveal our hearts. It is possible to admonish others to be the true church while enacting systems and practices that pervert it.

Article 29 notes that the false church is itself a persecutor. "It persecutes those who live holy lives according to the Word of God and who rebuke it for its faults, greed, and idolatry." The false church is busy distracting from its own necessary work of repentance and love by throwing darts. These darts are aimed at those who pursue personal piety by the power of the Spirit and promote neighborly love that forsakes greed and caste systems in obedience to the Word of God.

When the church does not apply discipline to matters of injustice and abuse, it becomes hard to distinguish the true church from the false church. Ultimately, Christ alone discerns the true from the false. His watchful eye looks into the visible church and sees the invisible church within it. "His winnowing fork is in his hand to clear his threshing floor and to gather the wheat into his barn, but he will burn up the chaff with unquenchable fire" (Luke 3:17).

However, that does not take away the collective church's calling and each Christian's individual mandate to search ourselves to see if we truly are in the faith. So here is the question for us—across countless churches, hundreds of traditions, and varying forms of polity: How do we engage the necessary work of church discipline? How do we restrain the misuse of power and the overprioritization of certain sins based on leadership's priorities and not the word of God? How do we guard against legalism and abuse of power?

The first answer and gut check is that the motivation behind our discipleship is love.

Here are some themes to consider and prayerfully discern as you think about your own discipleship and correction.

## Love Matters

Love must motivate all elements of discipleship. Even among Christian antiracists, we cannot correct and call out white people ensnared by white supremacy unless we have love. Not love abstractly or esoterically but love practically. A love that dogmatically resists denying people intrinsic dignity, even when they act a fool. A love that tells the truth, sets boundaries, holds beloveds accountable, and rejoices at every expression of repentance.

## Power Matters

In a community that pursues fearless love, power is acknowledged *and* decentered. We do the work of seeing and hearing each other acknowledging the internal temptations and social forces seeking to stratify us. Power is the force that creates change or compliance. It is the fuel behind the influence. We need not pretend it isn't there. Each community ought to name aloud the forces and influences operating implicitly and explicitly within it. Bring these forces under the light of scripture to see if they are in order with the moral will of God.

## God's Word Matters

While I don't worship the Bible, and certainly not any one person's interpretation of it, I believe God has uniquely revealed the plan of salvation and God's character in scripture. People far more spiritually gifted and knowledgeable about church history and biblical languages have debated about Christians' holy text for generations. Those debates will rage until Christ returns. Yet, I am comfortable saying that in scripture there is a God-ordained and upheld truth, even if I only see it dimly. My inability to perceive a truth does not negate its existence. My personal understanding and even agreement are not what makes truth *true*.

This is critical for both progressives and conservatives to acknowledge, since many of their battles are not only about what truth is but who gets to decide. It is a question of power and authority. Conservatives will claim it is a question of scriptural authority; progressives are right to push back and question if it's about the authority of the interpreter or God's authority.

God the Creator, and God alone, decides what is God's truth. We the created, on the other hand, in humility seek God, and in God we find what we need. We are given what God has for us. The goal, then, is not to know scripture better than the next person, or throw around verses like daggers, or ignore scripture like the plague. The goal is God. The goal is knowing God.

Our Bible-reading is a pursuit of love. How do I love God on God's terms? When we are sharpening, discipling, and challenging one another, we sit with scripture that speaks by the power of the Spirit today. In church discipline, we ask communally and individually: are we loving God, neighbor, and self on God's terms?

And why, we might ask, are God's terms the priority? God is love.

### Reputation Matters

Christians are not judges but rather witnesses. A witness is only as influential or useful as they are credible. The Bible asks us, "What good is salt that loses its saltiness?" The response is that it is trash, useless, maybe even a poser. The Bible goes further to say this salt gets trampled on. Likewise, our witness is trash when we spend time judging the world and ignoring our sins. We secretly make ourselves feel good and pious with our shock at others who avoid blood-bought, godly grief and transformation.

Christians continually need grace. No need for shame. And the gospel shows that we are not called to performative perfection. Consider what it means for the church to pursue each of its members in love, everyone calling one another out in order to call them in to greater fellowship and love. Imagine what our reputation would be if it was clear that our motive was love. Consider how powerful our witness can be before our neighbors when we don't make excuses for the unrepentant or minimize the sins in our pews. Fellowship with other believers does not mean covering up for them when they have done wrong, nor does it mean throwing them aside. The harder work is correction, not abandonment. God has not excused us from obedience just because we don't like or understand God's commands. God's ways are simply higher than ours. When our God's moral system and voice sound exactly like ours, it is a sign that we are making a god in our own image.

This is easy to see when our enemy makes a god in their own image, because we don't like our enemies, and therefore we reject the characteristics of their god.

But are we able to see the ways we attempt to speak for God with *our* own words, in *our* own interest?

### Submission Matters

We answer to one another. I cringe hearing leaders say "Follow me as I follow Christ" when I know they have no system of accountability in place. This can so easily turn into spiritual abuse, taking God's name in vain to enact one person's vision. While the Bible speaks to giving honor to God-given, competent leaders who are qualified through character, no part of the body is supreme over another. I cannot stress enough that we cannot lead those whom we will not learn from.

We cannot correct who we do not respect. When extending correction, it is God's moral will that guides our concerns and our love for each other, not our temporary and earthly positionality. I am grateful for leaders marked with humility and care for others. But to be clear, heaven has no pastors. Leaders, ordained or not, must govern themselves in ways that acknowledge their eternal positions as children of God.

May we spur the church on to become what it is supposed to be. And for those of us on the fringes, ready to jump ship, may we be encouraged to challenge the church to be what we believe and hope it can be. After all, that's what love looks like.

May we boldly ask:

What is the precedent in the past of disciplining bigotry and mistreatment in the church?

What outside entities are leaders accountable to?

How do we ensure that retribution does not happen to those who raise issues within the church?

How do we actively address and attend to issues of inequities in the church that may cause some to be silent about mistreatment, and others to be emboldened to mistreat others?

How do we encourage accountability for leaders through our liturgical practices, like teaching and preaching?

How homogenous are the members on your leadership trajectory? Are the people who keep you accountable the same kind of people as you?

Are your leadership meetings open? Are meeting minutes

and notes available to members, to the congregation, to the public? What is behind closed doors and what is not?

When it comes to issues of church discipline, are there available examples, notes, or cases for members to review, to see how these matters have been addressed on a denominational level— from the local church to the council, etc.?

What do we do with complaints against leaders? What is our process for evaluating the credibility of these complaints and grievances?

How do you encourage members and attendees with less social power and status to confront leaders? And how do you ensure the protection of these members and attendees when they do speak up?

Does your church have a precedent for using NDAs (non-disclosure agreements)? Do you have a policy against this?

Do you know the different purposes of secrecy versus confidentiality? Secrecy favors those with power; confidentiality is on the agenda of those with less power. How does your church use these to protect those who are more vulnerable as opposed to adding additional layers of protection for the most powerful within the church?

How does your church talk about people who leave? How does your church follow up to seek additional feedback that could be valuable for the health of the church *and* for the good of the departing member?

How can I as a member contribute to a culture where accountability and transparency are expected from leaders and members? What is my continual role, as a member of this church, in cultivating the health of the church, resisting abuses, and helping our leaders make good decisions?

What feelings and temptations arise when you hear about bad news—especially bad news that makes you and your church look bad? Do you feel tempted to cover it up, to fabricate details, to spin the narrative, to silence those who have been injured? How do you resist these temptations, or repent when you've succumbed to them?

Questioning the church is not the same thing as questioning God. We honor God by holding one another in loving accountability and encouragement.

If you as a believer long to say among other believers:

We love people.

We love ourselves.

We love the Body of Christ.

We love God's moral will.

We love the witness of the church.

We love justice, healing, and real reconciliation.

Then you have embraced the messy work of church discipline.

Examine yourself to see whether you are in the faith; test yourself. Can't you see for yourself that Jesus Christ is in you—unless you actually fail the test? And I hope you will realize that we have not failed the test.

Now we pray to God that you will not do anything wrong—not that we will appear to have stood the test, but that you will do what is right, even if we appear to have failed. For we cannot do anything against the truth, but only for the truth. In fact, we rejoice when we are weak but you are strong, and our prayer is for your perfection.

This is why I write these things while absent, so that when I am present I will not need to be severe in my use of the authority that the Lord gave me. He gave it to me for building you up, not for tearing you down.

Finally, siblings, rejoice! Aim for perfect harmony, encourage one another, be of one mind, live in peace. And the God of love and peace will be with you.

(2 Cor. 13:11)

# PART III

## Liberation

EKEMINI: Whew, that was a lot. *(In my Grandmaster Flash and the Furious Five voice)* Love is a jungle sometimes; it makes me wonder how I keep from going under.

MICHELLE & CHRISTINA: Makes me wonder how I keep from going under. Ah-huh-huh-huh-huh.

EKEMINI: *(\*cackle\* \*cackle\* \*snort\*)* Fix it, Jesus!

CHRISTINA: You know what I'd love? Freedom.

MICHELLE: Good segue! As liberation is the last topic on the table today.

EKEMINI: Last but not least! I think it's time for us to dream together.

# Love & Justice in Multiethnic Worship

## By Michelle Higgins

> Music is our witness and our ally. The "beat" is the confession which recognizes, changes, and conquers time. Then, history becomes a garment we can wear, and share, and not a cloak in which to hide; and time becomes a friend.

> JAMES BALDWIN

I'VE STOPPED COUNTING THE TIMES I've visited Detroit, Michigan. I love that city. It's the home of Motown, y'all. Nuff said, I know. But it's also the home of the Black power monument to Joe Louis, and I love the Wright Museum of African American History. That's right, the "FUBU" museum before we had the Smithsonian's National Museum of African American History and Culture in Washington, D.C. And please don't get me started on the pizza. I can smash that rectangle pan for breakfast, brunch, lunch, and late-night. (But Saint Louis is my hometown; we go hard for a crispy thin crust, so I can't be acting out like that.)

A few years ago, I visited Detroit for a conference that helps Christian racial-justice organizations network to build power for the sake of community development. One evening, I took a long walk around the city with Charlene and Darren, a couple I'd always admired but rarely spent time with. Charlene and Darren are that couple whose collective cuteness is both ultra-cool and warmly welcoming. They know no strangers, protect their togetherness, and spur each other on to good works. It helps that their baby girl is adorable in all caps, but even before they had their daughter—the time where this story happens—they shared a dream.

For several years, Charlene and Darren dreamed of opening a restaurant called the Fattened Caf. They spoke of the direct reference to the parable of the prodigal son, and the communion experience of sharing a meal. Charlene talked about the intentionality of building a hybrid cuisine, harmonizing Darren's Blackness and her Filipino heritage.

As we walked around Detroit together, Charlene and Darren shared all the thoughts running through them. The only thing I could think about while they were talking was "This is worship." Beyond preparing food, their dream was for fellowship. They spoke of bringing people together to learn about one another through the love of food and culture. They were committed to hiring youth and working-class people and creating affordable menu options that allowed them to serve events that were important to them, no matter the budget limitations. Their testimony of cooking together and then filling people up was clearly grounded in creating community. Their intentionality inspired me and challenged me to rethink my own ministry of structuring and leading in worship spaces.

People are hungry, and we need to know where there's a feast prepared. This is the lens through which I wanted to build a framework for multiethnic involvement in worship. As with Darren and Charlene's plan for pop-up Fattened Caf feasts, participating in multiethnic worship requires interaction with different people for the sake of producing the worship experience.

Everyone who experiences worship plays a part in how worship is led. My multiethnic worship story is a multipurpose mixture. It's field notes from a forgiven failure; it's a love letter to Black women worship leaders, especially my sisters in marginalized spaces. Read me however you will, dear sister. But know that you were made to praise, so every piece of your praise matters. The people who prepare your community's worship space are hopefully doing so with you in mind. Knowing that I'm on my way to a feast makes me want to learn all I can about the menu and the chefs who prepared it. Loving my life as a worshipper makes me long to learn all I can about how this particular feast is made. My hope is to provide my sisters at the banqueting table a quick tour of the farm and a short glimpse into the kitchen.

In various training resources on multi-*anything* ministry from the past twenty years, majority-culture ministry leaders are instructed to befriend someone who can explain the underrepresented culture and then shepherd (or coach) them through constructing more inclusive elements to be presented in public worship. On the part of the cultural shepherd, there is little expectation of lasting connection outside the named ministry goal.

The responsibility of leading God's people into an experience of surrender, amid and in spite of life's worries—and threats, for people in marginalized groups—is an especially high calling. Worship leaders often carry many responsibilities, from directing music to designing the worship service. They are tasked with setting an atmosphere of total adoration for the same God who conceived of our existence, controls every situation, and comforts us through the highs and lows. Often, they must work with a team of pastors who have authority over them in the space they co-create. Let me be plain: representation and inclusivity, no matter how important, are very difficult to achieve in every worship experience. Even worship teams who work with the most affirming and accepting pastoral leadership can become discouraged when desires for a multiethnic worship ministry are met with reality. Congregations that want many cultures represented in worship are not always thinking about the challenges of expanding the music repertoire of ethnically homogenous volunteer pools, the unpredictability of ongoing access to quality equipment, or retaining multitalented artists without breaking limited budgets. Nearly none of these pieces plays a role in the examples I will share, but all of them have some impact on my story.

I've been leading music for congregations in some capacity for over twenty years. After fourteen years of worship leadership, I realized I would never satisfy my longing to learn the best way to make space for multiethnic worship. I've been on a decades-long quest for the best way to build a framework I could customize as needed. My eventual realization was that multiethnic worship has no meaning and bears no fruit without justice and love at the root.

Years ago, I taught a Sunday-school class about Black gospel music and global worship. During one of the sessions, I spoke about the beauty of Pentecost as a precursor to the coming of the Kingdom of God. As I was listing the languages I imagined we would hear in the Kingdom, I shared my excitement about hearing and speaking my native language, which my family and many Black families had been robbed of by trafficking in the transatlantic slave trade. One of my Spanish-speaking friends, Tia, from Central America, conversed with my ideas and named similar feelings.

I did a double take.

"Wait, isn't Spanish your heart language?" I asked.

"Nah, sis, it's the colonizer's tongue, just like the English language for you."

My heart sank. I was stunned and shamed by how obvious the truth was. We talked together for a while after the class. Tia was open to speaking with me and receptive to my apology for making an assumption and asking the question in the manner that I did.

She was not part of the music ministry that I was leading at the church. But I often asked her to help me with teaching new songs. I'd consulted her for translation, pronunciation, and background information on different types of Spanish-language music, and I felt we'd built camaraderie and rapport in the process. I asked her to describe her experience and told her that if at any point these requests made her frustrated, I truly wanted to know. She told me that she did enjoy our time overall, as no meeting was exclusively about work. But it became clear that when we talked on and on about Spanish speakers, she was showing me grace and doing me a favor.

Tia made it clear to me that singing in Spanish was still a joy to her. The closest comparison we discovered to my monolingual life was the experience of having a worship service saturated in Black gospel music. English is the language that I know only because of centuries of injustice, but the Lord was working through it nonetheless.

Still, by assuming Tia's true native tongue was Spanish, I had participated in an ignorance that came from centering a norm of my own construction, supported by a colonizing mindset that I needed to continue to dismantle. I had followed a practice of presuming that singing in any language besides English would provide diversity credibility. But I hadn't considered the relational and educational cost. And I'd paid the price: I'd missed out on an opportunity to make space to hear about the tribes she was descended from. I'd missed out on the opportunity to learn with my staff and volunteers about the complexities of colonized Central and South America, much akin to the colonizing of Africa and Australia—for most Black and Brown populations in the world have a story about being weighed down by whiteness.

For Black multilingual worship leaders, the practice of leveraging relationships with diverse nonwhite people bears a glaring resemblance to tokenism and carries the potential for exploitation. Multiethnic worship is meaningless without a commitment to justice and love. Through my search for a framework for connecting Christian worship across cultures and global liberation struggles, I was challenged, changed, disappointed, and formed in ways that will never leave me.

## HERE ARE SOME OF THE THINGS THAT I LEARNED

And when I say learned, I mean it, sis. I mean that I learned these things because I needed to learn them, not because I needed to know them in order to teach or to lead. (Though, trust me, that helped!) But I learned how truly I needed to be led in order to cling to God's power and call beautiful my own limitations.

## Define Those Buzzwords You Use All the Time

I define worship, broadly, as the practice of connecting with God through prayer, praise, music, making art, making noise. But worship is also a synonym for that weekly congregational event. "Multiethnic worship," in this essay, generally refers to the latter definition. But I am inspired more and more by the broader definition to expand my view of worship and change my mode of leadership. God's people have beautiful experiences when our vision encounters the vastness of God's imagination, which is evident in the many cultures and ethnicities God gathers together for worship. But what is the difference between these definitions?

In his book *Many Colors,* Soong-Chan Rah describes the church's "dysfunctional relationship with culture." In more ways than one, the good pastor-professor asks the reader to consider that every church has a culture that must be identified and audited. He also quite seamlessly makes distinctions between the terms "ethnicity" and "culture." As I read through his work, I realized how often I mix the terms and use one when I mean the other, viewing them as the same. But these terms are quite distinct, and knowing the difference between them can help pastors and church leaders who are committed to creating a space of welcome for all manner of cultures *and* ethnicities.

We refer to a person's *ethnicity* when we discuss ancestral origins: traditional lands, tribe or people group, and language associated with the people. But *culture* is the things you do in order to exist in your world. It's learned behavior that is associated with a place where particular actions work for or against your best interest. It's a group of people who assign importance to or pass judgement on certain behaviors.

Professor Rah writes, "Your church has a culture." I doubt any congregation can start the journey toward multiethnic worship without first realizing the culture they are inviting people into.

I believe that worship leadership is dynamic, so I am always learning. I have learned a lot, and I have a lot to learn. What I can say in earnest, without a doubt, is that multiethnic worship is meaningless without a commitment to justice and love.

## Worship Must Be Inclusive

In Black churches, ethnicity often dictates culture. Because the two are not always defined separately, there is little differentiation, especially in North American Black cultural expression. But Black cultural expression is vast. Black cultures are numerous enough to include people who do not express our shared ethnic roots in a uniform way. The Black church has always been diverse. Liberating worship through justice and love leads us to make church inclusive.

Whether or not you're part of a church that uses the term "multiethnic," Black people are multicultural, and many Black churches are multiethnic. I grew up in Black churches that were common ground for Kenyans, Jamaicans, Black Germans, Nigerians, Colombians, Egyptians, and Black Texans alike. The fact that "Blackness is not a monolith" should make us both proud and humbled. Many of the worship spaces built through-out the Black diaspora have multiple ethnic roots represented. We use the term "Afro-Caribbean" to describe an extended family of music styles based in at least four languages and twenty rhythms. And when Black people say "African music," we are talking about at least fifty-four distinct ways to praise. The more I learn about the massiveness of all that "multi" truly means, the more I see the vastness of the God who put the "multi" in multitudes. God is not a monolith. This too is evident in every corner of every culture who sings His praise.

If worship is our expression of adoration for someone above us who makes us equal to one another, then how much more welcoming might we be to one another as the liberated survivors of oppressive forces who despise our ethnicity and pit our cultures against one another? This is not a call to watered-down worship based in Black absolution of white guilt. Nor is it a superhuman expectation, covered in the sheep's clothing called "forgive everyone as Christ forgave you," which we know has been used to guilt Black churches into welcoming abusive white people and calling it a ministry of reconciliation.

I envision a more faithful, embodied expression of the bold-ness that Blackness requires. In the worship space, the truer any person can be to self and Spirit, the more they welcome people from every place the Spirit lives. This picture of multiethnic worship is possible only through *enjoining* our intersectional struggles. In white-centered worship, the value and validity of liberation struggles is measured by their perceived morality, i.e., how well their leadership or purposes match up with a white heterosexual norm.

Not long after graduating seminary, I joined a networking-

and-support group for women-of-color worship leaders. One of my sisters in the group, whom I will call Ella, served a multilingual, majority white congregation that had regular attendees whose primary language was Lingala. This group comprised two Black families—about twelve people—and occasional guests. Ella was praised for providing multilingual music and spoken elements, projected for the congregation on the sanctuary walls during worship. While Ella was required to display English translation for every Spanish language element, her church leaders told her on a few occasions that it was unnecessary, confusing, and "at times uncomfortable" to have Lingala translation on every English-language slide. The reasons given were logistical: it was seen as more orderly to "only display Lingala when necessary." Her pastor told her, "During the call and response reading, the congregation won't know whether to answer in Lingala or English, and it will be messy."

When changing our ways in worship is too complex, too messy, the compromise of making it happen "only when necessary" is still a marginalizing act. If it's unnecessary for non-English speakers to fully understand a worship service, is it also unnecessary for them to be fully dignified, fully welcomed, fully empowered? If their participation is only partly necessary, is their presence fully valued? Cultural superiority, which is merely a courteous cover for supremacy, is evident when humans dictate the necessity or non-necessity of other humans. Ella's place of worship was more haughty than humble. Welcoming the Holy Spirit of liberation is the only way to transform our hearts and homes into places that worship God, who fully welcomes us all.

Because liberated worship embraces every global struggle,

multiethnicity is neither forced nor mitigated. A congregation need not guilt or explain itself if multiethnicity is not happening, because worship is always a preparation for inclusivity. When churches commit time and leadership development to the practice of inclusivity, our congregations naturally long for multiethnicity, and we find ourselves comforted by diversity rather than made anxious by it. In white-normative spaces, which are fundamentally noninclusive, multiethnicity is a defense mechanism. In conferences and trainings I have attended or led, I am accustomed to churches with all white pastors saying, "I want to apologize for the fact that we have all white people in leadership." I cannot list the number of people who have said those words in almost twenty years, across the United States. Often, they follow the apology with bold statements about how many nonwhite people are in their membership, or how often they support and partner with people of color who lead other organizations and churches. Rather than making room for inclusive leadership, they highlight their selective activity with multiethnicity.

But I'm too Black to believe that these apologies and statements denote a commitment to inclusivity in everyday life.

In inclusive spaces, worship offers a welcome so warm and natural, it's spiritually disarming.

One of my brothers in worship leadership is Eric Lige, who lives in California and works around the world. He and I met after applying for the same leadership position on the worship team for an international missions conference, and I am so gloriously glad that he got the job! Eric is an astoundingly charming presence. He deftly commands his worship teams and defers with authenticity and warmth to their skills when they complement his. I also know him to be absolutely fantastic at the Electric Slide (in the Blackest way, *okay*? If you know, you know).

A few years ago, Eric and I were invited to join a cohort of Black and Brown worship leaders discussing the future of the multiethnic church. We gathered in Michigan in wintertime. I came from Missouri and he flew in from Cali. While I was more prepared for the elements, the event was much more his scene than mine. And yes, y'all, we clowned in the most Holy Ghost "iron sharpening iron" kind of way. Eric introduced me to some people I have come to respect as heroes in and survivors of the white-centered worship wildness machine. One evening, one of the event's organizers joined us for dessert and fellowship in a common area of the conference center where the event took place. The organizer, Syreeta, was a Black Girl Magic firehouse event designer, vocalist, and administrator. We gathered around a piano and harmonized through every traditional gospel song we could name. We talked about the similarities in our experiences of worship leadership and creating "hush harbor" spaces within white-majority places.

People in the cohort heard the fellowship and joined in to share stories and songs as well. Others sat nearby and carried on conversations over our joyful background noise.

We all spoke freely, sometimes awkwardly, but always vulnerably. Cohort members asked questions about song origins, the meaning of different lyrics, or different versions of a song they'd heard in a different place. A few people vamped into preaching and teaching. While the room was ethnically diverse, all the people sharing music were Black. When we asked to hear music from other traditions, our colleagues expressed satisfaction with "just being in the room." The day after our fellow-ship time, we talked about how that felt like one of the richest worship services we'd had in a while. I told Eric that I wondered if we could have been more intentionally inclusive. He said, "That was really inclusive. How many times have we filtered conversation because non-Black people were in the room? How often have quote-unquote global worship leaders felt put on the spot to perform without the option to relax and enjoy not carrying the vibe for a change? Nobody but God was in charge, so to me that was some good worship!" Eric delivered this word from the Lord in casual camaraderie. But I was disarmed in that moment.

Our impromptu worship gathering was not based on winning each other's admiration or insisting on strict parity for appearance's sake. We did not have multiethnic worship per se, but it was inclusive. Inclusivity is liberative. None of us were expected to be anything but ourselves. None of the non-Black singers felt left out. Inclusivity creates comfort, invites confidence in asking questions, upholds humility in receiving feedback, and plants patience in the work of unifying many voices without forcing uniformity. There was no question of mess or confusion. We felt needed and desired, no need to apologize for who we were. We all participated in glorious worship because everyone was worshipping God. There was only one God in the room.

## Remove Tokenizing from Worship Ministry

The mere existence of Blackness as an ethnicity is a witness to God's creative, redemptive power. This power is our inheritance.

When we share our worship practices, we express the gifts that we believe God has given our ethnicity and the cultures that represent it. In their book *Worship Together,* Nikki Lerner and Josh Davis describe the different ways that God can show leaders how to become more open to more ethnic expressions in their worship service. God can send a dream or a vision, a book recommendation, a conference, or a surreal worship experience. "His options are limitless," they write. And they right! God's liberating purpose is present in His limitless options for making multiethnic worship a possibility. This sacred potential makes me mindful as I work in diverse spaces.

I have found it important for people of color to maintain a posture of protest if they are few in number at a "multiethnic" church, especially if that church is white-led. We become the worship leaders even if we can't sing. We become the token scripture reader even if we lack stage presence. I have seen this done in earnest desperation to "live out" the vision of Revelation today. I have also been invited, and myself been complicit in inviting and elevating people of other ethnicities simply because they give the church credibility. Diversity in music, ministry leadership, and buffet choices at the church potluck do not a just ministry make. Plantation owners ate fried chicken, Islamophobes smash felafel, and Cinco de Mayo does not magically make us hip to Latine community concerns. Justice isn't cheap. Without love and justice, our worship has no witness and does not nourish or disciple us at all. We must love and continue learning to love the ethnicities we claim to honor. This learning will lead us to stand in the way of anything that hinders their liberation—a freedom deeply connected to our own.

Anything else is tokenism.

Lemme tell you why.

## Multilingual Worship Is Often Courteous Colonizing

If we take our cues for multiethnic worship expression from the scriptures in Revelation where all the nations are singing and celebrating together, we're going to need a reason for leaving out the stories of liberation victory and the total defeat of oppressive powers that appear in the same book. Without an ethic grounded in the justice that brings all nations to the throne, it might be harmful to sing in different languages and act like we have the entire storyline of Revelation in view. If we want to worship together and feast together but never address oppressions, we need to rethink our priorities.

Not too long ago, my mother was asked to give a sending prayer during Sunday worship to cover a pastor from West Africa. He was departing the United States, where he and his family are loved and respected, to return home to work. As Mom prayed, she asked the Lord to "anoint your servant from the top of his head to the soles of his feet," as many Black Baptist and Pentecostal preachers are known to do.

After mom prayed, she took her seat in the pews. Another pastor at the church—the one who had asked her to pray—walked up on stage and said he enjoyed the times when Mom prayed. "It's always so fun," he said. He added that it was extra fun on this occasion, as he and others were discussing how "tickled" they were by her phrase. He was white, and so were the tickled people he referred to. We were all part of this congregation known for multiethnic worship, diversity in leadership, and regular civic engagement—a clear justice commitment was present in their mission and vision statements. But that commitment was not evident in this moment.

For if shepherds are too busy being amused by Black women's prayers to receive a baptism in head-to-toe anointing, our churches are not participating in the diversity of language that Pentecost offers. Black people are resilient enough to "sing Zion songs in strange lands," like the Old Testament stories of God's people in exile, but we shouldn't find those strange lands in the church.

After the worship service, the pastor who was prayed for approached my mom. He said he wanted to show her reverence and gratitude, and he was especially thankful for her "claiming a full-body anointing" for him. The phrasing reminded him of the worship services in his hometown.

Without a commitment to love and justice, our worship is no witness at all. Worship must feel like welcome, not fabrication. To lead worship requires enough humility to sit down at a table where the meal and ingredients might be a surprise—and faithfulness enough to find flavor and nourishment even in the unfamiliar dishes. Every time we serve communion to one another, every time we greet one another, we are practicing participation in God's expansive story, which calls each of us essential. We don't need to be entertained or shown something fun in order to denounce exploitation, embrace mutuality, and pray for God's anointing. Worship is the place where we are asked to welcome surprises, to be nourished by people with different abilities, and to join ourselves to causes we might not take up on our own.

## Seek the Beloved Community

People of God, open up your Bibles. Today we're in 1 Corinthians 12:12–27.

*Clears throat*

I have been singing in church for as long as I can remember. When my sister Mary and I were four and five years old, our mother taught us to harmonize when we sang. We spent almost three hours a day practicing music. I spent every Sunday of my childhood in church for most of the day. Morning worship, afternoon fellowship, evening worship and choir rehearsal. My mother and father are preachers and teachers. My uncle is my presiding bishop, my cousins are pastors and ministry leaders. I have served the worship arts in some capacity for half my life.

Under my leadership, a dozen different congregations, community choirs, conferences and special events have been served. Almost every artist, musician, and volunteer that I have worked with closely has testified to me or someone else that I failed them. I believe them. I don't know the details of every disappointment. What I do know is that leaders must learn how to live: liberated from the perfectionist machine, free from the presumption that multicultural work makes no messes. It is possible to be fallible but not fragile. I don't know anyone who hasn't wrestled with failure. I do know that we can fail without making failure our name.

Leadership has taught me that I am a learner. When I teach these lessons learned about the different members of God's body, I often talk about the lifetime it might take for a person to realize what part they are. I am they. They are me. I thought I was the brain's right temporal lobe, but I am more likely the soft underside of a pinky toe. The work is different over here, but no less important. My mode is movement, my testimony is praying with my feet.

1 Corinthians 12 says that the body of Christ "is not made up of one part, but of many," and that "God has placed the parts in the body, every one of them, just as God wanted them to be." Fellowship at God's table, living as distinct members of God's house, is a nourishing action that involves different people with different perspectives, experiences, and abilities. This truth applies to different parts of the church. Not all nonwhite persons were born to sing and dance, teach cultural intelligence at the cookout, and build dioramas for the missions month info table. Congregations need more than multiethnic worship, which functions only within constraints that are manageable for white mediocrity. A partial list of questions guiding these constraints are: Is it "necessary" (as discussed earlier)? Can we control it? Will we gain cash or cultural capital?

Multiethnic worship is meaningless until white-centeredness—and therefore whiteness—is cast out. Worship is liberated by a commitment to the things that God is committed to: love and justice—the flourishing of righteous relationships and right action. The collective activity of God's diverse household is a purposeful part of reaching this ultimate goal. That goal is unity in the body of Christ. If the whole body was the hand, how would the mind function? If every member of the Ugandan body is presumed to be a dancer, we miss out on the climate-justice leadership of Leah Namugerwa and Vanessa Nakate. Inclusive worship is more than music; it is more than multiethnic. It welcomes the eyes and ears of the body, the slender and short, the curvy and the cane-carrying. Meaningful multiethnic worship is intentionally interdependent. When God's body moves as a unified whole, each part freed from trying to be another, our worship is inclusive, and the body is liberated.

> But God has put the body together, giving greater honor to the parts that lacked it, so that there should be no division in the body, but that its parts should have equal concern for each other. If one part suffers, every part suffers with it; if one part is honored, every part rejoices with it. Now you are the body of Christ, and each one of you is a part of it.
>
> 1 CORINTHIANS 12:24–27

By connecting our freedom struggles across ethnic and cultural divides, our acts of worship both testify to and ready us for the work of justice that the struggle for freedom requires. I served as an organizer for a local prison-abolition campaign in 2018. Let me tell you, we sang or meditated before every protest, because social justice without steadfast love swiftly turns to hopeless stress. The church in the United States has a parallel testimony. We claim to have steadfast love for people whose fight for justice means nothing to us. What purpose can our worship serve if we don't mean anything we are singing? What is the point of proof-texting Revelation 7:9 if we aren't going to talk about Revelation 7:16?

In the first passage, we see people from every nation, tribe, and language group streaming around the throne. When the Prophet asks, "Who are they?" our answer must move us into ministry. They are our neighbors, our ancestors, they are us. We are them. We are the ones whose tears will be wiped away, whose hunger will be met with filling, and whose tribulations will be overcome. This is the multiethnic multitude who will be saved by God's justice. Thus multiethnic worship will come from a place of liberation, when we are finally free from all constructs—including the ones built by white people who just want to have more fun while they praise.

Much like the lessons learned in my time with Darren and Charlene, God's vision of multiethnic worship feels like a feast prepared in more settings than just the sanctuary, for more tastes than just the ones we recognize. Different members of the body of Christ function in different places, with various strategies, writing different stories, by God's design. So worshipping God is designed to bind us together across distance and difference. I haven't seen Eric in almost two years. I don't know if I will ever work with my former colleagues again. And though we all live in the same city, I don't see Darren and Charlene regularly. We do not attend the same church, hang out on weekends, or text like homies. I hire them for catering events as often as I possibly can. The Fattened Caf's Filipino-style longganisa is now available in my local grocery store, and my church's Juneteenth cookout was blessed by Darren's smoked chicken and made-from-scratch potato salad. No matter how far apart we are, whenever the family of God gathers for worship, there's always a feast prepared, and every bite feels like communion.

After this I looked, and there before me was a great multitude that no one could count, from every nation, tribe, people and language, standing before the throne and before the Lamb. They were wearing white robes and were holding palm branches in their hands. And they cried out in a loud voice: "Salvation belongs to our God, who sits on the throne, and to the Lamb."

All the angels were standing around the throne and around the elders and the four living creatures. They fell down on their faces before the throne and worshiped God, saying: "Amen! Praise and glory and wisdom and thanks and honor and power and strength be to our God for ever and ever. Amen!"

Then one of the elders asked me, "These in white robes—who are they, and where did they come from?"

I answered, "Sir, you know."

And he said, "These are they who have come out of the great tribulation; they have washed their robes and made them white in the blood of the Lamb. Therefore, "they are before the throne of God and serve him day and night in his temple; and he who sits on the throne will shelter them with his presence. Never again will they hunger; never again will they thirst. The sun will not beat down on them, nor any scorching heat. For the Lamb at the center of the throne will be their shepherd; he will lead them to springs of living water. And God will wipe away every tear from their eyes."

REVELATION 7:9–17

# POSTLUDE

Please allow me to nerd out for a moment. One of my favorite worship-planning resources is the family of works in *Songs of Zion*, a hymnal written for and by the Black church. Released in 1981, it is a record of the tunes and background of musical elements in the tradition of Black Christian worship in the United States. In *Come Sunday*, the liturgical planning volume that accompanies the hymnal, William B. McClain reflects on the wholeness of God as represented in the Black worship tradition: "Worship in the Black tradition is celebration of the power to survive and to affirm life, with all of its complex and contradictory realities." McClain goes on to discuss how Saturday night and Sunday morning experiences blend together in the world of Black Christian worship. The "sacred and secular" meet in the sanctuary. Oftentimes, our church music can be heard on the same radio stations that play dance music and love songs. I suspect this is because Blackness reshapes worship to embrace every identity that white-centered worship traditions might cast out. Where whiteness divides, Blackness welcomes. I hesitate to trust a framework for worship based on oversimplifying ethnic expression to a binary of *white* and *other*.

Black church leaders must interrogate the purposes of multiethnic worship, especially when it's framed as an ethic that makes white churches relevant. Our ethnic roots are in freedom and struggle, in every beautiful expression of praise, every prayer poured over our pains. Every silent tear, through every weary year, was part of our ethnicity being built into countless expressions of culture. Nikki Lerner and Josh Davis are right: God's possibilities are limitless. Because they are as vast as God's justice. They are as freely accessible as God's love. There will never be a need to use an image-bearer as a tool to make our churches relevant. I don't know that a true commitment to collective identities in Jesus and Blackness would ever allow that.

It is not for us to decide who lives in the beloved community. Our assignment is to welcome one another by worshipping God. There are many meanings for the word "worship," many ways to make worship out of our various works. To dance, sing, and sway; to look after young people and care for aging people; to make church buildings accessible for all bodies; to embrace multilingual families—this is worship. Every part of God's body is built to partake in worship that is as welcoming as the world is wide. Answering God's invitation to dwell and thrive in this community means believing that every part of us is welcomed, individually and communally.

Whether sharing celebrations, airing frustrations, carrying grief, or giving gratitude, living in community teaches us to trust in God's plans and purposes above our own. The more I learn about people, the more I lean on the Lord.

When Jesus gave the greatest commandments, he was teaching people how to live with each other and how to obey God. In Mark 12 and other gospels, Jesus says to love the Lord, our God, with everything that we are, and love our neighbor as we love ourselves. Even this teaching grounds us in worship. To love the Lord with our everything means to give our everything to what God loves.

The Lord loves to liberate people, and God draws near to the oppressed. The more we worship the God who loves justice, the more we will join God's work for justice, rooted in love. This is what makes multiethnic worship meaningful; a unified purpose is communicated by a multitude of different expressions.

Multiethnic worship is right in front of us. It's a vision, a handshake, a block party, a movement, a cookout, a cause. Multiethnic worship is a preview of God's promise to unify the history and future of time.

For the origin of every ancestral line shares the same liberated conclusion.

# Reborn to Resist

## By Christina Edmondson

*An epistle to the wounded, worried, and*
*wondering church in America*

THERE SEEMS TO BE A LOT of religious remixing these days. I get it. If the face and economic engine of American Christianity is *actually* right-wing Christian nationalism, we ought to hightail it away from there. For that religion is no more than white men hell-bent on not being figured out as insecure and in possession of illegitimate power. The faith of the biblical and first-century followers of Jesus was very different from the Christianities we might see around the world and across the street from us today.

Being able to distinguish between these different Christianities has been a part of the survival story of Africans since my ancestors were trafficked to these shores. Yet, somehow unacknowledged in Christian propaganda is a truer Christianity shaped in the hush harbors that turned slaves into abolitionists, silenced women into prophetesses, and those once in shackles into choreographers. It is in this Christianity that we are reborn to resist. Ours can be a Christianity that stands in the tradition of Tubman and Douglass, with clarity and conviction.

> I love the pure, peaceable, and impartial Christianity of Christ; I therefore hate the corrupt, slaveholding, women-whipping, cradle-plundering, partial, and hypocritical Christianity of this land. Indeed, I can see no reason, but the most deceitful one, for calling the religion of this land Christianity. I look upon it as the climax of all misnomers, the boldest of all frauds, and the grossest of all libels.
>
> FREDERICK DOUGLASS, *Narrative of the Life of Frederick Douglass, an American Slave /
> Incidents in the Life of a Slave Girl*

The "boldest of all frauds" is the taking of Jesus's name for the advancement of evil and oppression.

For the last few years, I have been up to my eyeballs in religion and race research, trying to reckon with the question of how Christianity in America can make one group so committed to freedom, even for the good of their enemy, and another complicit in their neighbor's bondage. We know it is not that clean of a dichotomy, yet my spirit longs to know more and more of what the rebirth in Christ really means now, as we long for the just and holy future to come.

So many of us long for a reset, a fresh start, a clean slate. A new beginning. Ever wish you could start all over again?

When I talk about rebirth, I'm not talking about some vague new beginning. I'm talking about the fresh, new wind of full dependency on Christ, and the pathway of justification—being made right with Christ—that sanctifies all of who we are. Rebirth does not remove nor dismiss any of us; rather, rebirth puts all our identities on the agenda of sanctification. Rebirth does not acknowledge only our helplessness but also the limitations of our own understanding. And yet we don't need to fear the not knowing, because we aren't saved by our intellectualism. In other words, to be reborn is to see the world with fresh, new eyes. Rebirth sees our limitations and knows we are in need. Rebirth need not know it all, for it rests in the provision and comfort of the one who does know all things.

This stands in sharp contradiction to the reputation of Christians as know-it-alls and judgmental culture warriors. And so it is under these pains that I've wrestled with the idea of the Christian's rebirth, the temptations to resist our necessary dependency on Christ, and the believer's fixation on the sins out there, at the expense of the internal repentance that is also required of us.

While reading and reading, I could hear my old graduate school professors remind me, "Check your biases!" One mentor in particular, Dr. Castle, taught me, "Researchers have to check their biases by declaring them and relying on peers to see or question what they cannot." For example: I for one have a host of biases about race, shaped by lived experiences, intergenerational storytelling, and media influences. Our biases aren't necessarily morally wrong or inaccurate, but the core problem with biases is that they are untested largely because they are hidden. Add some social power and insecurity to unchecked bias and we have legalism and unjust laws running amok. When a faulty bias is finally exposed and challenged, we too often resist correction, turning a bias into a guarded conviction.

We wear our false sense of knowing like armor, believing it will protect us.

That armor, the armor used to cover up the vulnerability of ignorance, fails us at the wrong moment and under the right conditions. The sword of suffering, church hurt, national crisis, or whatever it might be cuts through, and we find that our faulty convictions cannot heal or hold us. As a matter of fact, they betray us, and we find ourselves looking for someone or something to blame. We might even reach out for another untested bias, a new conviction to replace the ones that failed.

Our biases are also impacted by our burdens. Erykah Badu told us we gonna hurt our backs dragging all them bags like that. When I am hurt by something or someone, I can find myself embracing a black-and-white way of looking at the world. For example, when I find myself physically sick yet still doing work, and am not offered help or slack, I'll start thinking that nobody sees my pain. Something that is actually nuanced can become all bad or all good. I know I am not alone in this as I sit in a nation where fears, legitimate and orchestrated, drive neighbors to polarization. Seeing this dichotomous thinking applied to the church has been painful but understandable.

These burdens, and the impact they've had on us, reveal the tensions and insufficiencies we feel in the church today. The church was supposed to be good, but when it fails us, the church has failed, period.

As Black women, we get the burden of loyalty deep down in our bones and our spirits. Or at least it feels that way. We are loyal to customs, identities, people, and institutions. We represent both the most religious and the most caricatured, othered, and disrespected group in the United States. Through centuries of white-supremacist patriarchal Christianity, still we rise. Through chauvinistic and traumatized Black male minimization, rejection, and muleification, still we rise. Through in-group bitterness and colorism, still we rise. Maya Angelou's poetic brilliance still spurs us on to rise and rise, although sometimes that rising looks more like hobbling or leaning, depending on the day or maybe hour of the day. But we going to rise. Even if broken, exhausted, and bitter inside. That's the brand, the burden, and the beauty.

For Black Christian women, this contrast of being morally esteemed and morally reviled, hyper-ignored and yet hyper-seen, is taxing, to say the least. Black Christian women live under a stereotype of either moral perfection or moral corruption. We are either the dutiful mammy or the tempting Sapphire.

But the formulas of moral perfection no longer work. And maybe they never did.

The rewards people were able to get—or thought they'd get—in exchange for their religious perfectionism are no longer guaranteed. Nor are they even necessarily attractive to the new generation. A woman in the 1960s may have been able to tolerate the patriarchal practices of a church in order to pursue and create a particular family, for example. A young student might take out thousands in tuition loans for a college degree and the promise of an economically stable future. But the social guarantees for compliance are defunct, and the rules do not apply.

Each generation holds up a new mirror for the church and society. So, among members of Gen-Z and millennials, who are more likely to be institutionally disloyal and unimpressed with status-quo Christianity, the response can be a quest for self-

discovery and even self-deification unimaginable to most Gen
X-ers. This generation has felt war on its shores—from 9/11, to
the trauma of seeing America turn from Obama to Trump, to
the mental health challenges ravaging too many young bodies,
and so this generation requires more evidence of hope. Whether
you wanna call it leaving loud, deconstruction, or being spiritual
instead of religious, the trauma of religious life in America has
triggered a crisis of faith and a freeing from faith in many. Many
are now singing, "Don't give me that old-time religion. It's not
good enough for me." This is good for the church, for this generation is demanding more than just the cultural Christianity
many are comfortable with. At the extreme end, some are reim-
aging a God wiped of white supremacy but still made in another image of humanity. But the fact that they are pushing
Christians at large to give a reason for the hope that they have?
This is a gift for the Church.

To be clear, to the extent that old-time religion is a pyramid
scheme or political cover-up for our exploitation, it's not good
enough for me *or* you. Moreover, it's not what the God whose
throne is justice and grace wants for us.

> Righteousness and justice are the foundations of
>     your throne;
> love and faithfulness go before you.
> Blessed are those who have learned to acclaim you,
> who walk in the light of your presence, Lord.
> They rejoice in your name all day long;
> they celebrate your righteousness.
> For you are their glory and strength,

and by your favor you exalt our horn. Indeed, our
   shield belongs to the Lord,
our king to the Holy One of Israel.

PSALMS 89:14–18

## THERE IS ANOTHER WAY

Christian nationalism, or any other form of Christian pagan-
ism, creates mini-gods meant to kill us. When we see it, we
should reject, denounce, and run. Why? Because death is sin's
endgame. Whether it's the pet sins that hold you in bondage to
please others and satiate yourself or the systemic sins that
plague communities, its endgame seeks to drag us to the grave.
And this ain't Marvel, y'all; this is real life. Sin's goal is not only
to kill our culture by putting us in whiteface; it ultimately wants
to wreck our bodies, minds, and souls. Fake Christianities and
real oppression are busy wrecking our collective Christian witness. The empire of Christian nationalism is naked, and even
through tear-stained eyes, let us see its legalism, abuse, and manipulation.

There is a Christianity, and much more marvelously, a Christ,
who offers us a faith of both acceptance and resistance. We are
reborn to resist. This Christianity is the one that makes African
Americans resist racism and injustice and reject pie-in-the-sky
theology. I know that when hurt by the representatives of the
church, some of us will be tempted to throw the baby Jesus out
with the corrupted bathwater. But if we do not pursue healing,

wisdom, and justice, we will deconstruct ourselves into self-destruction.

What inclines us to listen to voices of destruction more than to voices of empowerment? What makes us pay more attention to the instruction of the Church of "Our Kind of People" than the God of Fannie Lou Hamer? Which god is dictating our thoughts? The Jesus that needs *you* to make him credible? Earthly power is wrong about who Jesus is. So why do we believe its lies? Some of us want to sanitize the idea of Jesus, and others want to rush to defend Jesus. Like the apostle Peter, who in the span of twenty-four hours went from defending with a sword to denying with his mouth.

But there is another way: to learn the transformative ways of Jesus. This is what sanctification means. And together in sacred community, we can seek this out. Together, we must see to it that we do not live as if unwittingly agreeing with white supremacy that Jesus is a white man who upholds the caste systems in our awakening.[1] Together, we resist—from continent to continent, generation to generation—whispering truth to one another.

So here are questions for us to reckon with, questions that come from a faith that produces necessary resistance: Can Christ be corrupted? Is there a Christ who predates whiteness and America and our present-day political factions?

As we sit with these questions, we must consider our surroundings. All things are but a vapor, yes, but there's a difference between that and a noxious gas. We must be wary of the fumes we breathe.

We must be born again through the real Jesus, who calls us to resist sin and rest in grace.

Listen to the real Jesus's words to this crowd, and to our crowded hearts:

> Again Jesus called the crowd to Him and said, "Listen to me, everyone, and understand this. Nothing outside a person can defile them by going into them. Rather, it is what comes out of a person that defiles them."
>
> MARK 7:14–15

Jesus's words here matter. In a world sick with injustice, this matters. For the one in three women abused before age eighteen, this matters. In Christ, even under the weight of trauma and bigotry, we stand uncorrupted. So we do the work of guarding the heart, which is revealed by what comes out of it. Christ knows this matter intimately, as he is accused of being a tool for the enemy when he draws near to the sinful and the sinned against with great compassion. Yet sinful people and systems don't contaminate him. He has enough righteousness to clean the dirty feet of the disciples. Enough holiness to stand between guilty men dying. Enough purity to eat with prostitutes. What Christ alone makes clean is clean forevermore. So we need to lament the evil co-opting of Christ's name for purposes of domination, but we need not fear that somehow the real Jesus is no longer divine, just, and full of grace toward us. Greater is he that is in you than the enemy that is in the world (1 John 4:4).

It bears repeating: Jesus's love for the beloved predates earthly caste systems, whiteness, misogyny, and every kind of injustice.

God's love will outlast every wrong. The Creator's agenda of grace is upheld by a mighty arm of power and sovereignty. Christ is greater than the corruption all around us and within our hearts, and most importantly, he is unintimidated by it. In the face of environmental injustice, multigenerational trauma, and medical racism, Christ draws near even now. In the face of the self-idolatry, rebellion, unforgiveness stewing in our own hearts, Christ draws near even now.

Emanuel means "God is with us," and God is with us in the midst of the evils, addictions, and traumas that plague us. He will also be God with us in our deliverance and eternal wholeness. Yes, God was there feeling the full weight of suffering in the bottoms of slave ships. Yes, God was there among the children desperate to escape the powerful hoses knocking them to the ground. Yes, God was there when they hurt you, silenced you, and blamed you for your own persecution or abuse. And we were there with him. The apple of his eye and the center of his heart, we were there as he died at the hands of an oppressive government, an unrepentant religious order, and rebellious humans. We were in the breaths that uttered the words "Forgive them, for they know not what they do." It was his love and remedy to our sins and shame that kept him on the cross. We were there because we were on his mind and in his heart. God is with us, so we are reborn to resist.

Yet, in this present age, while sin and injustice wreak havoc around us, Christ grieves.

Christ grieves as he prepares to put all this sin and injustice under his feet. In a world of posers and faux vulnerability, we want a savior who is strong enough to weep with us. Someone who believes our story and gets it in a way we once thought and

still believe our fake gods would. Christ reigns over his cove-
nanted siblings—that's us—with grace and healing for every
form of abuse, dehumanization, injustice, and idolatry that
harms the beloved. He also sits with and washes the feet of
those who run from him and deny him.

Though Jesus is our great high priest, his intercession is not
only inflamed by his power but also by his great compassion
and empathy. After all, what good is power apart from love?
Power, sovereignty, and providence bring no comfort without
holiness, grace, justice, and fidelity. Power without compassion
and a secured path to redemption is frightening. Power without
justice and love is the weightiness that we feel daily from misogynoir. Jesus knows intimately the sting of injustice and the
temptation it brings. He experienced the injustice of hunger,
loneliness, and the abuse of power—and he was tempted on
every side. Tempted to live by something other than the word
of God. Tempted to pledge allegiance to the devil in order to
reign and rule. Tempted to use his power outside of God's mission to rescue people.

But Jesus resisted these temptations, knowing there was no
love in these façades of power.

And so Jesus calls us away from both the personal and the
social consequences of spiritual rebellion. The covenant-
making-and-keeping God ends our need to compromise, de-
spair, and rebel. Y'all remember TLC, the bestselling girl group
of all time? Remember the way their music videos played
around the clock on the Video Jukebox Network and Black
Entertainment Television (BET)? Growing up, I'd cram them
in between homework and phone calls. And in 1994, T-Boz,
the late Left Eye, and Chilli brought us the hit song "Creep."

You might remember the lyrics, and the crimson-red satin pajamas they wore as they bopped from side to side.

> So I creep, yeah, just creepin' on,
> But I'll know. 'Cept nobody is supposed to
> know . . .
> And no attention goes to show.

Nearly three decades later it's abundantly clear in my very grown mind that this song is about a noncommittal relationship. There is a woman who doesn't want to let go of the unfaithful man she loves but is persuaded that, because of her loneliness and unfulfillment, she must now "creep." She creeps to unnamed partners, attempting to satisfy herself under a cover of deception. At bottom, she does all this creeping because she's holding on to a cheater and finds temporary solace in a new partner because she "needs some affection," as the song goes.

The song's protagonist feels justified in her creeping because she's been wronged. Her hopes are unfulfilled. She becomes unfaithful, deceptive, and deluded—eventually becoming the very source of her pain. She knows she has been wronged, but she is still willfully entangled with her partner. She doesn't let go of a bad thing; instead, she attempts to add to the mix by medicating with poison.

I've lost count of how many times I have been tempted to a type of entitled rebellion because of real mistreatment or injustice. Have you ever held on to something or someone that does not, will not, and cannot love you? Do you love or long for it and claim it as yours even though it doesn't mean you well? You might even redefine what love is in order to claim that you are loved by that person. You might even convince yourself it's all fine and good. But if you look closely, you might find that your loyalty and commitment are really a form of bondage. You won't let it go, and the truth is, it won't let you go, either. So you creep.

Instead of doing the hard work of cutting it off or calling it out, we dabble with another to satisfy our affections.

We so easily live unsatisfied lives with a gaping longing. We numb it and ignore it as long as we can.

But we don't need to settle for this life of grasping and compromising, despairing and rebelling. Instead, we really can rely on Jesus, with his steady fidelity and powerful compassion.

We must be born again.

This question of being born again has been debated among denominations for generations. We can see its origins in the book of John, in an exchange about the necessity and consequences of the rebirth in Christ. In chapter 3 we find the story of a creeping, noncommittal Pharisee: Nicodemus, a member of the Jewish ruling class. He comes to Jesus at night, in the dark, where he seeks out the satisfaction of answered questions. He wants revelation without risk. He wants fulfillment without fidelity. He wants to know more than he already does without challenging what he already believes. What Nicodemus finds is a light so bright that no deception goes unseen. When Nicodemus encounters Jesus, he meets someone whose answers are impossible yet compassionate; someone who is exposing truth yet is caring and covering. So even though the sun is down, the Son is actually up, illuminating and cleansing away self-deception.

Here are Nicodemus's words to Jesus, the mysterious one from God: "Rabbi, we know that you are a teacher who has come from God. For no one could perform the signs you are doing if God were not with him" (John 3:2–15).

Jesus replies, "Very truly I tell you, no one can see the Kingdom of God unless they are born again."

"How can someone be born when they are old?" Nicodemus asks. "Surely they cannot enter a second time into their mother's womb to be born!"

Jesus answers, "Very truly I tell you, no one can enter the Kingdom of God unless they are born of water and the Spirit. Flesh gives birth to flesh, but the Spirit gives birth to spirit. You should not be surprised at my saying, 'You must be born again.' The wind blows wherever it pleases. You hear its sound, but you cannot tell where it comes from or where it is going. So it is with everyone born of the Spirit."

"How can this be?" Nicodemus asks.

"You are Israel's teacher," says Jesus, "and do you not understand these things? Very truly I tell you, we speak of what we know, and we testify to what we have seen, but still you people do not accept our testimony. I have spoken to you of earthly things and you do not believe; how then will you believe if I speak of heavenly things? No one has ever gone into heaven except the one who came from heaven—the Son of Man. Just as Moses lifted up the snake in the wilderness, so the Son of Man must be lifted up, that everyone who believes may have eternal life in him."

> For God so loved the world that he gave his one and only Son, that whoever believes in him shall not perish but have eternal life. For God did not send his Son into the world to condemn the world, but to save the world through

him. Whoever believes in him is not condemned, but whoever does not believe stands condemned already because they have not believed in the name of God's one and only Son. This is the verdict: Light has come into the world, but people loved darkness instead of light because their deeds were evil. Everyone who does evil hates the light, and will not come into the light for fear that their deeds will be exposed. But whoever lives by the truth comes into the light, so that it may be seen plainly that what they have done has been done in the sight of God.

JOHN 3:16–21

You should not be surprised at my saying "You must be born again."

Jesus describes people as "loving darkness rather than light." Darkness in this context is not simply a shade or tone or color; it is a cloak used to hide, conceal. It is self-delusion. When our actions are evil, out of step with the love of God, self, and neighbor, and we have no intention of stopping them, we avoid the light because we don't want our wrongdoing exposed. But when our deeds and misdirected loves are brought into the light, we are reminded that all that has been done, avoided, and thought is visible in the sight of God. God, through Jesus, sees us not to condemn but to deliver us by faith.

Our blindness in no way hampers God's sight. There is something about the cover of night that fools us into thinking that we are unseen. We are like a child hiding under blankets, a big lump that is clearly visible to onlookers, no matter how convinced the child is that what they cannot see others cannot see as well. In our idolatry and narcissism, often rooted in real pain, we project our character, insecurities, limitations, and priorities onto our created and constructed god. We make a god in our own image and in our own pain. Nicodemus is taken a back by the idea that he must be born again. Yet it is Jesus's words that imply that Nicodemus should know better.

When we are deluded, we can find ourselves eager to teach instead of learn. Insecure people thirst for buy-in to their ideas and ways. Did you notice how in the passage, Nicodemus first attempts to *enlighten* Jesus? Maybe you have found yourself among others being the self-appointed mic dropper, politically or theologically. I know that there are people who see me and my co-hosts this way. Have you ever tried to show how your thoughts, ways, and beliefs are more evolved or gracious than God's? Do you find yourself "schooling" the eternal God in matters of the present moment? *"God, that Scripture was for then, but not now. God, if you had power, you would do something about the injustice in the world."* Yet, whenever we communicate or pray, we tell God nothing that is unknown to the Divine. Nicodemus tells Jesus something that Jesus already knows and tries to extend the tokens of his group's approval. *"We know who you are, and we approve."* Huh?

The temptation to only see God in ways that are preapproved by the group that we want to be in, whether legalistic conservatives or litmus-test progressives, is real. But God does not need our faith or acknowledgment. He is not Candyman or Beetlejuice. God doesn't exist by our belief. Our faith does not make Him real. God is the god over our existence, not the other way around. We need to believe in God. The benefit is ours alone. Yet how many of us lean into groupthink, parroting catchphrases and approved ideologies that our group has allowed us to believe about Jesus? In this text Nicodemus, speaking with a communally approved voice, is relatable. Yet Jesus is still asking, "Who do you say that I am?"

Being around the church or churchy folks is not enough to answer this question correctly.

"'But what about you?' he asked. 'Who do you say I am?'

"Simon Peter answered, 'You are the Messiah, the Son of the living God'" (Matt. 16:15–16).

Nicodemus is coming to Jesus not knowing the most important truth: that Christ is the Messiah. We know Christ only when we see Him as our Messiah, our Savior, and Son of the living God—the living God who has an actual say over our eternal life and how we live now. Jesus is the one who publicly rescues those who cannot rescue themselves from sin and delusion. Jesus is not a medication for our woes or a supplement to an unfaithful partner that we won't let go. He knows us, He sees us, and He doesn't let go. He sees us truly and deeply. He knows all about our needs and fears, and the things that are hard for us to admit.

In the freedom of being fully known and loved by Christ, we are no longer corrupted by social curses, no longer bound to them. In Christ we are empowered to resist them.

After Nicodemus's self-exposing opening statement, Jesus follows with a greater revelation. This is refreshing, because our wrong or partial answers cannot change God's truth. Jesus's words blow Nicodemus's mind. Jesus tells the Pharisee what He tells all of us, despite how well we think we know Jesus.

"You must be born again."

Nicodemus is flabbergasted with this statement and revelation, but instead of turning to wonder and humility, he responds with more lecturing and self-assurance. *Let me tell you how things are supposed to work, Jesus. Grown people cannot return to the birth canal.* The Pharisee becomes so upset that he raises his voice, exclaiming, "How dare you attempt to send me back to my mother's womb? How dare you make me vulnerable, small, dependent, and unseen? I cannot be born again"—a statement possibly masking a conviction that one does not need an entire overhaul, restart, or rebirth.

Again, Jesus the Rabbi schools Nicodemus, the teacher of the law. "Why are you surprised by these words and saying?" Jesus asks Nicodemus. Those who think they know God and religion find themselves wanting what Jesus has, apart from Christ's conditions: a rebirth. "Flesh gives birth to flesh but the Spirit gives birth to the spirit." Jesus is inviting us, through rebirth, into a new way and a new identity. Again, we should not be surprised at Christ saying that when we get close to the light, we must be born again.

Yet we live as if we are surprised by the necessity of being born again—not only surprised but shocked and offended. We want God to reign wonder and renewal out of our old flesh. We want to stay as we are, with our list of entanglements, without surrendering to a new way, a renewed way. We continue to hold on to unfaithful loves and live as if permissible to creep to God as our pick-me-up, cultural validation, or self-help remedy.

It's likely we don't see ourselves as Nicodemuses. After all, he represents the male religious elite. We might be the opposite of an esteemed leader in our faith community. Culturally, we might be used to being ignored and having our spiritual insights and wisdom dismissed. Yet the idea that Nicodemus represented the faithful of that day does resonate with the narratives of Black women in America. Black women are superwomen, the people who are asked to bear the burden of social disenfranchisement with a smile and Negro spiritual. The ones who encourage others and remain by the book.

Like Nicodemus, when we claim to know God, making a case for our own discernment or faith credentials, we are held to a higher standard. This is one of the things that first stands out to me about Nicodemus's interactions with Jesus that night. He provides his credentials: that he knows the Lord. He says "we" know who Jesus is and where he came from. However, coming to Christ at night and without reverence reveals that he doesn't really know who he is talking to beyond the thoughts of the "we."

Jesus says to Nicodemus, "You should not be surprised."

Should we be surprised? People ain't right. This idea is that we have deep, intrinsic dignity and are fearfully and wonderfully made, but we are desperately in need of new birth core to Christianity. Jesus is saying to us, even now, "You should not be surprised by this."

We want to look pious and be in the know and in the in-crowd with our social validators. You should not be surprised by this. We want to flex the religious jargon and litmus tests. You should not be surprised by this. We wanna rightly call out others' complicity with systemic sin but cover our own sins from the light of transformation. You should not be surprised by this.

Nicodemus represented the religious ruling class. You should not be surprised by this, either. The greater the height of our performative piety, the deeper the fall we take in true Christ-given revelation.

We must be born again.

Christ is not just offering us relationship over religion. Christ is telling us what we ought to already know, with our religious credentials. We must be born again. Our rebirth is not a change of our humanity but a return to the fullness of it. We don't cast off our providentially given culture or design in our rebirth. We are not reborn into mythological whiteness or caricatures of womanhood, but rather into the journey of all that God has for us to be and become.

Jesus makes the case that when we come to Him, deceptions and entanglements will not be tolerated. But our very being gets a restart. In Christ we are born again. Jesus loves us too much and is too worthy to allow us to have Him as an add-on. As a matter of fact, because of how loyal we are to our old loves and hates, we will need to surrender all those lies and attachments. It can be painful, like ripping off a Band-Aid. We will need to become a new person, someone who is born again. However, the unearned rewards for us beyond rebirth are manifold. We find ourselves with a love that forever claims us, is faithful to us, and brings us into the fullness of God's very best for us.

When we are reborn, we can see the world anew. We have new eyes to see and behold the beauty in our neighbors' humanity and the wickedness of the sins that crush them. We are reborn to resist every expression of lovelessness in our hearts and in the systems that impact friend, neighbor, and foe. Our rebirth in Christ—a product of the Father's resolute love, the Spirit's transformative pursuit and the Son's merciful sacrifice—makes us able and willing to do that which was once impossible: resist sin.

We are born again to resist.

Perfection is elusive, but godly grief for sin is obtainable. Resistance against personal and systemic sin isn't self-righteous piety or loyalty to the flavor-of-the-week partisan conviction, but rather a resting in God's Word, promises, and power. Our rebirth is evidenced by resounding resistance and a full embrace of Christian freedom. Our rebirth comes with a prescription to rest. We are literally reborn to rest. To rest from our rat races, our legalism, and our desire to be god to ourselves and our neighbor.

The very sins that once entangled and oppressed you no longer define you. You are reborn to resist. Coming to Christ fully dependent on His grace alone doesn't make us docile and compliant to injustice. Rather, our rebirth results in holy convictions and empowerment to speak truth to power and grace to the crushed.

With reborn eyes we see our former distractions, addictions, and idols for what they truly are: worthless chains. By faith we are born again, and we don't have to pretend that we have all the answers, or that we are superwomen or have no hurts and scars, because like the infant who is just born, we can depend on God alone for our nurturing care.

With the soul-healing that Christ gives, we stop creeping around.

And we start walking in the light.

# The Keys to the Kingdom of God

## By Michelle Higgins

There are Black people in the future.

ALISHA B. WORMSLEY

IF OUR CONFIDENCE IS EMBEDDED in the truth that God made us, and we exist by the delight and imagination of our Creator, our freedom, then, becomes integral to our image-bearing.

Black existence is impossible to contain. The African diaspora testifies of itself that Black people are built for abundance without limit. We thrive amid constant threat. We spin gold despite our chains. When nobody but God holds us together, that alone is proof of the reparations that we ourselves are owed. We defend a liberation fully deserved that yet must be demanded. It's that Joseph-style, God-ordained goodness born out of pain. We are not manmade; we are God-orchestrated. We cannot be man-handled or man-maintained.

Blackness in United States history has often been defined as the opposite of whiteness. I define whiteness as the norm to which all things are compared, making Blackness a base identity that must be denounced. For much of the history of global colonization, our defiance in the face of anti-Blackness has been a testament to our rights. Dwelling on delight, imagination, and the struggle for freedom, we know that we were made for more than comparison. So we work toward Black pride born of biblical humility, not defined by the people whose identities threaten our destruction. We strive to reflect God's purpose and identities. And I believe that Black people are meant to make use of every tool God gave us. As I ponder our journey from the struggle to the Kingdom, I see the gospel story tracing the same path. Through God's word, I am inspired by three aspects of Blackness that are each akin to a holy attribute of God:

Delight.

Freedom.

Imagination.

### Creator God's Gift of Delight

God's delight calls creation good. Blackness delights in the blessing of being called good by our Creator. Psalm 1 tells us that when we delight ourselves in the Lord and meditate on God's law, we will be planted like a mighty tree beside the waters, and nothing can move us.

### Redeemer God's Gift of Freedom

Jesus paid the full price for our freedom, making our Blackness a blessing and not a curse, a testament to the power of resurrection, and a threat to the forces that try to dictate our deliverance. Our freedom is sealed in the "now and not yet," as Jesus has completed his work that brings liberation to the cosmos. Blackness, then, is emboldened by the expanse of Christ's freedom. If it is for freedom Jesus set us free, then we can face each protest and police threat with a boldness that cannot die and will not perish under the weight of racism. We were made to be free, and whomever the Son sets free is free indeed.

## The Holy Ghost Imagination

I was six years old when I first heard a preacher say they were using their "Holy Ghost imagination" to picture and preach about the future for the people of God, meaning that the Holy Spirit allows us to look ahead in our hearts for the sake of moving our bodies and setting our minds on God's promise of a future where the last are first, the oppressed are avenged, death and war are no more, and every tear is bottled up, never to be cried again. A Holy Ghost imagination grants us the daring to imagine the world that God is making a reality.

Undoubtedly, Black power has an enemy in white supremacy. We are battling with a dominant system whose sinister acts can be deceptively sweet. White supremacy is a terrorist ideology; it is not the human enemy we are called to love. It lacks the attributes that trace their origins to the divine mind. Neither imagination nor freedom nor delight in goodness is available under white supremacy in any of its forms. Supremacy seeks to eschew equality, so it is incapable of sensing delight in fellow created things. As for freedom, it is fueled by the opposite of liberation power, because white supremacy cannot survive without Black subjugation. The previous points thus prove the last—supremacy is utterly unimaginative. Dreaming of a future where all people are flourishing and free is not only too much work for the supremacist, it is heretical to them.

Much like the supremacy it upholds, whiteness as existence begets no godlings. That is, God is not the author of its origin story.

Whiteness is a shape-shifting culture that exists to soften the blow of the functions of supremacy. It conceals the true impact of tokenizing and rewards the colonized with social advancement dressed up as relational currency. In the story of whiteness, Blackness is meaningless—which is the only thing that makes whiteness meaningful. As Blackness is empowered, whiteness cannot exist. And this is good news, for there is no room for whiteness in the economy of God.

More than the increasingly unsurprising mess that is white supremacy, whiteness is the real adversary in our battle. While it presents as a contrasting equal to Blackness—an ethnicity built by history, defined and redefined over time—whiteness is an identity devoted to kingdom obsolescence. Whiteness seeks to make the Kingdom of God obsolete. But in the Kingdom, God makes whiteness obsolete. Both white supremacy and whiteness are on the long list of oppressions that, in the Kingdom of God, will cease to exist. Supremacy might be the organized religion of people who uphold whiteness, but whiteness is the breath of life for the worshippers themselves.

And when all you breathe in is wickedness, you must be born again.

In *The Sum of Us*, Heather McGhee describes the reasons that the U.S. economy fails everyone, domestically and internationally. This comprehensive volume will take up extra space in your Black Girl Magic tote bag, but it is a must-read. You can't pass the first chapter without hearing what most Black women already know, what Black economists like McGhee have *been* telling us: the zero-sum idea of whiteness vs. everyone plays a lead role in both the mythology and the tragic ending of the economy of the United States. Whiteness appears to defend democracy but is ultimately destructive, making democracy impossible. She writes, "I sensed that this core idea that's so resonant with many white Americans—there's an us and a them, and what's good for them is bad for us—was at the root of this country's dysfunction." Ms. McGhee ponders the possible reasons that this idea took root. Is it that humanity is just naturally competitive? Is this "us and them" based in ideology—something that participants in the zero-sum game must commit themselves to and might therefore denounce at any time? Whatever the reason for its prevalence, we know this much: the worldview of whiteness is worthless, but it is costly to our collective future.

Devastating proof of the deadliness of whiteness surrounds us.

And our spiritual realities are not protected from our social realities.

Often in our pursuit of a church united across race, class, nationality, and social structure, Black Christians forget that whiteness is yet a deadly enemy, no safer than white supremacy— one that orders our democracy, dictates the dollars we deposit, and shortens the number of our days. Christians of color often expend energy on education and moderation for the sake of white people who "need to understand" racial justice before organizations can pursue it in earnest. This underscores the power

of seemingly harmless whiteness. Where God's attributes expand, the worship of whiteness restricts. Whiteness instructs us
to delight and even take pride in caution, suppresses our innate
freedom to be ourselves without explaining ourselves, which
then stifles our collective imagination. This is all part of the
playbook of white supremacy.

The deception of this white-centeredness surrounds us, even
when we may not immediately recognize it. But it is dangerous.
It is dangerous because it dictates our lives, from culture and art
to policy. For example, when we say "music" it is often distinct
from Black music, and "art" from Black art. State governments
are passing the CROWN Act, a law prohibiting discrimination
on the basis of hair textures and styles that are widely associated
with Black people and people of color. Why do we need a law
that protects people who want to wear locks and afros? Because
we live in a society where coaches cut locks off athletes' heads.
Students are docked letter grades for wearing hair beads. Em-
ployees are gossip fodder for changing their hair so often that
"people can't recognize you." That's a real and repeated story,
y'all.

Even our national identities are hyphenated. "American"
means white. While I could not be more proud to add the word
"African" to American in order to identify myself, I know that
there's only one group of Americans that do not hyphenate
their national identity, and it ain't the Native Nations.

And don't get me started with the violent white-supremacy-
stained faith that oozes from so many pulpits in our country.

In theology and church history classes, our ancient creeds
are interpreted by European church fathers. Our contemporary global outreach ministries are founded on the testimony

and cultural biases of white missionaries. Many of the institutions trusted to interpret Scripture are built on racial terror and gender discrimination. And they passed it down to us, calling it holy. Christian colleges require classes with names like "Christian Heritage of the West," which never include Western regions like Mexico, the Caribbean, or South American countries—effectively ensuring that all nonwhite Christianity is optional, leaving learners to conclude that nonwhiteness cannot display Christianity at all.

I want to say we aren't missing out by avoiding white Christian colleges and similar institutions, especially for theological education. But I have to admit that much of what we know about our faith and eschatology—the ultimate future of the faithful—comes from scholars who were educated in and continue to protect these institutions. The views of these gatekeepers sound like sarcasm in response to the idea of a Palestinian Jesus from an oppressed, occupied land, and the prevalence of these views as moral guideposts skews our vision of God's Kingdom.

Whether we accept or deny what these institutions tell us about who God is and what God is saying, we all must examine how we allow whiteness to inform our Blackness and interpret our faith.

What will the saints who worship white Jesus do when they see a brown-skinned Savior lifted up above Creation? What will we do when Jesus tells us his dwelling place was with the poor all this time, that his gospel—as he told us—was good news for them? When the last become first, what will we do? The time is now (and the time was a while ago) to grapple with the log we've set in our own eye. It is time to confess that America's addiction to deception is keeping us from the truth that would set us free. The church's refusal to decenter whiteness is the primary reason we have failed to address its cultural impact.

What happens when we don't decenter whiteness?

In August of 2017, a rally called "Unite the Right" was planned in response to dispute over Confederate monuments in Charlottesville, Virginia. The night before the event, a torchlight procession took place. Hundreds of white people, mostly masculine in appearance, uniformed in khaki pants and white polo or button-down shirts, carried flames across a field at the University of Virginia. According to journalists and historians, the torchlight procession was meant to be an homage to Hitler Youth parades. Police and law enforcement were supposedly planning to surveil the rally, but no law enforcement was visible during the procession aside from one campus police officer. The white people were chanting, "White lives matter. Our blood, our soil. Jews will not replace us," and making noises to imitate monkeys when they passed by Black people and other people of color.

Thirty days before the rally on Saturday—which Black movement organizers, counterprotesters, clergy, and politicians had planned for—armed KKK groups had begun gathering publicly in anticipation of the torchlight procession. Multiple sources confirmed that these same armed militias would be present and not policed.

On August 12 at 1 P.M., James Alex Fields, Jr., plowed his vehicle into a crowd of people protesting the rally to Unite the

Right. Thirty-two-year-old Heather Heyer was killed and nineteen people were injured. Fields has admitted his actions were intentional.

On the same day, also in Charlottesville, a group of white men followed DeAndre Harris and his friend, threatening them with a flagpole. Harris and his friend began to run. His friend was speared by the pole; they both fell down and then got separated. DeAndre ran into a trap inside a parking garage. Six white men surrounded him and brutalized him. At the time of this writing, DeAndre is still living with medical issues because of his injuries.

By the end of the weekend, reporters and residents were calling the events of August 12 the Charlottesville Massacre.

Home to poet and auntie Rita Dove, actor Dwayne "The Rock" Johnson, and ancestor-survivor Sally Hemings, Charlottesville is located on land once stewarded by the Monacan and Manahoac tribes. This quiet college town found itself in an identity crisis in 2017, one that surfaced the city's entrenched whiteness and willful ignorance, buried for so long. But even after the rally, few locals had any awareness that they were suffering from an issue much older and deeper than the presence of rally-goers and counterprotesters.

The crisis was whiteness, long unaddressed and continually defended. Layla Saad, author of *Me and White Supremacy*, spoke on the subject in an interview with *Time* magazine. She said that while the phrase "white supremacy" "conjure[s] up images of men marching in Charlottesville," it is not always as obviously threatening, and it is not locked in to the historical past. She goes on: "It still shows up today in interpersonal relationships, in what we see as the norm in the media, or the norm in companies, or the norm in schools. And so, dominance doesn't have to just be enslavement." Charlottesville is one example of the natural participation of whiteness in white supremacy. They are distinct but cannot exist without each other.

Since the United States was conceived, whiteness has been the good-cop enforcer and evangelist of supremacy. It shrouds the history of enslavement and colonization in a mythology of racial and sociopolitical progress. It builds a system of socially acceptable apologetics. Racial reconciliation becomes the face of allyship, and privilege and patriarchy become protection—all allowing "everyday" whiteness to breed.

For the average person of faith who finds their identity in whiteness, what happened in Charlottesville might seem an unlikely outburst of extremism. But for many Christians of color—and honestly, the world over—what happened in Charlottesville was an inevitable outcome of whiteness breeding.

The City of Charlottesville—and the entire country, for that matter—knew to mourn the murder of Heather Heyer (a white woman). They knew to denounce the "hatred that killed her." They even knew that this hatred included white supremacy. But what this city and this country could not do was examine white identity, which is exactly what the hundreds of rally supporters were claiming to lay hold to in Charlottesville that weekend.

Bloodshed and violence, and a country pretends to look away. The perfect picture of whiteness.

After that weekend, many Church leaders demanded a call to dismantle white supremacy, regionally and nationally. But for every church leader who denounced white supremacy, there was another church leader who insisted that the Charlottesville rally was not an accurate picture of all that white people could be. For this leader, it wasn't the latest event in a history of racial terrorism. No, this leader, whether mainline or evangelical, *believed* in white culture, that it could be redeemed. That it had to be redeemed.

But there is no redeeming whiteness. It is a weapon used by (sadly) people of all ethnicities to enforce white supremacy. Whiteness in raw form exists to diminish the power and beauty of nonwhite identities. Whiteness is dissatisfied without a badge, spotlight, or bruise to boast.

After the violence in Charlottesville, I received multiple, almost daily invitations to join calls to discuss what must be done. The more I got into the work of facilitating and participating in these conversations, the more my discomfort grew about white people uplifting the fact that a white woman gave her life for the movement.

And I noticed something else. Almost overnight, churches began using the term "white supremacy" in their worship services. These were the same churches that, just a few months earlier, had been warning me and other Black movement activists and organizers that the term was too inflammatory and too judgmental. I really about fell out, y'all. Everywhere I looked, I thought, am I missing something? What made faith leaders suddenly bold enough to denounce white supremacy in that moment? Why not in 2014 when a Black teenager was murdered by a police officer in Missouri? Why not in 2016 when a public-school lunchroom employee was murdered execution style by police? Why wait for an army of well-pressed white people moving with tiki torches to surround a Confederate monument?

The answer, I discovered, was disappointing but not complicated. Before the events in Virginia, white faith leaders—the
kind who only live around other white people; the kind who
live completely white-centered lives—had few distinctions to
draw between themselves and the average person who attended
the rally. When seemingly suspicious Black people are killed by
police, there is less of an outcry from the people who allegedly
believe that every human bears the image of our divine Creator.
Whiteness does not see Michael Brown, Jr., as a victim of white
supremacy. For whiteness cannot see itself, and therefore cannot free itself, from the presumption that it is entitled to set
global norms. The person that whiteness was built to protect
was that person kicking DeAndre Harris, or the person who
drove a car into a crowd.

These are the people that white Christians scramble to disas-
sociate from.

But hurriedness to conceal the kinship between whiteness
and white supremacy is still the work of anti-Blackness, because whiteness is merely refined, not rejected. The only
reason "white supremacy" became a popular phrase among
white-centered organizations I was working with is that white
evangelical Christians are identical to white-supremacist
churchgoers in their social, political, fiscal, and moral lives. The
only way for Bruce Wayne to hide that he was Batman was to
speak as if his own alter ego was a scourge in the community.


But the call of the Kingdom is deeper and truer. God would
have all of us liberated from whiteness, so that no one should
claim an identity based in subjugation.

The call of God's Kingdom is to confront any system that insists on inequality; any identity that insists on exclusivity; any culture fueled by the success of one group at the expense of another. The Kingdom of God tears these systems down for the sake of building a truly liberated community. Because the Kingdom that God is building requires all God's children to be joined together—not siloed, not segregated, not arranged by income or intelligence, not pit against one another by ability, gender or sexuality, or body-mass index but joined, inclusively, together. Now, that is some cosmic good news.

Now, what is beginning to happen, and in spite of all the things that have happened to all our brains for all these generations, to divide black people from black people, to divide Indians from West Indians, to divide me from you, to divide whites from whites, it is absolutely true, *absolutely true,* that if George Jackson and Angela Davis and my child have no life, have no future, no one in this room has any future.

JAMES BALDWIN, 1971 speech

For people of faith, seeing the way forward means becoming unintimidated by taking ownership of our co-creation in God's Kingdom. We are empowered by the Holy Spirit to practice both protest and patience. This means demystifying the knowable aspects of eschatology in order to plant social, political, and spiritual investment into the future reflected from God's promises. It requires us to cling to the gifts of delight, freedom, and imagination. These are the basis of our guiding framework for seeing the future of Blackness through God's attributes. Eschatology is creational, and Creator God promises renewal for all the things he made that bring him delight. Eschatology discusses the ultimate end of oppression, and Jesus is the God who brings freedom to all people who have suffered. Eschatology is concerned with existence and power. Who is judged and who judges? Who sees eternity and why? The Holy Spirit both broadens us and humbles us so we can partake in God's grand imaginations. Overall, our delight is grounded in God's goodness—best experienced through freedom in Jesus, limiting nothing that grows from the Holy Ghost imagination. In this reality, whiteness cannot survive the eschaton. But the result for the future of Blackness is the full right to be called family in the household of God.

God's household is an eternal, global family, both already formed and yet being built. The Kingdom of God is a mosaic of creative majesty that joins people together as many parts in one body. In Jesus, people from diverse nations share the same spiritual location, now identified as Christ's body. Each of us has been grafted onto a family history revealed in the story of Scripture. In Ephesians 2:19, the Kingdom of God is described as a now-and-future reality of unified identity: "You are no longer foreigners and strangers but fellow citizens."

This new identity has an impact on every identity we claim, both individual and collective. It challenges our perceptions of division—and unity.

When identity in the family of God reconfigures our core perceptions of self, our imaginations expand to embrace God's vision for Blackness as part of our eternal being. Any sense of

Blackness as dependent upon whiteness is utterly dismantled by the equalizing truth that the existence of Blackness is justice, as is the obsolescence of whiteness.


A few months after the Charlottesville Massacre, I preached at a conference in some attempt to answer the question everyone seemed to be grappling with: what is the future of the church? I was specifically asked to preach on racial justice. For me, the good news I felt led to preach was this: along with sin and death, which Jesus defeated, whiteness, too, would be cast into hell. Around that time, I'd been searching for a text to help round out this perspective that I'd been called to by the Spirit. Multiple institutions had been asking: how do we pursue justice when so many of our institutions were formed in racial violence?

I pondered these realities until 2020, when I read the critical work *After Whiteness: An Education in Belonging,* by Willie James Jennings. I'm wowed by the fact that a Black man wrote the best book I've ever read on whiteness. But as Baldwin taught us, Black folks know white folks better than white folks know themselves. Jennings writes: "The most urgent questions are about how we should rethink the work of building so that we can move away from the cultivation of an institutional persona that is soul killing and death dealing." As I read the pages, I was struck with a challenging vision. I am not sure it is possible to form institutions that do not have suffering at their root. The question weighed on me: what institutions exist that are not part of a testimony of suffering?

These questions are indeed urgent, as Jennings says. Why?

What much of human history shows is that successful systems are built by colonizing. The United States might be the most influential country in the world, but this nation was built by terrorizing native people. By that time, the empire method had long been perfected by Great Britain and other global powers. But even systems and institutions that were not formed by subjugation have some amount of suffering involved in their birthing.

The best examples of system-building without subjugation at the root come from the communities whose freedom struggles oppose colonizing powers. Geechee clans in Mississippi were said to be made up of "unbreakable slaves" and castaways that had no "market value." They developed a common language, and raided plantations to find lost loved ones and bring them back to islands they'd built towns on—places where white folks had discarded them, once realizing the Geechee communities couldn't be controlled. Similarly, the trade systems of Gullah people in the Carolinas created a solidarity economy based in bartering and charitable giving. These two systems have suffering in their roots only because the people building power were the same ones who had suffered oppression. They knew firsthand that subjugation would lead to destruction, not success.

The Black church was very similar. Because white oppressors dictated that Black people were not permitted to boldly express ourselves, we were brutalized for protecting ourselves, punished for presuming our own humanity. We experienced enslavement and lynching at worst, and appropriation and tokenizing at best. We were not seen as delightful, certainly not worthy of freedom, and were presumed to lack both imagination and intellect.

There's a powerful distinction between the Black and white worshipping communities founded in the United States. The Black church was built in response to suffering, with God's ultimate vengeance in view. We created a space where our bodies and minds were not on high alert from constant threat to our well-being, because we focused on prophetic purpose that freed our spirits even if our bodies were yet bound. The white church was built to defend systems that *caused* suffering and framed oppression as a generative force. They gathered to rehearse a mythology that teaches every generation how to protect themselves from the truth. Jennings has something to say about this, too—what he brilliantly names "the convening power of whiteness."

> Whiteness was formed in the colonial theater with a convening power unprecedented in the world not only in its scale but also in its utter disregard for the convening abilities of other peoples. In the hands of Europeans, the good of convening joined the bad of imperialism, and from it came a vision of the universal controlled by Europeans.[1]

Whiteness does not even account for Black people in the denouncement of white supremacy. Before the violence in Charlottesville, in June of 2017, a white evangelical denomination was having difficulty passing a resolution to denounce alt-right ideology at one of their mass gatherings. The denominational committee that facilitated resolutions claimed to appreciate the purpose of the resolution but took issue with some key phrases. The resolution was drafted by a Black pastor. The revisions were made by the resolutions committee, all but one of whose ten members were white. The author of the resolution is quoted in *The Atlantic* as saying he had no issue with not being consulted during rewrites.[2] He calls their decision—of not inviting him into the rewrites—customary. This is a commonplace kind of margin making. Whiteness will take control and go so far as to marginalize the architect and his vision of healing for the future. And whiteness will rewrite any consensus plan for the future, on their terms. And they will call it "custom." When nonwhite people in a white-centered system resolve to denounce the evils that whiteness generally allows, it is white people who dictate the manner and result of such a denouncement. Whiteness will communicate its own boundaries, thank you very much. Whiteness convenes only itself.

What whiteness does not account for God will clarify and exalt. Yes, the convening power of whiteness has had centuries of success, but whiteness does not convene without an agenda—and that agenda has a paywall. A costly one.

In the Kingdom of God, the convening power of the Holy Spirit fuels our capacity to reflect God's attributes as the redemptive features of society. The Spirit empowers God's colaborers by reassuring us that there is no action required for us to be worthy. Because Jesus paid the full price for our freedom, there is no cost in the Kingdom of God. God's agenda is public.

Whiteness convenes to deny God's attributes in all things nonwhite by diminishing their brilliance. For instance, Black creativity brings criticism instead of delight; our music is called seasonal, too performance-driven and "not congregational." Black freedom is feared: our demands for social justice are tempered with calls for moderation and explanation. The Holy Spirit casts the vision for how God himself will reverse every white curse. God delights in our worship; Jesus's story shapes our struggle for freedom, and the Holy Ghost imagination guarantees a future where we are among the many nations, singing proud praises as we lay down our crowns at God's throne. What whiteness defies we must not deny. And that is this: the glory of God is displayed through us, not because of us. God's power does not come from us, and it is not exclusive to us.

Where whiteness insists that no other identity holds the intelligence or wherewithal to convene, Blackness is proof that the only convening power required is based in Spirit and in truth. Once our eyes are set on watching God, we will be enriched by God's presence and delivered from wondering about whether we are valuable to anybody else. Because anti-Blackness is the same thing as whiteness, the gospel as told by whiteness is no gospel to us at all.

But there is good news for Black Christians, and it begins with the comfort of God's love for us. God's plan for Black people around the world is the same as for those of any nation: He will welcome all who call upon his name to sit at his table. He will break our chains and bless us with crowns of glory that we will lay at His feet. And we will sing in native tongues that time and injustice took from us—but not from God.

Black liberation is a returning to original identity for all people. It is the ultimate revelation of our true story, the perfected joy that this world didn't give us and the world can't take away. Sometimes I feel far away from this good news. I am discouraged to the point of doubt. Whiteness is so loud, y'all. I remember the witness of the old preachers who taught me about "the already and the not yet," that all-encompassing phrase that connects present to future. And what the old folks taught me the young folks embodied. I think of the phrase "no justice, no peace" as a warning and an invocation. Our future peace depends on the presence of justice; and until justice comes, we won't stop disturbing the peace.

In the protests during the Ferguson Uprisings, we repeated "no justice, no peace" as a protest chant. I often use the phrase when I preach, because it might as well be the subject line for half of the prophetic books in the Bible! In Ezekiel 36, the Lord gives the prophet a word for the mountains that have been plundered and fought over for their natural resources. God promises the people the same restoration that will come to the mountains. God will take them out of the hands of their oppressors and restore them. God will put to shame all the nations that brought shame upon others. Instead of perishing in ruins, the mountains and the people thrive, and God's favor is bestowed on them as a new heart, from a cleansing Spirit, that brings them rest. In this picture, which is often repeated through the Bible's prophecies, it is God's work to bring the justice that settles people and lands into legacies of peace.

When I look at the crisis and corruption plaguing my people today, crying out "no justice, no peace" is more than a warning that we will not stop making noise; it's stating where we are "already," because what we deserve is still in the "not yet." No justice: evictions, gentrification, and inhumane wages. No peace: homelessness, starvation, and crimes of desperation. No justice: race-based placement of prison waste stations, toxin-producing factories. No peace: low property values, trafficking hideouts, working-class Black people ignored and underinsured. Until we see God's justice, there will be no peace.

Humanity is living in a peaceless time. We despise and destroy each other; assume that we can possess each other and call it success. Then we realize we are all wounded from devouring each other and the earth. We need transformational change, which requires systemic justice to bring about peace. This known need for revolution in our time is similarly described in God's word. Ezekiel 36, Isaiah 66, Jesus's ministry, Revelation 21, and the broader story of Scripture narrate the intersection between movements for biblical justice and Black liberation. We know that there are Black people in the future, that God's good creation exists beyond whiteness, and that we have a future of building beyond suffering.

But what is that future to include?

What do we live on for?

How does that "not yet" reality keep us energized for the constant struggle we are in "already"?

The passion that keeps us protesting in the present is the same drive that delivered our ancestors in the past and empowers our perseverance into the future. We press on by the power of God's promise. We exist as a critical part of God's plan.

The Bible teaches us that ethnic identity is part of God's eschatological purpose. Blackness is critical to the global fulfillment of God's promise to renew all things. For in no other extended time throughout history has an ethnicity built itself. God ordained Blackness as the answer and antidote to whiteness. We have been protected from possible extinction—through trafficking, medical testing, exclusion from healthcare access, and countless conditions of poverty and scarcity. Though we yet suffer, we bear witness to the resilience that our story reveals.

## ABOLITION AND COVENANT JUSTICE

Soon the Black body politic will thrive in liberated economies governed by and unified through the same all-powerful Jesus who made Himself poor. The last shall be first. We must hold on to this vision—and holding on to this vision means working now as if it is truly on the way. In my years working in the Black liberation movement, I have often noticed and gratefully experienced the presence of the Holy Spirit in organizing meetings. Many organizers in the Black radical tradition describe our guiding ethic as "deep, abiding love." Hearing this always inspires my sense of God's *hesed,* an unfailing, covenant love— often translated as steadfast love—that Christians know as the predominant preview of a renewed society. *Hesed* is expressed through fellowship, relationship, worship, childlike faith, and adoration of God.

Love is both the root and the fruit of God's liberative mission. God's love leads us to delight in each other and all of the goodness that has been created. It is love that fuels our fight for freedom, no matter how constant our struggle may be. God's love is the source of the Holy Ghost imagination, which inspires us to work as we wait with expectancy for a future where perfect love casts out all fear of threat and bondage. That future is the Kingdom of God.

When Jesus was teaching about repentance, he often said, "The Kingdom of God is near you." Accountability and change are foretastes of the coming Kingdom. So too is abolition work a preview of the full liberation from sin and struggle that is to come. Abolition requires creative purpose, a commitment to finding ways for people to be free, and an imagination that casts its vision beyond a system of punishment that strips humans of their sense of connection to God.

Prisons and policing as we know it in the United States were built largely to segregate Black people from society. Police forces evolved from fugitive slave patrols, and prison was designated as a space where it was lawful to enslave people. In 2020, scholar and author Darnell L. Moore gave a speech called "Let's Get Free." In it he discusses the radical imagination that abolition requires. Moore emphasizes "practice, practice, practice" as the activity we can take now while we commit to envisioning the not yet. He says in a 2015 article, "Not Yet Here: A Case for Abolition Theology," "I insist that the black imagination must also be used to dream that which is not yet. It must be used to deny normativity its power. Black imagination requires nothing less than a transgressive counter-hegemonic force if it is to bring about a future of true liberation."

The Black liberation movement is necessarily committed to a twenty-first-century abolition ethic. This belief that the carceral state is irreparably corrupt interacts with God's ultimate justice, especially as it pertains to racist violence, by creating a space where people are truly equal, and oppression is not even part of the framework of punishment. Abolition insists that it is possible to build a world that has no dependence on or origins in suffering.

Abolition ethic bears the markers of God's attributes. Thus, at its core, it moves in eschatological opposition to whiteness. In God's economy, there is no human who lacks creative purpose, and everyone is worthy of receiving a share in God's delight. There is no human who cannot feel the light of liberation. Everyone is worthy of freedom. There is no limiting the ways we can build community and keep one another safe. Everyone is worthy of imagining a flourishing future.

This future leans into Moore's prophetic call to "deny normativity its power," for very little has flourished under the current system of norms. In no small way, dismantling white supremacy and abolishing whiteness are part of the plan for God's redemption of the cosmos. This might be most evident in the covenant of justice present in the work of Jesus, and in the promises of God throughout the biblical story. In Luke 18, Jesus tells the story of the persistent widow who refused to give up her campaign for the dignity she was owed. She received what she demanded from an unrighteous judge, who was pushed into right action by her tenacity. Jesus commented on his own story: "And will not God give justice to his elect, who cry to him day and night? Will he delay long over them? I tell you, he will give justice to them speedily."

In Genesis 16 and 21, the Lord allows Hagar to name him "the God who sees" when he appears to her in the wilderness. An African woman was scorned by the family of a patriarch who forced her to participate in their impatience with God's promise. But she was the first to speak a name for God. She received a promise from God that she and her son would not die in the desert. God's deep and abiding, steadfast love, promised a justice that Hagar would never have found in the tents of Abraham. She was brought out to build a nation free from enslavement, and free from the threat of her body being misused. Covenant justice means that the Lord sees us. All of us. The healing of the nations does not leave out Black people simply because we do not know the nations of our origin. God cares about the material conditions of people in the African diaspora.

When we know this truth, we can approach the glory prefigured by God's people through the Spirit's presence today. The not yet is here already. But the revolution can't be televised or seen by human eyes. Faith is the sense of the Spirit that will make us see. "For we walk by faith, not by sight" (2 Cor. 5:7).

## BLACKNESS NOW CAN PREFIGURE GOD'S GLORY TO COME

Walking by faith means challenging our own sight. Faith is the radical force that gives substance to the renewal we hope for, and evidence of the not-yet that we cannot perceive. Faith is not only the way of life for the righteous, it is the foundation for our works that God uses to build the Kingdom.

By faith we recognize the grace of God in disruption—in protesters on highways warning us to go home a different way when the empire has decreed death for our children. Disruption challenges our pride in preaching against marriage equality while forgetting the families separated by immigration issues.

As a balm to some and a warning to others, God disrupts our earthly sight with a vision of redeemed reality. This is no time for polite perspectives bound by social convenience. Freedom won't wait; "time will tell" nothing that God has not already revealed. Anthems and flags are muted and made invisible. The displaced will see their home. The most marginalized Black people we ourselves refuse to welcome will be guests of honor at the Lord's table.

Our journey has hardly begun, and the path of our existence is eternal, as it is for the rest of the household of God across the globe. Blackness requires boldness now, but the Word of the Lord to the African diaspora is that Black struggles have a sure and triumphant end. While we're taught to hope like Mary of Bethany that on the last day, our human value will be resurrected, the resurrected Jesus is staring us in the face. He is pulling his people into his bosom of blessing.

The Kingdom that is to come is already at hand. We can find it in the blessings of Blackness that prefigure the "not yet" that is "already" here, through worship and fellowship, leaning together on the everlasting arms of a God whose plan is perfect.

We can thrive in our reason for being by the gift of our Creator's delight.

We have access now to freedom in its fullness by the work of Jesus our Redeemer.

Though today we see only in part, the Holy Ghost imagination gives us a vision of God's global family.

Our faith is already evidence of a glory that is not yet seen. Our Blackness is bestowed by the triune God. Black life, love, and liberation are originally and ultimately the work of our triune God, showing us how beautiful the Kingdom is, how glorious it will be.

For the Lord takes delight in his people; God will crown their long-suffering with victory.

PSALMS 149:4

# Diaspora Dreams

## BLACKNESS AS THE IMAGE OF GOD

## By Ekemini Uwan

WHEN BLACKNESS GETS WRITTEN ABOUT, it is often framed in contrast to whiteness. I get it. I've done this. And there are times when this framing is necessary, due to our history and the present racist exigencies. Many of us are trying to make sense of our social locations by writing in ways that are liberating.

Yet I submit that if Blackness is perpetually in conversation with whiteness, these discourses do not become *liberating* but *limiting*, as they serve to tether us to that which continues to oppress us.

In the words of the Commodores:

> I may be just a foolish dreamer but I don't care.
> I'm searching for that silver lining. Horizons I've
>     never seen.

Oh, I'd like to take just a moment and dream my
dream. Ohhh, dream my dream.

"Zoom"

I believe we can tell better stories of ourselves—stories that
are hopeful, life-giving, joyful, loving, and restorative; stories
that are void of oppression. This is the future that awaits us in
Christ, so now is an opportune time to share my eschatological
dreams and foretell our future.

Moreover, these stories of future hope are just as true and
real as our Black history and Black present. As the apostle Paul
reminds us in 2 Corinthians 4:18, "So we fix our eyes not on
what is seen, but what is unseen, since what is seen is temporary,
but what is unseen is eternal." My hope and prayer is that as I
take this moment to dream my diaspora dreams, we may lay
hold of the coming glory. It's a glory that has already arrived,
but its full manifestation has yet to be revealed. It's a glory that
beckons us to dream. Will you dream with me?

## BLACKNESS AS THE IMAGE OF GOD

Before we delve into my Black diasporic dreamscape, it's imperative that we go back to the Garden of Eden as it is recorded in the book of Genesis, for within it is the portal to the
future glory that we read about in the book of Revelation. It is
in the Garden of Eden that God declares His decision to bring
all of humanity into being. God says, "Let us make mankind in

our image, in our likeness, so that they may rule over the fish in the sea and the birds in the sky, over the livestock and all the wild animals, and over all the creatures that move along the ground."

> So God created mankind in his own image,
>     in the image of God he created them;
>     male and female he created them.
> God blessed them and said to them, "Be fruitful and increase in number; fill the earth and subdue it. Rule over the fish in the sea and the birds in the sky and over every living creature that moves on the ground."

GENESIS 1:26–28

There is no shortage of theologians who have proffered countless theories on what it means for human beings to be made in the image of God. Some say the image of God is functional, in that it is what we *do,* and not necessarily who we are. Others say it is immaterial, citing the souls within human beings as the location of the image of God. And then there are those who equate the image of God with either righteousness or holiness; so, when the Fall occurred, according to them, we *lost* the image of God. I think it best to focus on what is conspicuous about the image of God within humanity. And as we seek the truth of what this means for us, we can trust that, by faith, we will understand the mysterious aspects *by and by.* For the secret things belong to the children of God (Ps. 25:14), and John reminds us that when we see God, we will be like Him (1 John 3:2). Soon, and very soon, we will understand all these things, but not a moment before.

Although presently we see through a glass dimly (1 Cor. 13:12), it doesn't mean we cannot see at all. What is evident about the image of God is that this glorious endowment has been given to human beings *exclusively*. Nothing in all creation is made in the image of God except for humanity: not the vegetation, nor the birds, nor the livestock, etc. Which is why God blessed Adam and Eve and, according to Barnabe Assohoto and Samuel Ngewa, why God "assigned a two-fold mission: to increase in number and fill the earth (Genesis 1:28a) and to rule over creation and to subdue the earth (1:26c, 28b). This mission was not a heavy burden but a gift from God. Human beings were to occupy and enjoy, not fear creation.... It is important to note that men and women were permitted to rule over other living creatures, not over other human beings."[1]

This message bears repeating: we don't rule over each other. Period.

Once again, the Godward hierarchy—the reality that humans are made in God's image and likeness, thereby being set apart and placed above the animals, the plants, the vegetation, etc.—comes into view when we see the dominion over creation that God gave to our first parents, Adam and Eve—and to us, as their progeny. The image of God within humanity is our sine qua non; without it, we cease to be human. Concretely, the whole person is made in the image of God. The image of God, also known as the *imago Dei,* is not a supplementary gift or addendum, nor is it incidental. The *imago Dei* is irrevocable. This is critical, because it means that not even the intrusion of sin in Genesis 3 can nullify the image of God within each of us.

That's good news, because what the image of God also means is that we not only are *made* in the image of God, we also possess some of God's attributes. We have the capacity to love, create, and reason, among the other "transferable" divine attributes.[2]

This has significant implications for Black people globally.

Our dignity is made in the image of God.

Our humanity is made in the image of God.

Our physical appearance is made in the image of God.

Thus, the denial of the *imago Dei* within Black people is the very site of our oppression.

In the words of Toni Morrison, "What does not love you has trivialized itself and must answer for that."[3] And we know America continues to trivialize itself.

But we do not. We know that loving ourselves is no trifling matter. And when we affirm the image of God within ourselves, we agree with our liberating God that what God made is good. Blackness is our inheritance.

We would do well to agree with God on everything, but especially on this matter.

Blackness as the image of God involves our entire being—soul and body—and that includes the variegation of our skin tones, from the rich melanin that begets an onyx hue to the aureate complexion that looks as though one were kissed by the sun. The image of God extends to our many hair textures, running the gamut from coily to curly to kinky to nappy and every texture in between. The *imago Dei* is reflected in our beautifully defined bone structure, the stride in our step, and the tenacious "souls of Black folks." The image of God is embodied in our Blackness.

Some of you may have heard the oft-repeated adage "I'm Christian before I am Black." At face value, this assertion may seem innocuous. Some might even conclude that it's commendable, because the speaker is declaring their singular devotion to the Christian faith while holding ethnocentrism in abeyance. However, when you take a moment to think about it critically, you'll see that the saying creates a false dichotomy that pits two beautiful realities against each other. God has never presented us with this false choice between our Christian faith and our Blackness. God doesn't make us choose—because God chose to send Jesus Christ to us embodied as a brown-skinned Palestinian Jewish man. And at this very moment, Jesus is seated at the right hand of God, in that very body.

I've heard this false dichotomy repeated so many times by Black Christians, in a variety of church spaces, that I've come to call this phenomenon the "bleachification of Christ." This occurs whenever Jesus Christ is likened to a bleaching agent. It's as if the moment a Black person comes to faith, the bleachification of Christ is activated. As if Jesus Himself douses Black Christians with a bottle of bleach, eradicating our culture, language, vernacular, and our collective, embodied Blackness.

But that is not so.

Run away from that spiritual skin bleach: white supremacist Christianity. It'll destroy you from the inside out.

Our Blackness is not a result of the Fall; it is evidence of God's goodness. Our Christian faith does not erase our Blackness. On the contrary, it accentuates, affirms, and confers on it a transcendent significance we cannot fully appreciate apart from our faith.

God made us Black on purpose and with intention, as a testament to the intractable truth that Black people—soul and body—are inherently, fearfully, and wonderfully made in the image of God, and shall remain so. In this way, our Christianity is expressed through our embodied Blackness, and speaking eschatologically, we will retain our Blackness in the new heavens and new earth (according to Revelation 7:9). God delights in our Blackness, and so should we.

As mentioned earlier, the portal to future glory was in the Garden of Eden. Given the state of the world, you might be tempted to say, "I wish we could go back to the Garden of Eden!" Which reminds me of that old Donald Lawrence bop: "Let's get back to Eden, live on top of the world. . . ." But Eden was never God's goal for humanity. Although Eden "was very good," it was not perfect because it had not reached its ultimate goal, which was eschatological fulfillment: life together with God for eternity.

So what kept Eden from being perfect? The answers are found in Genesis 2:9 and 16:17, and in Genesis 3:1.

Genesis 2:9 reads, "The tree of life was in the midst of the garden, and the tree of the knowledge of good and evil." In verses 16 and 17 God commands Adam, saying, "You may surely eat of every tree of the garden, but of the tree of the knowledge of good and evil you shall not eat, for in the day that you eat of it you shall surely die." So we have two trees: one that will confer life and one that will confer death. In Genesis 3:1 we learn that there is something else in that garden that keeps it from being perfect. The Scripture says, "Now, the serpent was more crafty than any other beast of the field that the Lord God had made."

From these passages we can see that there are three features in the garden that indicate that Eden was *not* the highest goal for humanity:

1. **The tree of life** symbolizes an escalation of life that would have been conferred on Adam and Eve had they eaten of its fruits, moving them from the estate of innocence to the estate of glory. They would have advanced beyond life in Eden to future glory, receiving eternal life; and they would have been confirmed in righteousness and holiness.

2. **The tree of the knowledge of good and evil** is the probation tree, meaning that while they were in the garden, the obedience of Adam and Eve was tested temporarily. Adam and Eve lived under the threat of death; that is what the tree of the knowledge of good and evil symbolized. Death was the consequence for disobedience.

3. **The Serpent's presence** defiles the garden-temple of Eden, tempting Adam and Eve to sin against God. Remember, God gave Adam and Eve dominion over everything he made. Guarding the garden-temple meant that Adam and Eve were to exercise dominion and crush the serpent for profaning the garden-temple. So long as the serpent remained in the garden, Adam and Eve could not advance beyond probation.

These elements exhibit the way Eden in and of itself was not a picture of God's highest vision for humanity. Beyond just the *presence* of these elements, Genesis tells us that Adam and Eve chose to disobey God by eating the forbidden fruit, effectively failing to exercise responsibility for their dominion over the serpent. We also know they did not obey God's one prohibition, though they had the capacity to do so as image-bearers who were sinless. We know this not only because it is written in Genesis 3 but because we live with the consequences of sin every day: stratification, discrimination, subjugation, inequity, and iniquity abound. You know it. You feel it. You see it. You live it.

The current state of the world causes us to long for something greater. I find much resonance and consolation when I read the Scripture in Ecclesiastes 3:11 that says, "He has also set eternity in the human heart." As image-bearers, we have this longing and knowledge that God has embedded within us, that there is more beyond this world. Although we are finite, we were made for eternity.

## DREAMING IN DIASPORA

This longing for escape reminds me of "The Afrolantica Awakening," a fictional vignette in Derrick Bell's seminal book *Faces at the Bottom of the Well*. Bell captures the history of Black emigration movements as he describes a new continent called "Afrolantica" that mysteriously rises from the bottom of the Atlantic Ocean. Predictably, the United States—among other countries—stakes a claim to the land, but the land turns out to be uninhabitable for all people except African Americans.

Bell writes:

> In an effort to determine whether other African Americans could survive on Atlantis—a possibility many believed,

given the new land's importance, highly inappropriate—the next helicopter expedition carried on board three African American men and, as pilot, an African American woman. An amazed world watched the landing, filmed by a crew member and beamed back via satellite for televising. After a cautious first few steps, the crew discovered that they needed neither their space suits nor special breathing equipment. In fact, the party felt exhilarated and euphoric— feelings they explained upon their reluctant return (in defiance of orders, they spent several days exploring the new land) as unlike any alcohol- or drug-induced sensations of escape. Rather, it was an invigorating experience of heightened self-esteem, of liberation, of waking up. All four agreed that, while exploring what the media were now referring to as "Afrolantica," they felt *free.*[4]

In Bell's story, the discovery of Afrolantica and the newfound revelation that only Black Americans can inhabit the would-be "promised land" galvanizes millions of Black Americans, sparking another iteration of the Black emigration movement. The fourth of July is the date the first Afrolantica armada was to set sail, with the first wave of thousands of Black settlers. However, just as quickly as their hopes had risen, along with the ships' anchors, they are dashed by peculiar weather reports.

Within hours of their departure, they received weather reports of severe disturbances in the ocean around Afrolantica. The island that had stood for a year in clear sunlight, a beacon of hope to long-besieged blacks, was—for the first time since its emergence—enveloped in a thick mist. . . . Then the mist rose. The sight that met the eyes of the black settlers on the emigrant armada was amazing, terrifying. Afrolantica was sinking back into the ocean whence it had arisen.[5]

As Bell continues his narrative, I'm struck by the counterintuitive response by the would-be Afrolanticans upon seeing their new continent sink into the ocean from whence it came. Although Afrolantica disappears before the eyes of the eager would-be Black settlers, their hope and resolve prove impervious to Afrolantica's descent. For they have experienced an "Afrolantica Awakening": they realize that the liberation they were seeking in the *promised land* already dwells within, since liberation is in the mind. They return with steadfast confidence, saying, "It was worth it just to try looking for something better, even if we didn't find it."[6]

The quest for a Black utopia on this side of glory continues to come up short; but I hear the Staple Singers belting, "I know a place ain't nobody cryin', Ain't nobody worried . . . I'll take you there." This glorious place, free from pain, worry, tears, and oppression, is not a figment of imagination, nor is it subject to climate change: it exists not only in the mind and heart of faith but beyond this earthly realm. This place is heaven.

If I was a betting woman, I'd wager quite a bit of money on the guess that when we are encouraged to think about heaven, the infamous saying that "some people are so heavenly minded, they are no earthly good" probably comes to mind. But as my co-host Dr. Christina Edmondson has often said on *Truth's Table,* "We are heavenly minded to be of earthly good."

It is through our minds that heaven-inspired liberative dreams are seeded and cultivated, before they ever sprout on this side of heaven. Which is why I have a great appreciation for the brilliant imagery that Derrick Bell gave us in the eyes of the Black settlers who experienced the *Afrolantica awakening,* demonstrating that liberation is in the mind.

Bell's fictional vision reminds me in turn of the biblical author John, who wrote in the book of Revelation a prolonged prophetic vision of all the things that will take place someday on earth and in heaven. It reads like sci-fi, but it's far from fiction. The book of Revelation is intimidating to many, because its imagery can be esoteric, cryptic, and downright scary. Nevertheless, it speaks of heaven, the glorious future to come, with a new heaven and new earth, and the holy city coming down from God, where God will dwell with those of us who hold fast to the testimony of Jesus Christ.

There is no way I can do the book of Revelation justice in this chapter. Nevertheless, I invite you to unleash your eschatological imagination as I reveal my own by sharing my diaspora dreams through the portal of the book of Revelation.

Revelation provides us with an incisive view of what the restoration of all things will look like and be like for us in heaven. When people talk about the reconciliation of all things, they are usually referring to the vision described in Revelation 7:9: "After this I looked and there before me was a great multitude that no one could count, from every nation, tribe, people, and language, standing before the throne and in front of the Lamb. They were wearing white robes and were holding palm branches in their hands."

What we see here is a beautiful glimpse of a legion of people from every ethnic group and language, worshipping God in unison. Then verses 15–17 describe the unbridled satisfaction that this multitude of people are partakers of, because they kept the faith and persevered through tribulation:

> Therefore, they are before the throne of God and serve him day and night in his temple; and he who sits on the throne will spread his tent over them. Never again will they hunger; never again will they thirst. The sun will not beat upon them, nor any scorching heat. For the Lamb at the center of the throne will be their shepherd; he will lead them to springs of living water. And God will wipe away every tear from their eyes.

When I meditate on this chapter in my sanctified imagination, I consider how the restoration of all things includes the restoration of the ethnic identities and native tongues of the descendants of Africans who were stolen and brought to the Americas and the Caribbean during the transatlantic slave trade.

I am a descendant of the Ibibio ethnic group, which was one of many ethnic groups that were taken during this reprehensible time of history. And in my eschatological imagination and deep within my soul, I believe that we will be reunited with our kin and kinsmen. Every ancestor who was stolen. Every spouse that was separated. Every neighbor, artist, writer, healer who was shipped, beaten, maimed, and disappeared as a result of this evil institution of slavery.

Mother and child,

cousins,

friends,

siblings.

Reunited and restored to wholeness around the throne of God, who is our Redeemer.

This great reversal—the fulfilled promise of the Gospel—fuels my diaspora dream. It reminds me of the final scene in the movie *The Color Purple*, when sisters Nettie and Celie are reunited after being violently separated for many years due to the abuse in the household. Nettie, Celie's younger sister, goes on to become a missionary to the Olinka people, a fictional tribe in Africa. For many years, Celie thinks that her sister Nettie is dead and gone, because Celie's abusive husband, Mister, would intercept Nettie's letters and keep them hidden from her.

Then, one glorious day, a car appears a long way off. Celie assumes it is just a lost driver stopping for directions. The car parks at a distance, and as the mysterious passengers exit and stand outside it, their beautiful violet-and-crimson scarves dance in the wind, signaling to Celie a distant familiarity she has yet to fully realize. She draws closer, with steps of determination, and as she recognizes her sister Nettie, she belts out, "NETTIEEEEEEEE!" from a place of deep ancestral perception, knowing that it is indeed her sister.

Celie's determined steps now quicken to a run-turned-hobble, which communicates to the audience the length of time that has passed, and how that time has marked Celie. Nettie runs with the same determination, only time hasn't yet caught up with her. They stop an arm's length apart from each other to behold the miracle of this reunion. Within seconds they pull each other in for a kiss on the lips and then pull away for a moment to caress each other's face and hair, and with exacting eyes examining each other's faces, they draw close for another embrace. Nettie then introduces Celie's now adult children, Adam and Olivia, who greet their mother Celie in the Olinka language through smiles and tears, in awe of this miraculous reunion.

In my eschatological imagination, Celie represents the descendants of Africans who were trafficked to the United States but *remained*. Nettie represents the descendants of Africans, like the Ibibio people who were stolen from Ibibioland, kin, and culture and were trafficked to the United States, a land they knew not, but who *returned* to Africa. Adam and Olivia represent continental Africans turned Black immigrants who come from the countries from which the highest concentration of Africans were stolen in the transatlantic slave trade, and who were left behind to contend with colonial forces while their distant relatives were brought here as chattel. Due to the devastation wrought by colonialism in their homelands, they emigrated to the United States.

Regardless of our entry point into this history, reunion, renewal, reclamation, redemption, and the restoration of all things await those of us who have kept faith by holding to the testimony of Jesus Christ.

As the sun sets in the final scene of *The Color Purple*, Nettie and Celie's silhouettes drape across the horizon as they play a hand-clap game called makidada. A song that conjures our ancestral connection and interconnectedness as a people.

In my sanctified imagination, I envision a God-ordained cosmic pan-African family reunion that culminates in us playing and singing makidada in unison around the throne of God.

I dream in diaspora, for the good of our people made in the image of God, and for the glory of God.

> Blessed are those who wash their robes, that they may have the right to the tree of life and may go through the gates into the city.
>
> REVELATION 22:14

# Conclusion

WE WANT TO THANK OUR SISTAS for sitting at the table with us! As is our custom at *Truth's Table*, we'd like to leave you with a prayer of blessing.

Let us pray.

Merciful God, the Creator God who masterfully designed the human frame, hear our lament.

How long will Black girls be denied their humanity? Treated as if they have no pain or as though they cannot feel pain? How long will Black pain be punished? Our creativity cursed, success blocked, or drive pathologized by being given standards to meet that are unattainable to others? How long will Black women's grief and anxiety be ignored as they are labeled irresponsible or haughty?

God of Hagar, see, restore, and avenge Your daughters. Grant healing and protection.

God of the tired and misused Black women, hear our prayer.

God of wonder, God of hope, God of joy, the One who made

us Black women. The God of Harriet, Ida, Fannie, Helen, Yvonne, and Arit, we give You praise because we are fearfully and wonderfully made. You have claimed us in a world that ignores us. We give You praise because of Your promises. Promises that carry us through lament and into hopeful expectation. Make us steadfast witnesses to Your Truth, as we become living epistles for Your glory.

It is in You that we live and move and have our being. How good and pleasant it is to know that we are Your daughters. May our lives reflect the overflow of grace that You have granted to us.

We pray this in the name of the Father, Son, and Holy Spirit. Amen.

# Acknowledgments

First, giving honor to God who is the head of our lives.

We would like to thank our sistas at the table and our standing-room-section listeners. We are so thankful for your presence, encouragement, and engagement with us through the years and seasons.

We'd also like to thank our production staff, Beau York, Joshua Heath, and Darryl Bradford.

A big thank-you to our administrative staff, Kiara Allison, Emani Young, Alicia Quan, and Praise Weru.

We can't forget our *Truth's Table* Patreon supporters; without their financial support, this table would cease to exist.

A big shout-out to our growing community of sistas in our *Truth's Table*'s Black Women's Discipleship Facebook group.

Writing a book ain't easy and it's not for the faint of heart. A good editor is like a skilled doula, and our editor, Ashley Hong, helped us birth this baby into the world. We greatly appreciate the patience and prowess in activating our words "one degree more."

We are grateful for our literary agent, Chris Park. From day one you have taken all the pieces learned from your varied experiences in the world of publishing to guide us to this point. May the Lord bless all your endeavors.

This book would not be what it is without our collective and individual support from our village.

## EKEMINI WOULD LIKE TO THANK

God for His steadfast love, care, and grace over my life. I am blessed to be a servant of the Lord. As hard as this calling has been, You are walking with me and guiding me. Truly, one day in Your courts is better than a thousand elsewhere.

Thank you to my sweet mother, who sacrificed her time and flew out to help support me in writing this book. I had several family obligations in the midst of writing this book, and if she had not stepped in, I would not have been able to write my chapters. I love you strong, Mommy!

To my Grandma-o! Thank you for being my first and favorite theologian and for raising me up in the fear and admonition of the Lord. You modeled the faith and life of a First Lady and a true evangelist who is never ashamed of the gospel of Jesus Christ. You always said to me and my sisters, "Be ready to meet Jesus. We don't know the day and hour of His return. I don't want any of you to miss heaven." I try to live with this theological truth in mind on a daily basis and I let it guide my public ministry. Thank you, Grandma-o! You shall wear a crown.

To my sisters, my brother, and my nieces, I cannot thank you all enough for your sacrifices, your care through the pandemic by giving me a soft place to land so I wouldn't be alone in this world. I thank you all for your love, care, prayers, sacrifice, and support. May God bless you all exceedingly and abundantly above all that you can ask or think for what you've given me.

To my mentor, Stefnie Evans, thank you for walking with me since I was a babe in Christ. I came to faith eighteen years ago and you have mentored me through every season. You see me, know me, and love me. Thank you for your wisdom and rebukes, but above all else thank you for your love for Jesus and holiness. You've had a profound impact on my life, and I thank God for you.

To my late father, Victor Uwan, whom I have never forgotten and will never stop grieving over until we meet in Glory. Thank you for the gifts you left me. Gifts I didn't know I had until God presented them to me much later in life. Most of all, I thank you for your love. You were a good father. You loved me so well, and when I think about you daily, I remember your abiding love for me, Mommy, and my sisters. I can't wait for that glorious day when we will worship around God's throne together. Until then, enjoy that never-ending Holy Ghost party. You always did love a good party!

To my co-hosts, sistas, and friends, Michelle and Christina, there is no way *Truth's Table* the podcast and now the book would have come to be without y'all's love, care, encouragement, commitment, and jokes. There is no one else I'd rather build this table with than the two of you. I love you both very much.

## MICHELLE WOULD LIKE TO GIVE THANKS

To the Creator, Redeemer, Spirit of Life, Love, and Liberation—thank you for every person and place that I call home.

To my mother and father, my sister and my beautiful babies: how I cherish you every day. My gratitude for your grace is unending.

For all the Black womxn who bless me, I give thanks. Stephanie, Kayla, Jam, Brie baby, my Michael of multitudes as always, and the coolest cousins a girl could never deserve.

Nonstop praise for my movement family who have become my political home, the Crew chat, Action, and all my St. Louis loved ones—you are built for abundance. Thank you for rebuilding me.

Prayers without ceasing have gone up from my church family who I am grateful to call my spiritual home. To the disciples, staff, and leadership at St. John's Church—The Beloved Community: I am the most passionately pastored Pastor I know! You are the reason for that.

And to the communion of Rock, River, Tree—thank you for lifting my eyes to see the horizon leaning forward, for teaching me that no God-graced face needs a hiding place. Thank you will never be enough, so I bless you in the words of Mama Maya: "And say simply with hope . . . Good morning."

## CHRISTINA WOULD LIKE TO THANK

God.

Yup.

Full stop.

I am in awe, God, of how You have sustained me in the midst of this incredibly difficult, complex, and surprising season of life. God, I am convinced of Your promises even as I lament. Let us run on to see what the end is going to be.

Additionally, I am grateful for the future Black women in my home. My beloved daughters, my broke best friends, you are magic, confetti, and hard questions. Like the Queen of Sheba, I hope that you never stop asking hard and necessary questions, even of the kings of the land.

I am eternally grateful for my mother and mother-in-love. What a gift to be mothered. I am old enough now to know that you always need a mother, and I have my beloved mother, mother-in-love, and mothers of the faith. I am blessed.

To my only and older sister, Nichole, I love you to pieces and I am glad you were my first conversation buddy. Thanks for never leading me astray. You are a woman of integrity and creativity.

Of course, my love grows each year for my sweet-face husband, Mika. Thank you, pastor-husband. Your integrity and compassion are beautiful.

To my insanely smart and hilarious co-hosts, E and M. Look at God! Can you believe this? All of this from a group text. By all of this I mean tears, cheers, cackles, and creativity. I am praying that the Lord will continue sanctifying you and granting each of you the desires of your hearts.

# Notes

## THE AUDACIOUS PERSEVERANCE OF COLORISM

1. Sarah Webb, "Recognizing and Addressing Colorism in Schools," *Learning for Justice,* January 25, 2016. www.learningforjustice.org/magazine/recognizing-and-addressing-colorism-in-schools.
2. Dr. Sarah L. Webb, "Colorism Healing: Learn. Transform. Resist," Colorism Healing, accessed July 27, 2021. colorismhealing.com.
3. Yaba Blay and Théard Noelle, *One Drop: Shifting the Lens on Race* (Boston: Beacon Press, 2021).
4. Arthur H. Goldsmith, Darrick Hamilton, and William Darity, Jr., "From Dark to Light: Skin Color and Wages Among African-Americans," *Journal of Human Resources,* 42, no. 4 (Fall 2007), 701–38. doi.org/10.3368/jhr.xlii.4.701.
5. Jess McHugh, "Denied a Teaching Job for Being 'Too Black,' She Started Her Own School—and a Movement," *The Washington Post,* February 28, 2021. www.washingtonpost.com/history/2021/02/28/nannie-helen-burroughs-black-teacher/.
6. Nannie Helen Burroughs, *Nannie Helen Burroughs: A Documentary Portrait of an Early Civil Rights Pioneer, 1900–1959,* ed. by Kelisha B. Graves (Notre Dame, Ind.: University of Notre Dame Press, 2019), xxiii.

7. Ibid, 59–60.

8. Ibid, 63.

9. Randy J. Sparks, "Two Princes of Calabar: An Atlantic Odyssey from Slavery to Freedom," *William and Mary Quarterly* 59, no. 3 (July 2002), 555–84. www.jstor.org/stable/3491465.

10. Lester Davids, "Skin Lightening: The Beauty Industry's Ugly Billion-Dollar Secret," *International Business Times UK,* October 9, 2017. www.ibtimes.co.uk/skin-lightening-beauty-industrys-ugly-billion-dollar-secret-1579218.

11. Kathy Russell, Midge Wilson, and Ronald E. Hall, *The Color Complex: The Politics of Skin Color Among African Americans* (New York: Anchor Books, 1993).

12. Eona Harrison, "Skin Color Differences in Stratification Outcomes: Colorism over Time and Across Race," University of Maryland. paa2015.princeton.edu/papers/153085.

13. Tanzina Vega, "Schools' Discipline for Girls Differs by Race and Hue," *The New York Times,* December 11, 2014. www.nytimes.com/2014/12/11/us/school-discipline-to-girls-differs-between-and-within-races.html.

14. Topher Sanders, "The Lighter the Skin, the Shorter the Prison Term," *The Root,* July 5, 2011. www.theroot.com/the-lighter-the-skin-the-shorter-the-prison-term-1790864659.

15. Monique Jones, "Vanessa Bell Calloway Says Colorism Cost Her the Role of Lisa in 'Coming to America': 'I Just Wasn't Light Enough'," *Shadow and Act,* February 17, 2021. shadowandact.com/vanessa-bell-calloway-says-colorism-cost-her-the-role-of-lisa-in-coming-to-america.

16. Burroughs, *Nannie Helen Burroughs,* 32.

## PROTEST AS SPIRITUAL PRACTICE

1. "ACLU News & Commentary," American Civil Liberties Union (website), accessed August 20, 2021. www.aclu.org/news/by/aclu/.

## DECOLONIZED DISCIPLESHIP

1. Frantz Fanon, *The Wretched of the Earth* (New York: Grove Press, 2005), 42.

2. Katie Geneva Cannon, "Christian Imperialism and the Transatlantic Slave Trade," *Journal of Feminist Studies in Religion*, 24, no. 1 (Spring 2008), 127–34. www.jstor.org/stable/20487919.

3. Ibid.

4. Fanon, *The Wretched of the Earth*, 43.

5. Patricia Hill Collins, *Black Feminist Thought: Knowledge, Consciousness, and the Politics of Empowerment* (New York: Routledge, 2015).

6. David D. Daniels, "Honor the Reformation's African Roots," *Commercial Appeal*, October 21, 2017. www.commercialappeal.com/story/opinion/contributors/2017/10/21/honor-reformations-african-roots/783252001/.

7. Juliany González Nieves, "23 Latin American Women and USA Latinas in Theology and Religion You Should Know About," The Global Church Project, accessed May 22, 2020. theglobalchurchproject.com/18-latin-american-female-theologians-know/.

## HIDDEN IN PLAIN SIGHT

1. Dianne M. Stewart, "2019 Marked 400 Years of 'Forbidden Black Love' in America," *The Washington Post*, December 26, 2019. www.washingtonpost.com/outlook/2019/12/26/marked-years-forbidden-black-love-america/.

2. My phrase. Cite Black women.

## REBORN TO RESIST

1. Colossians 2:8.

## THE KEYS TO THE KINGDOM OF GOD

1. William James Jennings, *After Whiteness: An Education in Belonging* (Grand Rapids, Mich.: William B. Eerdmans Publishing Company, 2020).

2. Emma Green, "A Resolution Condemning White Supremacy Causes Chaos at the Southern Baptist Convention," *The Atlantic* (online),

January 6, 2020. www.theatlantic.com/politics/archive/2017/06/the
-southern-baptist-convention-alt-right-white-supremacy/530244/.


## DIASPORA DREAMS

1. Tokunboh Adeyemo, ed., *Africa Bible Commentary: A One-Volume Commentary Written by 70 African Scholars* (Grand Rapids, Mich.: Zondervan, 2010), 11.
2. There are nontransferable attributes, also known as "incommunicable" attributes, that God possesses exclusively, like omnipotence, omnipresence, and omniscience, among others.
3. Toni Morrison, "A Knowing So Deep," *Essence* 5, May 1985.
4. Derrick Bell, *Faces at the Bottom of the Well: The Permanence of Racism* (New York: Basic Books, 2018), 35.
5. Ibid., 45.
6. Ibid., 46.

# My Musings

SISTAS, NOW IT'S YOUR TURN. WHAT ARE YOUR MUSINGS?

# MY MUSINGS

# MY MUSINGS

# MY MUSINGS

# ABOUT THE AUTHORS

EKEMINI UWAN is a public theologian, contributing writer for Hallmark Mahogany, and the Inaugural Theologian-in-Residence for the Black Christian Experience Resource Center. She has appeared on MSNBC and NPR. Her writings have been published in *The Atlantic, The Washington Post,* and *HuffPost Black Voices,* and her insights have been quoted by CNN, *The New York Times, The Washington Post,* and *The New Yorker.*

Dr. CHRISTINA EDMONDSON is an educator. She holds a PhD in counseling psychology and an MS in family therapy. A certified cultural intelligence facilitator with experience in nonprofit, higher education, and corporate sectors, Dr. Edmondson often consults with organizations about diversity and inclusion as well as mental health issues. Her work and insights have been covered in *The Atlantic, The Guardian,* Essence.com, and CBS News.

PHOTO: NICOLE ELLIS

MICHELLE HIGGINS is senior pastor of Saint John's Church (The Beloved Community) in St. Louis, where she co-founded Faith for Justice, a collective of Christian activists, and serves as board chair of Action St. Louis, a political home for Black communities in the St. Louis region.

TruthsTable.com
Twitter: @TruthsTable
Instagram: @TruthsTable

31901068111097